Course	Business Communications II
Course Number	**COMM 3202**
	DURHAM COLLEGE

http://create.mcgraw-hill.com

ISBN-10: 1259367959   ISBN-13: 9781259367953

Contents

Credits

Job Hunting

Job Hunting

UNIT 6

Researching Jobs

MODULE
24

Learning Objectives

After reading and applying the information in Module 24, you'll be able to demonstrate

Knowledge of

LO1 Job search strategies

LO2 Information interviews

LO3 The hidden job market

LO4 New job interview practices

Skills to

LO5 Begin to self-assess realistically

LO6 Find information about employers

LO7 Use the Internet in your job search

LO8 Find posted jobs and explore the hidden job market

LO9 Present your non-traditional experience positively

LO10 Prepare for job interviews

Employability Skills 2000+ Checklist

Module content builds these Conference Board of Canada Employability Skills 2000+

Communicate

Think and Solve Problems

Demonstrate Positive Attitudes and Behaviours

Be Adaptable

Work with Others

Participate in Projects and Tasks

The first step in any job search is to analyze and identify your own abilities and interests.[1] The second step is to establish and nourish contacts—online, and through friends, friends of friends, and family.

LO1 LO5 What Do I Need to Know About Myself to Job-Hunt?

Your need to self-assess realistically: identify your knowledge, skills, abilities, interests, and values.

Each person could happily do several jobs. Personality and aptitude tests can tell you what your strengths are, but they won't say, "You should be X." In preparation for the job search, and for the interview, you need to answer specific questions like these:

- What achievements have given you the most satisfaction? Why did you enjoy them?
- Would you rather have firm deadlines or a flexible schedule? Do you prefer working alone or with other people? Do you prefer specific instructions and standards for evaluation, or freedom and uncertainty? How comfortable are you with pressure? How do you manage multiple deadlines? How much challenge do you want?
- Are you willing to take work home? Are you prepared to travel? How important is recognition to you? How important is money compared to having time to spend with family and friends?
- Where do you want to live? What features in terms of weather, geography, and cultural and social life do you see as ideal?
- What do you want from your work? Do you work to achieve certain purposes or values, or is work "just a way to make a living"? How important are the organization's culture and ethical standards to you?

Once you have identified in writing what is most important to you, look at the job market to find what you want. For example, your greatest interest is athletics, but you aren't good enough for the pros. Your job market analysis might suggest several alternatives. You might

- Teach sports and physical fitness as a high school coach or a corporate fitness director
- Cover sports for a newspaper, magazine, TV station, or new digital medium
- Go into management or sales for a professional sports team, a health club, or a company that sells sports equipment
- Create or manage a sports website

What Do I Need to Know About Companies That Might Hire Me?

LO6 LO7 LO8

You need to know as much as you can.

Organizations always have room for people who demonstrate motivation, energy, and critical thinking. Preparation through research demonstrates all these skills. Moreover, to adapt your letter and resumé to a specific organization, and to shine at the interview, you need information both about the employer and about the job itself. You can find this information free through numerous resources (see Figure 24.1).

You'll need to know

- *Jobs available:* Start your research online, at the library or the college or university career centre. Libraries' research databases provide resources for every part of your job hunt: the best local and national companies to work for (www.canadastop100.com/fp10); postings on Workopolis, Monster.ca, and Working.com; trade and professional websites, crucial for knowledge of industry regulations, developments and conferences; municipal, provincial, and national labour market, apprenticeship, and skilled trades information—even salary averages and negotiation tips.

Social networking sites like Facebook, LinkedIn, and Twitter do not offer free job search tips, but are increasingly popular for networking itself: use them to connect with mentors and prospective employers.[2]

Notebooks at campus placement offices often have fuller job descriptions than appear in ads. Talk to friends who have graduated recently to learn what their jobs involve. Request information interviews to learn more about opportunities that interest you.

- *Contact information:* Check the ad or the organization's website, or call the company. An advantage of calling is that you can find out whether your contact prefers a courtesy title (Mr., Ms., or Mrs.).
- *At least four or five facts about the organization and what it does:* Knowing the organization's products and services enables you to describe how you can contribute. Understanding the

FIGURE 24.1 **Websites Covering the Job Search Process**

Human Resources and Skills Development Canada **www.hrsdc.gc.ca/eng/home.shtml**	The Rockport Institute **www.rockportinstitute.com**
Career Builder **www.careerbuilder.ca**	Simply Hired **www.simplyhired.ca**
Fast Company **www.fastcompany.com/guides/reinvent.html**	WetFeet.com **www.wetfeet.com**
The Five O'Clock Club **www.fiveoclockclub.com**	Workopolis **www.workopolis.com**
Job Search by Indeed **www.indeed.ca**	Vault **www.vault.com**
Monster **www.monster.ca**	Working in Canada **www.workingincanada.gc.ca**
Job Hunter's Bible (Dick Bolles) **www.jobhuntersbible.com**	Spherion Career Centre **www.spherion.com**
Eluta.ca **www.eluta.ca**	

Laura Archer, who completed her degree in nursing at the University of P.E.I., has spent her career in the United States and Africa, where she is regularly deployed with Medecins Sans Frontiers. When she is not overseas, Laura works as a visual artist in Canada.

organization's values, goals, market, and competition allows you to define specifically how your skills outshine those of other candidates

Useful facts include the following:

- Market share
- Competitive position
- New products, services, or promotions
- Technology or manufacturing equipment applications
- Plans for growth or downsizing
- Challenges the organization faces
- The corporate culture (Module 2)

You can find these facts on the Internet, including information about corporate culture and even anonymous statements from employees. Check blogs, professional electronic mailing lists, and electronic bulletin boards. Employers sometimes post specialized jobs online; they're always a good way to get information about the industry you hope to enter.

Industry Canada's free, searchable Canadian Company Capabilities database (CCC, at https://www.ic.gc.ca/eic/site/ccc-rec.nsf/eng/home) provides full data, including contact names, for over 60,000 national businesses.[3]

The directories listed in Table 24.1 provide information such as net worth, market share, principal products, and the names of officers and directors. Ask your librarian to identify additional directories. To get specific financial data (and to see how the organization presents itself to the public), get the company's annual report on the Web (www.orderannualreports.com). (*Note:* Only companies whose stock is publicly traded are required to issue annual reports. In this day of mergers and buyouts, many companies are owned by other companies. The parent company may be the only one to issue an annual report.)

Many company websites provide information about training programs and career paths for new hires. To learn about new products, plans for growth, or solutions to industry challenges, read business newspapers such as the *Globe and Mail*, *National Post*, *Wall Street Journal*, or *Financial Post*; business magazines such as *Report on Business*, *Canadian Business*, *Strategy Magazine*, *Fortune*, *Business Week*, and *Forbes*; and trade journals. Each of these has indices listing which companies are discussed in a specific issue. A few of the trade journals available are listed in Table 24.2.

TABLE 24.1   **Where to Get Addresses and Facts about Companies**

General Directories	Dun and Bradstreet
Canadian Business Directory www.canadianbusinessdirectory.ca	*Franchise Annual: Directory*
Canadian Federation of Independent Business www.cfib-fcei.ca	*Hoover's Handbook of American Business*
	O'Dwyer's Directory of Public Relations Firms
Directory of Corporate Affiliations	*The Rand McNally Bankers' Directory*
Dun's Million Dollar Directory	*Scott's Business Directory*
Standard & Poor's Register of Corporations, Directors, and Executives	*Standard Directory of Advertisers* ("Red Book")
Thomas Register of American Manufacturers	*Television Factbook*
	Traders
Specialized Directories and Resource Books	
Accounting Firms and Practitioners	
Directory of Hotel and Motel Systems	

TABLE 24.2   Examples of Trade Journals and Magazines

Advertising Age

BtoB Magazine

CAmagazine

Canada Employment Weekly

Canadian Auto World

Canadian Business

The Canadian Firefighter

Canadian Musician

Computer Dealer News

Computing Canada

Direction Informatique

Essence (Canadian Federation of Chefs and Cooks)

Farm & Country (Ontario commercial farmer trade)

Financial Analysts Journal

Graphic Arts Monthly

HR Focus

Information Highways

Medical Post

Northern Miner (mining news)

Quill & Quire (publishing news)

The Western Producer (Saskatoon)

LO7 How Should I Use Social Networking Sites?

Consider your purpose and audiences: post a specific profile on appropriate sites, keep it updated, nurture your contacts, and tend your digital tattoo.

Although social networking will not replace the power of face-to-face meetings, savvy job searchers use all the tools available to reach their target audiences. Such tools include social media communications—blogging and networking sites—that now attract a diverse demographic.[4] Recruiters and employers routinely search social networking sites for likely candidates.

Career coach professionals recommend using specific sites and strategies to attract recruiters' attention:[5]

- Network on those sites that would most likely attract people (and employers) in the industries you are most interested in.
- Join in the online discussions whenever you have an opportunity to share your knowledge.
- Network on those sites offering the most technological advantages, and use them for positive influence. For example, LinkedIn permits you to post relevant information and create presentations to showcase your skills.
- Use the Internet for instructions on how and why job searchers should use these sites (www.youtube.com/watch?v=y7pSDD5IRPs, http://learn.linkedin.com/what-is-linkedin, and www.askdavetaylor.com/how_do_i_use_linkedin_to_find_a_job.html).
- Be discreet. Many recruiters and potential employers check candidates' online presence:
  - Limit your digital networking to career-related sites.
  - Keep your profile updated.
  - Check your privacy box.

Be aware that your digital identity is accessible to anybody, anytime. "With options like Pipli or Persona or Spezify it's a breeze to look someone up. Persona is an interesting and frightening experience because it uses key words like character and sports and education and genealogy and management to create a character timeline of who you are. It's never too early to take control of your digital identity."[6]

LO2 What Is the Information Interview?

Information interviews are a sophisticated form of networking.

Although you will want to use every medium possible to demonstrate your desirability as an employee, remember that people tend to hire people they know, and no technology can match the sense of familiarity that face-to-face time brings.

In an **information interview**, you talk face to face with someone who works in the area you hope to enter. The interview allows you to find out what the day-to-day work involves, and how you can best prepare to enter that field. However, when you're prepared, you can use the information interview to make a positive impression, and to self-recruit. ("I want to work for you!")

An information interview can

- Establish a positive image of you in the mind of the person, so that he or she thinks of you when openings arise
- Help you decide whether you'd like the job
- Give you specific information that you can use to present yourself effectively in your resumé and application letter

To set up an information interview, phone or write a letter like the one in Figure 24.2. If you write, phone the following week to set up a specific time and to begin to establish that all-important personal contact.

In an information interview, you might ask the following questions:

- What are you working on right now?
- How do you spend your typical day?
- How does what you do make or save the organization time or money?

FIGURE 24.2   **Letter Requesting an Information Interview**

774 Sherbrooke Street East
Montreal, PQ H8S 1H1

April 18, 2013

Kam Yuricich
Clary Communications
1420 Sherbrooke Street East
Montreal, PQ H3G 1K9

Dear Mr. Yuricich:

You-attitude focuses on the reader's importance.

Your talk to McGill's PRSSA Chapter last week about the differences between working for a PR firm and being a PR staff person within an organization really interested me. Your advice would be invaluable to me as I find my niche in the workforce. — *Emotional appeal flatters the reader.*

Information establishes the writer's credibility.

Last summer I enjoyed a co-op placement with Management Horizons. Although some of my assignments were gofer jobs, my supervisor, Jason Correila, gave me the chance to work on several brochures and to draft two speeches for managers. I enjoyed this variety and would like to learn more about the possibility of working in a PR firm. Could I schedule an information interview with you to learn more about how public relations consultants work with their clients? — *The specific request makes a logical appeal.*

Emphasizes the reader's expertise.

Perhaps we could discuss the courses you think would best prepare me for PR work. I have a year and a half left before graduation and would like to choose electives that would make me most employable.

Tells the reader the limits of the request.

When convenient for you, I would greatly appreciate 30 minutes of your time. I'll call you early next week to set up an appointment. — *Makes it easy for the reader.*

Sincerely,

Lee Tan

Lee Tan

- How have your duties changed since you first started working here?
- What do you like best about your job? What do you like least?
- What do you think the future holds for this kind of work?
- How did you get this job?
- What courses, activities, and/or jobs would you recommend to someone who wanted to do this kind of work?

Immediately after your interview, mail a handwritten note thanking the person for his or her time and information. A graceful thank-you letter demonstrates your emotional and social intelligence—critical interpersonal skills when employers are making hiring decisions.

LO3 LO8 What Is the "Hidden Job Market"? How Do I Tap into It?

The hidden market—jobs that are never advertised—is open to those who know how to use networking techniques. Referral interviews and prospecting letters can help you find it.

Most great jobs are never advertised—and the number rises the higher up the job ladder you go. More than 60 percent of all new jobs come not from responding to an ad but from networking with personal contacts.[7] Some of these jobs are created especially for a specific person. These unadvertised jobs are called the **hidden job market**; creating your own opportunities to meet and work with others informally—through on-campus political and social activities, and volunteer community involvement, for example—is the optimum method for tapping into this market.

Ex.
24.2
24.4
24.10

Referral interviews, an organized method of networking, offer another way to tap into these jobs. The goal of a referral interview is to put you face-to-face with someone with the power to hire you: the owner of a small company, the division vice-president, or branch manager of a big company, or the director of the local office of a provincial or federal agency.

Ask for a referral interview to learn about current job opportunities in your field. Sometimes an interview that starts out as an information interview turns into a referral interview.

A referral interview
- Gives you information about current opportunities available in your area of interest
- Refers you to other people who can tell you about job opportunities
- Enables the interviewer to see that you could contribute to his or her organization

Start by scheduling interviews with people you know who may know something about that field—professors, co-workers, neighbours, friends. Join your alumni association; network with alumni who now work where you would like to work. Your purpose in talking to them is to

1. Get advice about improving your resumé and about general job-hunting strategies
2. Become a known commodity and thereby get referrals to other people

Go into the interview with the names of people you'd like to talk to. If the interviewee doesn't suggest anyone, say, "Do you think it would be a good idea for me to talk to X?"

Then, armed with a referral from someone you know, call person X and say, "So-and-so suggested I talk with you about job-hunting strategies." If the person says, "We aren't hiring," you say, "Oh, I'm not asking you for a job. I'd just like some advice from a knowledgeable person about the opportunities in banking (or desktop publishing, technical services, etc.) in this city." If this person does not have the power to create a position, ask for more referrals at the end of this interview. You can also polish your resumé if you get good suggestions along the way.

Networking through information and referral interviews can lead to job offers.

Source: © BrandXPictures/Punchstock

Even when you talk to the person who could create a job for you, do not ask for a job. To give you advice about your resumé, however, the person has to look at it. When a powerful person focuses on your skills, he or she will naturally think about the problems and needs in that organization. When there's a match between what you can do and what the organization needs, that person may be able to create a position for you.

Remember the two truisms of job hunting: 1) *self-recruitment is still the number one way to get hired, and 2) people hire people they know.* Although the idea of cold-calling may seem daunting, you'll find most people receptive. You are likely to get the interview when you mention a familiar name ("So-and-so suggested I talk with you") and sound enthusiastic. Prepare as carefully for these interviews as you would for a job interview. Think of good questions in advance; know something about the general field or industry; learn as much as you can about the specific company.

Always follow up information and referral interviews with personal thank-you letters. Use specifics to show that you paid attention during the interview, and enclose a copy of your revised resumé.

LO9 How Do I Present My Non-traditional Experiences?

Address the employer's potential concerns positively.

Many people bring a variety of non-traditional experiences to the job search. These experiences often build on the transferable skills for which employers search. In a world where the ability to learn is recognized as the key to employability, your communication skills will determine whether you get the job. This section addresses various ways to present your previous experience positively.

"All My Experience Is in My Family's Business"

In your resumé, simply list the company for which you worked. For a reference, instead of a family member, list a supervisor, client, or vendor who can talk about your work. Since the reader may wonder whether "Jim Clarke" is any relation to "Clarke Construction Company," be ready to answer interview questions about why you're looking at other companies. Prepare an answer that stresses the broader opportunities you seek but doesn't criticize your family or the family business.

"I've Been out of the Job Market for a While"

You need to prove to a potential employer that you're up to date and motivated:

- Research changes in your field to identify prospective employers' priorities. When you can demonstrate that you can make an immediate contribution, you'll have a much easier sell. To do that, however, you need to know what the employer needs: What skills are employers looking for?
- Be active in professional organizations. Attend meetings, and read magazines, newspapers and trade journals.
- Learn the computer programs that professionals in your field use.

- Show how your at-home experience relates directly to the workplace. Multi-tasking, organizing food bank drives, managing projects, chairing school council/PTA meetings, dealing with unpredictable situations, building consensus, listening, raising money, and making presentations are all transferable skills.
- Create a portfolio of your work—even if it's for imaginary clients—to demonstrate your expertise and transferable skills.[8] Most of Canada's provinces and territories offer prior learning assessment and recognition (PLAR) to adults with work experience. Based on a demonstration of the requisite knowledge and skills, you can get credit for post-secondary courses. Most high-level courses require that candidates prepare a proposal and a portfolio of academic and work projects to demonstrate subject knowledge and skills.

"I Want to Change Fields"

Learn about the skills needed in the job you want. Learn the language of the industry. Then you can identify a good reason (from the prospective employer's point of view) for choosing to explore a new field. "I want a change" or "I need to get out of a bad situation" will not convince an employer that you know what you're doing.

Think about how your experience relates to the job you want. Jack is an older-than-average student who wants to be a pharmaceutical sales representative. He has sold woodstoves, served subpoenas, and worked on an oilrig. A chronological resumé makes his work history look directionless. But a skills resumé (Module 25) could focus on persuasive ability (selling stoves), initiative and persistence (serving subpoenas), and technical knowledge (working on an oilrig; courses in biology and chemistry).[9]

EXPANDING A CRITICAL SKILL

LO4 LO10 Selling Yourself in the New Work World

In the new world of work, non-traditional employment has replaced the cradle-to-grave job security of your grandparents. "Almost 40 percent of Canadians are earning a living as temps, part-timers, contract workers or self-employed consultants, and their numbers are growing."

Although small and medium-sized businesses offer the best employment opportunities for today's job seekers, all employers, regardless of company size, seek people who are well prepared, can think on their feet, and demonstrate values that match those of the organization.

To ensure that match, hiring processes are also evolving. Because the traditional employment interview has proven inadequate, employers are trying other methods, including multiple interviews, team interviews, behavioural interviews, and psychological testing. Aspiring candidates should prepare thoroughly to answer specifically the most important hiring question: What do you have to offer that will keep us competitive?

- Research the organization, the industry, and current challenges.

- Know the corporate culture, and be prepared to describe specifically how your skills and values fit that culture.
- Prepare to answer behavioural questions, such as "Describe a situation in which you diffused a potential conflict"; "Describe a situation in which you demonstrated leadership skills"; "Why did you apply for this job?"; "Give an example of a difficult situation you were in with people and how you handled it."
- Prepare for expert recruiters who will dig for unrehearsed answers (and character insights) with such queries as "When is it okay to lie? How far would you go to close a deal? What does independence mean to you?"

Astute interviewees understand that even the deceptively simple, kickoff question, "Tell me about yourself," translates as "Tell me specifically why I should hire you." Savvy employment searchers come prepared with specific examples to answer that question.

Source: Wallace Immen (2009, February 18), Job hunting 101, *Globe and Mail*, p. C1; Ron McGowan (2004, May 4), Forget a job: Grads must sell selves to new world of work, *Globe and Mail*, p. C1; Wallace Immen (2005, September 16), Thinking on your feet gets a foot in the door, *Globe and Mail*, p. C3; Andy Holloway (2005, October 10–23), Recruit right: A guide to finding the best fit, *Canadian Business*, p. 123; Arlen H. Hirsch (2004, November 10), 'Tell me about yourself' response is trickier than you might think, *Globe and Mail*, p. C9.

"I Was Fired"

First, deal with the emotional baggage. You need to reduce negative feelings to a manageable level before you're ready to job-hunt.

Second, try to learn from the experience. You'll be a much more attractive job candidate if you can show that you've learned from the experience—whether your lesson is improved work habits or the need to choose a job where you can do work you're proud of.

Third, suggests Phil Elder, an interviewer for an insurance company, call the person who fired you and say something like this: "Look, I know you weren't pleased with the job I did at company X. I'm applying for a job at company Y now and the personnel director may call you to ask about me. Would you be willing to give me the chance to get this job, so that I can try to do things right this time?" All but the hardest of heart, says Elder, will give you one more chance. You won't get a glowing reference, but neither will the statement be so damning that no one will be willing to hire you.[10]

"I Don't Have Any Experience"

You can get experience in several ways:

- Take a fast-food job—and keep it: If you do well, you might be promoted to a supervisor within a year. Use every opportunity to learn about the management and financial aspects of the business.
- Volunteer: Coach a community little-league team, join the PTA, help at your local food bank, canvass for charity. If you work hard, you'll quickly get an opportunity to do more: manage a budget, write fundraising materials, and supervise other volunteers.
- Freelance: Design brochures, create websites, do tax returns for small businesses. Use your skills—for free, if you have to at first.
- Write: Create a portfolio of ads, instructions, or whatever documents are relevant for the field you want to enter. Ask a professional—an instructor, a local businessperson, someone from a professional organization—to critique them. Volunteer your services to local fundraising organizations and small businesses.

Pick something in which you interact with other people, so you can show you work well in an organization.

If you're in the job market now, think carefully about what you've really done. Write sentences using the action verbs in Table 25.1 in the next Module. Think about your experiences and skills development in courses, in volunteer work, in unpaid activities. Focus especially on your communications skills: problem solving, critical thinking, managing projects, working as part of a team, persuasive speaking, and writing. Solving a problem for a hypothetical firm in an accounting class, thinking critically about a report problem in business communication, working with a group in a marketing class, and communicating with people at the seniors' centre where you volunteer are all valuable experiences, even if no one paid you.

If you're not actually looking for a job but just need to create a resumé for this course, ask your instructor whether you may assume that you're graduating and add the things you hope to do between now and that time.

Language FOCUS

The most successful job hunters are prepared: they seek opportunities to impress others positively and they understand that everyone they meet is both a potential employer and a potential customer.

"I'm a Lot Older Than the Other Employees"

Mature workers remain in demand for their sophisticated interpersonal and communications abilities. Uninformed employers are concerned that older people won't be flexible, up to date, or willing to be supervised by someone younger. You can counter these fears:

- Keep up to date. Read trade journals; attend professional meetings.
- Learn the computer programs your field uses. Refer to technology in the resumé, job letter, and interview: "Yes, I saw the specifications for your new product on your website."
- Work with younger people, in classroom teams, in volunteer work, or on the job. Be able to cite specific cases where you've learned from young people and worked well with them.
- Use positive emphasis (Module 12). Talk about your ability to relate to mature customers, the valuable perspective you bring. Focus on recent events, not ones from twenty years ago.
- Show energy and enthusiasm to counter the stereotype that older people are tired and ill.

MODULE SUMMARY

- Begin your job search by assessing your priorities, abilities, and interests. Do this assessment in writing, to make it real, and to note the information that might go on your resume.

- Use directories, annual reports, recruiting literature, business periodicals, trade journals, and websites to get information about employers, and job search tips.

- The most effective way to find the job you want is to self-recruit. The second most effective way is through a referral. Both these methods depend on your ability to network.

- Information and referral interviews can help you tap into the **hidden job market**—jobs that are not advertised. Collect contact names by networking: talk to friends,

relatives, salespeople, and suppliers; do volunteer and community work. Ask for an **information interview** to find out what the daily work involves, and how you can best prepare to enter the field. Or schedule brief **referral interviews** to learn about current job opportunities in your field.

- Prepare carefully for these interviews: these people know other people, and can offer suggestions and other referrals.

- Use social networking sites discreetly. Join business/industry-related sites, get involved in online discussions, update your profile frequently, and use the site's technology to showcase your skills.

ASSIGNMENTS FOR MODULE 24

Questions for Critical Thinking

24.1 What networking sites would be most relevant for a career in your field? Why?

24.2 Identify three community and/or volunteer activities that would expand your networking opportunities.

24.3 Suggest three reasons how knowing the corporate culture of a potential employer can make your job search much more successful.

24.4 What strategies can you use to build a compelling digital dossier?

Exercises and Problems

24.5 Beginning Your Self-Inventory

Initiate the job-hunting process on the nextSteps.org Job Search site (www.nextsteps.ca/career/start.php) by completing the inventory questionnaire. Note the results as part of the process of knowing yourself.

24.6 Assessing your Digital Identity

Research your digital tattoo to discover what employers can readily find online about you.

As your instructor directs

a. Share your findings with a small group of students.

b. Summarize your findings in a memo to your instructor.

24.7 Networking

Contact a friend, family member, or acquaintance who is already in the workforce, asking about one or more of the following topics:

- What jobs in your field are available in your contact's organization?
- If a job is available, can your contact provide information, beyond the job listing, that will help you write a more detailed, persuasive letter? (Specify the kind of information you'd like to have.)
- Who else can your contact suggest who might be useful to you in your job search? (Ask about any organizations you're especially interested in.)

24.8 Networking with Social Media

Social media experts suggest specific strategies for online job networking. Read Dave Fleet's blog post "13 Ways Social Media Can Improve Your Career," or find your own expert advice on using social media for your job search.

As your instructor directs

- **a.** Establish or revise your professional online presence according to your expert's advice.
- **b.** Present your new or revised professional presence to other members of the class.
- **c.** Based on class feedback, revise your professional social media profile.
- **d.** Write an email to your instructor summarizing the results.

24.9 Gathering Information about an Industry

Use six recent issues of a trade journal to report on three to five trends, developments, or issues that are important in an industry.

As your instructor directs

- **a.** Share your findings with a small group of students.
- **b.** Summarize your findings in a memo to your instructor.
- **c.** Present your findings orally to the class.
- **d.** Email your findings to the other members of the class.
- **e.** Form a group with two other students to write a blog summarizing the results of this research.

24.10 Gathering Information about a Specific Organization

Gather printed information about a specific organization, using several of the following methods:

- Use the most current edition of *The Career Directory*.
- Check the company's website.
- Read the company's annual report.
- Talk to someone who works there.
- Pick up relevant information at your local board of trade or chamber of commerce.
- Read articles in trade publications and online at the *Globe and Mail*, *National Post*, *Wall Street Journal*, or *Financial Post* that mention the organization (check the indices).
- Get the names and addresses of its officers (from a directory or from the Web).
- Read recruiting literature provided by the company.

As your instructor directs

- **a.** Share your findings with a small group of students.
- **b.** Summarize your findings in a memo to your instructor.
- **c.** Present your findings orally to the class.
- **d.** Email your findings to the other members of the class.
- **e.** Form a group with two other students to write a blog summarizing the results of this research.

24.11 Conducting an Information Interview

Interview someone working in a field you're interested in. Use the questions listed in the module or the shorter list here:

- How did you get started in this field?
- What do you like about your job?
- What do you dislike about your job?
- What three other people could give me additional information about this job?

As your instructor directs

- **a.** Share the results of your interview with a small group of students.
- **b.** Write up your interview in a memo to your instructor.
- **c.** Present the results of your interview orally to the class.
- **d.** Email a summary of your interview to other members of your class.
- **e.** Write to the interviewee thanking him or her for taking the time to talk to you.

POLISHING YOUR PROSE

Using Details

Details are especially important in reader benefits (Module 11), reports, resumés, job applications, and sales letters. Customers or potential employers look for specific details to help them make decisions, such as

what makes your product better than the competition's or how your experience would help the reader. Here's an example:

I can offer you more than ten years of advertising experience, including five years of broadcast sales in Ottawa, where I generated more than $19 million in revenue, as well as three years with J. Walter Thompson, Toronto's leading advertising company. For the first four years of my career, I also wrote advertising copy, including hundreds of local and regional radio spots for such diverse products as cookies, cat food, fishing tackle, and children's toys. I also wrote print pieces, including the entire 15-month campaign for Vancouver-based "Uncle Bill's Electronic Bazaar," which increased sales by nearly 37 percent during that period.

Reader Benefits

What features or experiences make your product or service unique? Useful? Cost-effective?

Weak: With the Stereobooster, your car will sound great.

Better: The Stereobooster safely gives your car audio system a full 30 watts per channel of sheer sound excitement—double that of other systems on the market—all for under $50.

The Five Senses

Describe sight, sound, taste, touch, and smell. Some sensations are so powerful that they immediately conjure up thoughts or emotions—the smell of fresh coffee, the sound of ocean waves, the feeling of sunlight against the skin.

Concrete Nouns and Verbs

Concrete nouns and verbs are better than more general nouns and verbs combined with adjectives and adverbs. For instance, *manager* and *15 months* are more concrete than *the person in charge* or *a while*. Concrete words make meaning clear and vivid:

Weak: At my last job, I typed stuff.

Better: As a clerk typist II for Hughes and Associates, I typed hundreds of memos, letters, and reports.

Increase your vocabulary by reading a variety of materials. Keep a dictionary and thesaurus handy. Do crossword puzzles or computer word games to practise what you know.

Adjectives and Adverbs That Count

Omit or replace vague or overused adjectives and adverbs: *basically, some, very, many, a lot, kind of, sort of, partly, eventually*. Increasingly, novice writers are using *so* as an adjective, as in "He was so happy about the promotion." Exactly how happy is this?

Conversational English, Not Jargon or Obscure Words

In general, choose the more conversational option over jargon or obscure words: *exit, typical,* or *second to last* rather than *egress, quintessential,* or *penultimate*.

Exercises

Add details to the following sentences.

1. I work for a company.
2. The person in charge of our department wants some files.
3. Sometime in the future I will get a job in my field.
4. It's been a while since I went there.
5. Our product will help you.
6. There are lots of reasons why you should hire me.
7. This product is so much better than its competitors.
8. We will have a meeting in the afternoon.
9. My experience makes me a good candidate for this job.
10. We plan to travel to a couple of provinces sometime next month.

Check your answers to the odd-numbered exercises in the Polishing Your Prose Answer Key.

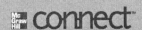

Practise and learn online with Connect. Connect allows you to practise important skills at your own pace and on your own schedule, with 24/7 online access to an eBook, practise quizzes, interactives, videos, study tools, and additional resources.

MODULE
25

Creating Persuasive Resumés

Learning Objectives

After reading and applying the information in Module 25, you'll be able to demonstrate

Knowledge of

LO1 Current resumé-writing practices

Skills to

LO2 Create the resumé that best showcases your qualifications

LO3 Make your experience relevant to employers

LO4 Increase the number of "hits" your resumé receives

Employability Skills 2000+ Checklist

Module content builds these Conference Board of Canada Employability Skills 2000+

Communicate

Manage Information

Learn Continuously

Demonstrate Positive Attitudes and Behaviours

A **resumé** summarizes your qualifications so persuasively that you get an interview. When you're in the job market, having a resumé prepares you for every opportunity. When you're employed, having a current resumé allows you to assess your skills' improvement; this ongoing inventory makes it easier for you to take advantage of other job opportunities that come up.

Even if you're several years away from job hunting, preparing a resumé now will make you more conscious of what to do in the next two or three years to make yourself a more attractive candidate. Writing a resumé is also an ego-building experience: the person who looks so good on paper is *you*!

FIGURE 25.1 **PAIBOC Questions for Analysis**

P	What are your ***purposes*** in creating a resumé? The resumé must display your knowledge, skills, and analytical abilities: you are recording your interpersonal and vocational aptitudes and shaping a persuasive story. Your ultimate purpose is to get the interview.
A	Who is your **audience**? Who will scan/read your resumé? What does your audience value, and how do you know? How can you create a resumé that will attract and hold your audience's attention?
I	What **information** should you include in your resumé? What information is the employer looking for? What do you know about the industry? The employer? What life/work experiences will make you stand out from other candidates? What keywords should you use to frame that information for immediate and maximum positive emphasis?
B	What communication and technical skills can you offer to **benefit** the potential employer immediately?
O	What audience **objections** do you anticipate? How can you create a resumé that stands out positively among all those others?
C	What **context** will affect your reader's response? Consider your relationship to the reader, the reader's values and expectations, the economy, recent organizational developments, current morale, and the time of year.

LO1 How Do Employers Read Resumés?

Your resumé can be screened in two ways: electronically or by a person.

If people do the reading, employers may skim the resumés quickly, putting them into two piles: "reject" and "maybe." In the first round, each resumé may get as little as 2.9 seconds of the reader's attention. Then the reader goes through the "maybe" pile again, weeding out more documents. If there are many resumés (and some companies get 2,000 a week), resumés may get only 10 to 30 seconds at this stage. After the initial pile has been culled, whether it's to one-half or one-hundredth of the initial pile, the remaining documents will be read more carefully to choose the people invited for interviews.

Alternatively, your resumé may be electronically scanned into a job-applicant tracking system. Then a computer does the first set of cuts. The employer specifies the keywords from the job description, listing the knowledge, skills, and abilities that the ideal applicant would have. Sometimes personal characteristics (e.g., *hard worker, good writer, willing to travel*) are included. The employer receives the resumés that match the keywords, arranged with the most "hits" first. The employer then chooses the interviewees.

LO2 How Can I Encourage the Employer to Pay Attention to My Resumé?

Show how your qualifications fit the job and the company.

Ex.
25.2
25.4–
25.6

You need both a paper resumé that's attractive to the human eye and an electronic resumé that serves your purposes in a job-applicant tracking system. You can do several things to increase the chances that a human being will pay attention to your resumé:

- Begin with a Skills or Summary statement: specifically describe your value to the organization (see Figure 25.3, Summary of Qualifications).
- Frame your skills and activities in measurable terms: "increased sales 10 percent"; "supervised five people"; "implemented a data entry system that saved the company $5,000."

Ex.
25.2
25.4

- Emphasize achievements that
  - ○ Are most relevant to the position for which you're applying
  - ○ Demonstrate your superiority to other applicants
  - ○ Are recent
- Use the keywords and technical terms of the industry and the organization; find these in the ad, in trade journals, and from job descriptions.
- Make your paper resumé attractive and readable by using
  - ○ **Plenty of white space:** Don't squeeze the margins to get more information onto a page.
  - ○ **A serif font:** Times New Roman, Century Schoolbook, or Bookman Old Style, for example.
- Left justify and bold the major headings.
- Include transferable skills: the ability to write and speak well, to identify and solve problems, to think critically and creatively, to work well independently and with others, to speak other languages, and to use a variety of computer programs.
- Design one resumé to appeal to the human eye and the second to be easily processed by an electronic scanner.
- Revise and edit your resumé to ensure it's error-free: grammar and spelling mistakes will cost you the interview.

The best resumés convey relevant details as concisely and attractively as possible. Most resumés use bullet points, omit *I*, and use sentence fragments that may be punctuated as complete sentences. Complete sentences are acceptable, as are *me* and *my*, if they are the briefest way to present information.

You may need to create several different resumés. But the more carefully you customize your resumé to a specific employer, the greater your chances for getting an interview.

What Kind of Resumé Should I Use?

Use the format that makes you look best.

Depending on their experience and the audience, people use one of three kinds of resumés: **chronological**, **functional**, or **combination**.

The chronological resumé summarizes what you have accomplished, starting with the most recent events and going backward: that is, using **reverse chronology**. It emphasizes dates. Figure 25.2 shows a chronological resumé. Use a chronological resumé when you have limited relevant work experience and your education and experience show

- A logical preparation for the position for which you're applying
- A steady progression leading to the present

EXPANDING A CRITICAL SKILL

Creating Attention-Getting Resumés

Keep your resumé simple and specific: you have only a few minutes to attract and hold a recruiter's attention. Follow these strategies to create a resumé that gets you the job interview:

Play with Layout and Design

If submitting a hard copy

- Use a laser printer to print your resumé on high-quality letter-sized paper. White paper is standard for business resumés; cream, pale grey, and parchment colours are also acceptable.
- Make your resumé readable and attractive:
  - ○ Use the Tables tool to create invisible columns.
  - ○ Use the same font throughout: Arial and Times New Roman are business standards.
  - ○ Vary font size: use 12-point for headings, and 11-point type for the text to get more on a page.
  - ○ Bold and italicize for emphasis; use bullets in lists.
  - ○ Highlight your desktop publishing skills: try smaller margins; use lines or borders.
  - ○ Use enough white space to make your resumé easy to read.
- Explore resumé templates to expand your range of options.

If emailing your resumé

- Attach it as a Word or PDF document.

- Save the document with your name included in the filename so that the recruiter can easily retrieve it among others.

Consider the Content

Employers want to interview eligible candidates. Ensure your resumé emphasizes your eligibility.

- Highlight skills relevant to the position and the organization.
- Be specific: reframe experiences into skills; provide facts and numbers.
- Be clear: use short, concrete nouns, and active verbs to describe your skills.
- Be honest. Even if potential employers don't check—and increasingly they do—lies and exaggerations are often glaringly obvious.

Proofread

Employers assume that the resumé represents your best work. Proofread, and then have at least two other people proofread for you, to ensure the document is perfect. Especially check

- Spelling of your college, university, and your employers
- Parallelism (Module 8)
- Consistency: headings, bullets, abbreviations
- Dates
- Phone numbers, email addresses, and URLs

FIGURE 25.2   **A Chronological Resumé**

Mohammed Shafer
210 Steeles Avenue West, Brampton, ON L6Y 2K3
905.555.3828 mshafe@bell.live

Objective

To find a challenging information technology position where my communication and technical
skills can make a contribution

Profile

Detail-oriented, analytical problem-solver
Experienced in customer service and negotiating skills
Experienced LAN, Internet, and Intranet user
Hardware certified: IBM and MAC
Trained in WHMIS and MSDS
Work well with others, without supervision, and to deadlines

Education

| 2013 | Diploma | Chemical Engineering Technology Co-op Program |
| | | Sheridan Institute, Brampton, ON |

Graduated with a GPA of 3.96/4.0

Work Experience

| 2009–2013 Summers | Assembly Line | FAN Personnel Solutions Brampton, ON |
| 2008–2013 Summers | Property maintenance | Self-employed |

Hobbies and Interests

Carpentry, electrical wiring, plumbing, canoeing, hiking, hockey

References

Upon request

Resumé
emphasizes
skills to
compensate
for limited
work
experience

The **functional resumé** emphasizes the applicant's most important (to the reader) job titles and
responsibilities, or functions, regardless of chronology. Use the functional/combination resumé if

- Your work experiences match the position responsibilities.
- Your skills and expertise match the position requirements.

- Your education and experience are not the usual route to the position for which you're applying.
- You want to de-emphasize your formal education.

FIGURE 25.3   **A Functional Resumé**

Dennis Crawford
65 Dunnet Drive
Barrie, ON L4N 0J6
705.555.4807
dcrawford@address.ca

Summary of Qualifications

- A highly skilled executive sales professional specializing in the CCTV/Video Surveillance marketplace
- Inducted into the company's President's Club four times for exceeding sales by 115% to 149%

Recognized for achievements in

- Regional & National Account Management
- Sales & Marketing Strategies
- Consultative Sales
- Product Management & Promotion

- Project Management
- Technical Sales Training
- Systems Design & Implementation
- Forecasting & Budgets

Professional Experience

Panasonic Canada Inc., Mississauga, ON
A global leader in consumer and industrial electronics manufacturing and sales

National Account Manager, Professional Imaging & Display Solutions Group *(2012–2013)*
Identified and managed high-profile national re-seller accounts while developing new growth opportunities through strategic networking with large national end-user accounts within Canada

- Developed a new national sales and marketing strategy while managing the Panasonic sales activities of 3 high-profile national re-seller accounts with over 35 sales professionals between them
- Identified, engaged, and closed new business opportunities with national re-seller accounts for a projected increase in sales of $500K within year one
- Successfully presented B2B strategies to high-profile end-user accounts securing net new business in excess of $1.5 million for select re-seller accounts
- Consultant to professional engineers, architects, sales professionals, and end users for the design and implementation of complex video solutions that exceed customer expectations
- Key liaison and consultant to product manager for industry trade shows and national marketing initiatives, often collaborating on booth design, marketing concepts, and product presentations for large industry trade shows, national technical sales seminars, and new product launches

Regional Account Manager, Central Division
Professional Imaging & Display Solutions Group *(2004–2012)*
Identified and managed regional re-seller accounts while developing new growth opportunities through strategic networking with Ontario regional and national end user accounts

- Developed sales and marketing strategies that successfully managed the Panasonic sales activities of 14 regional re-seller accounts with over 80 sales professionals
- Increased sales and market share within a territory that represented 40% of the department's annual sales forecast and budget
- Presented B2B strategies to several high-profile end-user and regional accounts resulting in a P.O. for over $1 million, setting a new record within the department
- Successfully organized, managed, and led an offsite national sales meeting on behalf of National Sales & Marketing Manager, opening channels of communication to a new level within the department; still considered by my peers to be the most effective and constructive sales meeting of record for the department
- Created and led successful product and sales training seminars, presenting at industry trade shows and technical product launches across Canada. Educated over 100 sales personnel and several hundred end users and consultants on the benefits of technology and products offered by Panasonic Canada Inc.

FIGURE 25.3   **A Functional Resumé (continued)**

Dennis Crawford
65 Dunnet Drive
Barrie, ON L4N 0J6
705.555.4807
dcrawford@address.ca

Product Manager, Professional Imaging & Display Solutions Group *(2003–2004)*
Technical product sales liaison among Panasonic factories, internal sales, service, and upper management
representatives, external sales, and end-user clientele

- Redesigned, developed, and deployed a struggling national product training program targeted at over
  35 Panasonic re-sellers with sales representatives in excess of 150 people; several hundred end users,
  consultants, and engineers; and over a dozen internal sales, service, and management staff across Canada
- Developed and presented strategies to factory representatives based on competitive product and market
  data, resulting in a more focused approach to product development for the North American market
- Managed product promotion and Regional Account Manager's involvement at industry trade shows
  both locally and nationally, aiding in the increase of product awareness and knowledge of our sales and
  customer base
- Successfully provided pre- and post-technical sales and system design support to over 35 re-sellers
  and three distribution accounts with a combined sales force of over 200 people, and over a dozen
  Panasonic internal sales, marketing, and technical service support people

KM Video & Security, Mississauga, ON *(2000–2004)*
*An industry leader in the design and implementation of complex video surveillance systems for medium and large
businesses*

Service Technician, CCTV Products *(2002–2004)*
Technical service representative responsible for maintaining complex video solutions for KM clientele

- Maintained a high level of customer service support by successfully diagnosing and repairing
  complex system/product faults, effectively reducing system downtime and maintaining the
  integrity of security solution
- Facilitated open communication between sales and customer service departments, resulting in more
  efficient customer service for our key clientele
- Designed, developed, and maintained weekly/monthly/yearly service contract schedule for key
  customers and successfully delegated work orders to service technicians for service contract clientele,
  increasing productivity by over 25%, which increased sales

Installation Technician, CCTV Products *(2000–2002)*
Installed complex video surveillance solutions

- Team lead, responsible for the installation and commissioning of complex video surveillance solutions
- Consultant to sales staff regarding installation estimates and project management, ensuring efficient use
  of installer's time and meeting strict deadlines to ensure project profitability
- Trainer of end users, internal sales people, and service staff on the operation of complex video solutions

Education

York University, Schulich School of Business

Sheridan College, School of Applied Arts & Technology
Architectural Technician Diploma (2001–2003)

Panasonic Canada Inc.

Canadian Professional Sales Association

FIGURE 25.4   **A Combination/Skills Resumé for Changing Jobs**

On the first page of a skills resumé, put skills directly related to the job for which you're applying.

The centred format is eye-catching but it can be hard to read. Here, bold headings draw the reader's eye.

Marcella G. Cope

370 Mahon Avenue
Vancouver, B.C. V7M 3E1
250-555-1997
mcope@postbox.com

Objective

To help create high-quality CD-ROM products in Metatec's New Media Solutions Division

Put company's name in objective.

Editing and Proofreading Experience

- **Edited** a textbook published by Simon & Schuster, revising with attention to format, consistency, coherence, document integrity, and document design.
- **Proofed** training and instructor manuals, policy statements, student essays and research papers, internal documents, and promotional materials.
- **Worked with authors** in a variety of fields including English, communication, business, marketing, economics, education, history, sociology, biology, agriculture, computer science, law, and medicine to revise their prose and improve their writing skills by giving them oral and written feedback.

Writing Experience

- **Wrote** training and instructor manuals, professional papers, and letters, memos, and reports.
- **Co-authored** the foreword to a forthcoming textbook (Fall 2012) from NCTE press.
- **Contributed** to a textbook forthcoming (Fall 2012) from Bedford Books/St. Martin's Press.

Computer Experience

- **Designed** a Web page using Microsoft Front Page (www.cohums.ohio-state.edu/english/People/Bracken.1/Sedgwick/)
- **Learned and used** a variety of programs on both Macintosh and PC platforms:
    Word processing and spreadsheets
    Microsoft Project
    FrontPage
    PageMaker
    Aspects (a form for online synchronous discussion)
    Storyspace (a hypertext writing environment)
    PowerPoint
    Email

Computer experience is crucial for almost every job. Specify the software and hardware you've worked with.

Other Business and Management Experience

- **Developed** policies, procedures, and vision statements.
- **Supervised** new staff members in a mentoring program.
- **Coordinated** program and individual schedules, planned work and estimated costs, set goals, and evaluated progress and results.
- **Member of team that directed** the nation's largest first-year writing program.

FIGURE 25.4   **A Combination/Skills Resumé for Changing Jobs (continued)**

Marcella G. Cope

Page 2

Employment History

- **Graduate Teaching Associate,** Department of English, University of Victoria, September 2008–Present. Taught Intermediate and First-Year Composition.
- **Writing Consultant,** University Writing Centre, Simon Fraser University, January–April 2007
- **Program Administrator,** First-Year Writing Program, University of Victoria, September 2008–January 2012

Honours

- **Phi Kappa Phi Honour Society,** inducted 2008. Membership based on performance in top 10 percent of graduate students nationwide.
- **Letters of Commendation,** 2003. Issued by the Director of Graduate Studies in recognition of outstanding achievement.
- **Dean's List**

Education

- **Master of Arts,** June 2013, the University of Victoria, Victoria, B.C. Cumulative GPA: 4.0/4.0
- **Bachelor of Arts,** June 2012, Simon Fraser University, Burnaby, B.C. Graduated with Honours

The **combination/skills resumé** (Figure 25.4) emphasizes skills you've acquired through work experience. Use a skills resumé when

- You want to combine experience from paid jobs, activities or volunteer work, and courses to show the extent of your experience in transferable and technical skills: administration, finance, public speaking, and so on.
- Your education and experience do not provide the usual route to the position for which you're applying.
- You're changing fields.
- Your recent work history might create the wrong impression (e.g., it has gaps, shows a demotion, shows job-hopping, etc.).

How Do Resumé Formats Differ?

They highlight you differently, depending on your experiences, your purpose (the job you're applying for), and your audience.

A chronological resumé, such as the one in Figure 25.2, focuses on *when,* then *what,* and emphasizes academic qualifications. Experience is organized by date, with the most recent job first. The functional resumé (Figure 25.3) highlights the applicant's qualifications according to relevant job functions or responsibilities. Extensive experience, not dates or academic degrees, is the focus. Seasoned and highly qualified applicants use this format.

A combination/skills resumé, such as the one in Figure 25.4, summarizes experience and acquired skills needed for the job. Under each heading, the resumé lists, in order of importance, paid and unpaid work (in classes, activities, and community groups). An Employment History section lists job titles (or functions), employers, city, and province.

Chronological Resumés

In a chronological resumé, start with the heading most relevant to the reader. Under Work Experience or Employment History, include employment dates, position or job title, organization, city, province, and other details: seasonal, full- or part-time status, job duties, special responsibilities, and promotions within companies. Include unpaid jobs and self-employment if they provided relevant skills (e.g., supervising people, budgeting, planning, persuading). If you've held co-op or intern placements (very significant to employers), include these under a separate heading such as Co-operative Placement Experience.

Normally, go back as far as the summer after high school. Include earlier jobs if you started working somewhere before graduating from high school but continued working there after graduation. However, give minimal detail about high school jobs. If you worked full-time after high school, make that clear.

If, as an undergraduate, you've earned a substantial portion of your college or university expenses, say so, either under Experience or in the Interpersonal or Skills Profile section with which you can begin the resumé (graduate students are expected to support themselves):

- These jobs paid 40 percent of my university expenses.
- Paid for 65 percent of expenses with jobs, scholarships, and loans.

Omit information about low-level jobs, unless they illustrate experience important to your reader.

Use details to display your attitudes, abilities, or talents. Tell how many people you trained or supervised, how much money you budgeted or raised. Describe the aspects of the job you did.

Too vague:	2010–2013	Sales Manager, the *Daily Collegian*, Mount Royal University, AB. Supervised staff; promoted ad sales.
Good details:	2010–2013	Sales Manager, the *Daily Collegian*, Mount Royal University, AB. Supervised 22-member sales staff; helped recruit, interview, and select staff; assigned duties and scheduled work; recommended best performer for promotion. Motivated staff to increase paid ad sales 10 percent over previous year's sales.

Verbs or gerunds (the *-ing* form of verbs) always create a more dynamic image than do nouns, so use them on resumés that will be read by people rather than computers. (Rules for scannable resumés to be read by computers come later in this module.) In the revisions below, nouns, verbs, and gerunds are in bold type.

Nouns:	2010–2013	Chair, Income Tax Assistance Committee, Winnipeg, MB. Responsibilities: **recruitment** of volunteers; flyer **design**, **writing**, and **distribution** for **promotion** of program; **speeches** to various community groups and nursing homes to advertise the service.
Verbs:	2010–2013	Chair, Income Tax Assistance Committee, Winnipeg, MB. **Recruited** volunteers for the program. **Designed**, **wrote**, and **distributed** a flyer to promote the program; **made presentations** to various community groups and nursing homes to advertise the service.
Gerunds:	2010–2013	Chair, Income Tax Assistance Committee, Winnipeg, MB. Responsibilities included **recruiting** volunteers for the program; **designing**, **writing**, and **distributing** a flyer to promote the program; and **presenting** to various community groups and nursing homes to advertise the service.

Note that the items in the list must be in parallel structure. Table 25.1 lists action verbs that work well in resumés.

TABLE 25.1   **Action Verbs for Resumés**

accomplished	calibrated	debugged	entertained	incorporated
achieved	canvassed	decided	equipped	induced
acted	carried out	decreased	estimated	inducted
adapted	categorized	dedicated	evaluated	influenced
addressed	caused	defined	examined	informed
acquired	changed	delegated	exchanged	initiated
activated	charted	delineated	expanded	inquired
adjusted	clarified	delivered	expedited	inspected
administered	classified	demonstrated	experimented	instituted
adopted	collaborated	depicted	explained	instructed
advised	collected	derived	explored	insured
advanced	combined	described	extracted	integrated
aided	communicated	designed	fabricated	interfaced
allocated	compiled	detailed	facilitated	interpreted
altered	completed	detected	filed	interviewed
analyzed	composed	determined	filled	introduced
announced	computed	developed	financed	invented
answered	conceived	devised	finalized	investigated
appointed	conducted	diagnosed	formed	justified
appraised	concluded	differentiated	forwarded	labelled
approved	condensed	directed	founded	licensed
arranged	conferred	discharged	furnished	located
ascertained	constructed	discussed	gathered	maintained
assembled	consulted	dispensed	generated	managed
assessed	contracted	displayed	graded	manipulated
assigned	contributed	disseminated	graduated	manufactured
assisted	controlled	documented	granted	mapped
assured	converted	drafted	guarded	marketed
attended	cooperated	earned	guided	maximized
audited	co-ordinated	edited	handled	measured
authorized	corresponded	educated	helped	mechanized
automated	corrected	elected	identified	mediated
began	costed	eliminated	illustrated	minimized
billed	counselled	employed	implemented	mobilized
budgeted	created	engaged	imported	modelled
built	cultivated	engineered	improved	modified
calculated	customized	ensured	improvised	monitored

TABLE 25.1   **Action Verbs for Resumés (continued)**

motivated	preserved	regulated	served	transferred
negotiated	presided	related	set	transformed
observed	prevented	released	set up	translated
obtained	priced	removed	settled	transmitted
officiated	printed	reorganized	sold	transported
operated	produced	repaired	solicited	transposed
orchestrated	programmed	reported	started	treated
organized	projected	represented	stimulated	tutored
oversaw	protected	researched	studied	updated
packaged	provided	responded	strengthened	upgraded
paid	published	restored	submitted	used
participated	purchased	retained	summarized	utilized
performed	qualified	retrieved	supervised	validated
persuaded	questioned	reviewed	supplied	valued
planned	rated	revised	supported	verified
positioned	received	sampled	surveyed	visited
practised	recommended	saved	taught	worked
precipitated	recorded	scheduled	tested	wrote
predicted	rectified	screened	theorized	
prepared	reduced	searched	timed	
prescribed	referred	secured	traced	
presented	refined	selected	trained	

Functional Resumés

The functional resumé focuses on the *what*; this format provides the flexibility to highlight relevant job responsibilities or functions, and to include a variety of experiences. Mature, highly skilled people with the right job credentials use the functional resumé to describe their extensive skills.

Begin with Career Achievements or Career Highlights, where you summarize your primary professional accomplishments. The Employment History is most important: describe your work responsibilities and subsequent skills as they relate to the position for which you are applying. Later in the resumé, identify conferences, clubs, and professional associations in reverse chronology to demonstrate your industry currency. Unless applying for a job for which your education credentials are paramount (like an academic position) and you have those credentials, place Education near the end of this format.

Combination and Skills Resumés

Combination/skills resumés use the *skills* or *aspects* of the job you are applying for as headings, rather than the category title or the dates of the jobs you've held (as in a chronological resumé). For entries under each skill, combine experience from paid jobs, unpaid work, classes, activities, and community service.

Use headings that reflect the jargon of the job for which you're applying: *logistics* rather than *planning* for a technical job; *procurement* rather than *purchasing* for a civilian job with the military. Figure 25.4 shows a skills resumé for someone who is changing fields. Marcella suggests that she already knows a lot about the field she hopes to enter by using its jargon for the headings.

Try to have least three headings related to the job in a combination resumé. Give enough detail to convince the reader that you have developed the requisite skill sets through a variety of experience. Put the most important category—**from the reader's perspective**—first.

A job description can give you ideas for headings. Possible headings and subheadings for skills resumés include

Administration	**Communication**
Alternatives or subheadings:	Alternatives or subheadings:
Coordinating	Conducting Meetings
Evaluating	Editing
Implementing	Fundraising
Negotiating	Interviewing
Planning	Speaking
Keeping Records	Negotiating
Scheduling	Persuading
Solving Problems	Proposal Writing
Budgeting	Report Writing
Supervising	

Many jobs require a mix of skills. Include the skills that you know will be needed in the job you want.

In a combination resumé, list your paid jobs under Employment History near the end of the resumé (see Figure 25.4). List only job title, employer, city, province, and dates. Omit details about what you did, since you will have already used them under Experience.

Checkpoint

A **chronological resumé** summarizes what you did in a timeline, starting with the most recent events and going backward (**reverse chronology**). Use a chronological resumé when your education and experience

- Are logical preparations for the position for which you're applying
- Show a steady progression leading to the present

Use a **functional** or **combination resumé** in these cases:

- Your education and experience are not the usual route to the position.
- You're changing fields.
- You want to combine experience from paid jobs, activities, volunteer work, and courses.
- Your recent work history might create the wrong impression.

What Parts of Resumé Formats Are the Same?

Increasingly all resumés begin with an attention-grabbing heading, such as Career Achievements, Career Highlights, Communication and Technical Skills, or Interpersonal Profile.

Every resumé should have an overview of your communication skills and an Education section. Career Objective, Honours and Awards, and References are optional.

Career Objective

Some job coaches and recruiters consider Career Objective statements irrelevant, and a waste of valuable space and placement.[1]

However, if you want to include a career objective statement, write it like the job description the employer might use in a job listing. Keep your statement brief—two or three lines at most. Tell what you want to do and what level of responsibility you want to hold.

Ineffective career objective:	To offer a company my excellent academic foundation in hospital technology and my outstanding skills in oral and written communication.
Better career objective:	Selling state-of-the-art Siemens medical equipment.

Including the employer's name in the objective is a nice touch.

As an alternative to writing a career objective statement, put the job title or field under your name:

Joan Larson Ooyen	Terence Garvey	David R. Lunde
Marketing	Technical Writer	Corporate Fitness Director

Career Achievements

Highlight proficiency in foreign and computer languages, and identify your outstanding communication skills, in order of importance to the reader:

- Excellent researcher, writer, and editor
- Conversant in all software applications
- Multilingual: speak, read, and write English, Arabic, and Punjabi
- Proficient in Internet, Intranet, and LAN usage

The functional or combination resumé uses career achievements to highlight measurable accomplishments:

- Started seasonal landscaping business Spring 2009; by Spring 2012 employed six full-time employees, generating revenues of $300,000
- Generated revenue of $2.5 million over quota as Western Division Sales Manager
- Implemented employee-mentoring program resulting in a 40% increase in retention
- Created new assembly procedure that cut production costs by 25%
- Developed procedures manual now used in every national and international office

Education

Education can be your first major category if you've just earned (or are about to earn) a degree, if you have a degree that is essential or desirable for the position you're seeking, or if you lack relevant work experience. Put Education later if you need all of page one to emphasize your skills and experience, or if you lack a degree that other applicants may have.

Include summer school if you took optional courses or extra electives to graduate early. Include study abroad, even if you didn't earn college credits. If you got a certificate for international study, give the name of the program and explain the significance of the certificate.

Professional certifications can be listed under Education, under or after your name, or in a separate category.

Include your GPA only if it's good. Because grade point systems vary, specify what your GPA is based on: "3.4/4.0" means 3.4 on a 4.0 scale. If your GPA is under 3.0 on a 4.0 scale, use words rather than numbers: "B average." If your GPA isn't impressive, calculate your average in your major and your average for your last 60 hours. If these are higher than your overall GPA, consider using them.

List the following in reverse chronological order: each degree earned; field of study; date; school, city, province, or state of any graduate work; short courses and professional certification courses; university, college, community college, or school from which you transferred.

> B.S. in personnel management, June 2012, University of Waterloo, Waterloo, ON
>
> A.S. in office management, June 2012, Georgian College, Barrie, ON

To fill a page, you can also list selected courses, using short descriptive titles rather than course numbers. Use a subhead such as "Courses Related to Major" or "Courses Related to Financial Management" that will allow you to list all the courses (including psychology, speech, and business communication) that will help you in the job for which you're applying.

> Bachelor of Science in management, May 2012, University of Guelph, Guelph, ON
>
> GPA: 3.8/4.0
>
> Courses Related to Management:
>
> | Personnel Administration | Business Decision-Making |
> | --- | --- |
> | Finance | International Business |
> | Management I and II | Marketing |
> | Accounting I and II | Legal Environment of Business |
> | Business Report Writing | Business Speaking |
>
> Salutatorian, Eastview High School, June 2008, Toronto, ON

A third option is to list the number of hours in various subjects, especially if the combination of courses qualifies you for the position for which you're applying.

> B.Sc. in marketing, May 2012, St. Francis Xavier University, Nova Scotia
>
> 30 hours in Marketing
>
> 15 hours in Spanish
>
> 9 hours in Human Resources Management

Honours and Awards

The Honours and Awards heading creates a positive impression even when the reader skims the resumé. Include this category for all awards that reflect your drive for achievement and recognition.

Include the following kinds of entries in this category:

- Listings in recognition books (e.g., *Who's Who in Web Design*)
- Academic honour societies (Specify the nature of Greek-letter honour societies so the reader understands that these are more than social clubs.)
- Fellowships and scholarships
- Awards given by professional societies and community associations
- Major awards given by civic groups
- Music accreditation and awards; varsity letters; selection to provincial or national sports teams; finishes in provincial, national, or Olympic meets (These might also go under Activities but may look more impressive under Honours. Put them under one category or the other—not both.)

Build your praise portfolio: keep a file of letters, emails, thank-you cards, and notes praising your job performance.

Omit honours such as "Miss Congeniality" that work against the professional image you want your resumé to create.

As a new graduate, you should try to put Honours on page one. In a skills and functional or combination resumé, place Honours and Awards on page two or three, depending on the space your Work Experience takes.

References

Ex. 25.3

Including references on a separate page anticipates the employer's needs and removes a potential barrier to your getting the job. You can omit this category on your resumé, however, since prospective employers now take it for granted that applicants will supply references when required.

When you list references, use three to five. Include at least one professor and at least one employer or advisor—someone who can comment on your work habits and leadership skills.

Always ask the person's permission to list him or her as a reference. Don't say, "May I list you as a reference?" Instead, say, "Can you speak specifically and positively about my work?" Jog the person's mind by taking along copies of work you did for him or her and a copy of your current resumé. Tell your references what points you'd like them to stress in a letter.

Keep your list of references up to date. If it's been a year or more since you asked someone, ask again—and tell the person about your recent achievements.

References the reader knows are by far the most impressive. In a functional and skills resumé, choose people to recommend you who can testify to your abilities in the most important skills areas.

What Should I Do If the Standard Categories Don't Fit?

Create new ones.

Create headings that match your qualifications: Computer Skills, Military Experience, Foreign Languages, Summer and Part-Time Jobs, Marketing Experience, Publications, Exhibitions, Professional Associations.

The items Education and Experience (if you use the latter term) always stand as separate categories, even if you have only one item under each heading. Combine other headings so that you have at least two long or three short items under each heading. For example, if you're in one honour society, two social clubs, and on one athletic team, combine them all under Activities and Honours.

If you have more than seven items under a heading, consider using subheadings. For example, a student who had a great many activities might divide them into Student Government, Other Campus or Extracurricular Activities, and Community Service.

Put your strongest categories near the top and at the bottom of the first page. If you have impressive work experience, you might want to put that category first after your name, Education in the middle of the page, and your address at the bottom.

Should I Limit My Resumé Length?

Don't limit the length if you have many qualifications.

The average resumé is now two pages, unless you need more space to emphasize your qualifications. Executive search firm founder Michael Stern (Michael Stern Associates, Toronto) says readability always trumps conciseness: "Someone with a lot of experience and expertise is better going to three pages than trying to fit everything on two pages of tiny, hard-to-read type."[2]

If you do use more than one page, the second page should have at least 10 to 12 lines. Use a second sheet stapled to the first so that readers who skim know that there's more. Leave less important information for the second page. Put your name and "Page 2" or "Cont." on the second page. If the pages become separated, you want the reader to know whom the qualifications belong to and that the second page is not your whole resumé.

LO1 LO4 How Do I Create a Scannable Resumé?

Take out all the formatting.

Figure 25.5 shows an example of a scannable resumé. To increase the chances that the resumé is scanned correctly

- Use a standard typeface: Helvetica, Futura, Optima, Times Roman, New Century Schoolbook, Courier, Univers, or Bookman.[3]
- Use 12- or 14-point type.
- Use the "ragged right" style—that is, do not use *justification* (which stretches each line out to the same length). Scanners can't always handle the extra spaces between words and letters that justification creates.
- Don't italicize or underline words—even for titles of books or newspapers that grammatically require such treatment.

FIGURE 25.5   **A Scannable Resumé**

Jerry A. Jackson

Keywords: family financial management; financial planning; retirement planning; investment sales; computer modelling; competitive; self-starter; hard worker; responsible; self-managing; collegiate athletics; sales experience

Campus Address
St. Mary's Road
Winnipeg, SK R2H 1J2
(306) 555-5718
Email address: jjackson@ccw.sk.ca
Created a Web page on saving for life goals, such as a home, children's education, and retirement:
http://hotmail.com/jackson.2495/home.htm

Permanent Address
2105 East Hill Avenue
Saskatoon, SK S7J 3C8
(306) 555-4108

Summary of Qualifications
High energy. Played sports during two years of college. Started two businesses.
Sales experience. Sold both clothing and investments successfully.
Presentation skills. In individual and group presentations, spoke to groups ranging from 2 to 75 people. Gave informative, persuasive, and inspirational talks.
Financial experience. Knowledgeable about stocks and bonds, especially energy and telecommunication companies.
Computer experience. Microsoft Word, Excel, SPSS, PowerPoint, and Dreamweaver.
Experience creating Web pages.

Education
A.A.S. in Finance, May 2012, Community College of Winnipeg, Winnipeg, MB
B Average
Comprehensive courses related to program provide not only the basics of family financial management but also skills in communication, writing, speaking, small groups, and computer modelling
Intermediate Accounting I and II
Business Writing
Consumer Finance
Financial Management
Interpersonal Communication
Investments
Microeconomics
Presentation Skills
Public Speaking
Report and Technical Writing
Sociology of Marriage and Family
Statistics

Sports Experience
Intramural Hockey Team (Champions, Winter 2011)
Two-Year Varsity Letterman, Community College of Winnipeg
Men's NCAA Division II Basketball

Use 12- or 14-point type in a standard typeface. Here, Times Roman is used.

In keywords, use labels and terms that employers might include in job listings.

Give as much information as you like. The computer doesn't care how long the document is.

Don't use columns. Scanners can't handle them.

FIGURE 25.5   **A Scannable Resumé (continued)**

Experience
Financial Sales Representative, Primerica Company, Winnipeg, MB, February 2010–present. Work with clients to plan investment strategies; recommend specific investments, including stocks, bonds, mutual funds, and annuities.

Entrepreneur, Winnipeg, MB, and Saskatoon, SK, September 2005–January 2010. Created a saleable product, secured financial backing, found a manufacturer, supervised production, and sold product—12 dozen T-shirts at a $5.25 profit each—to help pay for school expenses.

Landscape Maintenance Supervisor, Saskatoon, SK, Summers 2003–2008. Formed a company to cut lawns, put up fences, fertilize, garden, and paint houses. Hired, fired, trained, motivated, and paid friends to complete jobs. Managerial experience.

Collector and Repairman, ACN Inc., Saskatoon, SK, Summer 2008. Collected and counted up to $10 000 a day. Worked with technicians to troubleshoot and repair electronic and coin mechanisms of video and pinball games, cigarette machines, and jukeboxes. Drove company cars and trucks throughout Saskatoon metro area to collect cash, and move and repair machines.

Willing to relocate
Willing to travel
Canadian citizen

Don't justify margins. Doing so creates extra spaces that confuse scanners.

- Put the text in bold to make sure letters don't touch each other. Then remove the bold.
- Don't use lines, boxes, script, leader dots, or borders.
- Don't use two-column format, indents, or centred text.
- Put each phone number on a separate line.
- Use plenty of white space.
- Don't fold or staple the pages.
- Don't write anything by hand on your resumé.
- Send a laser copy. Stray marks defeat scanners.
- To increase the number of matches or "hits"
  - Use a Keywords section under your name, address, and phone numbers. Put the following in this section:
    - Degrees, job field or title, accomplishments
    - Interpersonal strengths and attitudes: *dependable, skilled in time management, leadership, sense of responsibility.*[4]
- Use industry buzzwords and jargon, even if redundant. For example, "Web page design and HTML coding" will "match" either "Web" or "HTML" as a keyword.
  - Use nouns. Some systems don't handle verbs well.
  - Use common headings such as Summary of Qualifications, Strengths, Certifications, as well as Education, Experience, and so on.
- Use as many pages as necessary.
- Mention specific software programs (e.g., Adobe Dreamweaver, Microsoft FrontPage) that you've used.
- Be specific and quantifiable. "Managed $2 million building materials account" will generate more hits than "manager" or "managerial experience." Listing Microsoft FrontPage as a skill won't help as much as "Used Microsoft FrontPage to design an interactive website for a national fashion retailer, with links to information about style trends, current store promotions, employment opportunities, and an online video fashion show."
- Join honour societies, and professional and trade organizations, since they're often used as keywords.[5]

- Spell out Greek-letter societies (the scanner will mangle Greek characters, even if your computer has them): "Pi Sigma Alpha Honour Society." For English words, spell out the organization name; follow it with the abbreviation in parentheses: "Canadian University Press (CUP)." That way, the resumé will be tagged whether the recruiter searches for the full name or the acronym.
- Put everything in the resumé, rather than "saving" some material for the cover letter. Although some applicant tracking systems can search for keywords in cover letters and other application materials, most only extract information from the resumé, even though they store the other papers. The length of the resumé doesn't matter.

LO1 LO4 How Should I Prepare an Online Resumé?

Follow these guidelines.

In your Web resumé,

Employability Skills

- Include an email link at the top of the resumé under your name.
- Omit your street addresses and phone numbers. (A post office box is okay.) Employers who find your resumé on the Web will have the technology to email you.
- Consider having links under your name and email address to the various parts of your resumé. Use keywords and phrases that tell the viewer what you offer: *Marketing Experience.*
- Link to other pages that provide more information about you (a list of courses, a report you have written) but not to organizations (your university, an employer) that shift emphasis away from your credentials.
- Be businesslike: link to other pages only if they highlight or demonstrate your abilities, and convey the same professional image as your resumé.
- Put your strongest qualification immediately after your name and email address. If the first screen doesn't interest readers, they won't scroll through the rest of the resumé.
- Specify the job you want.
- Specify city and province for educational institutions and employers.
- Use lists, indentations, and white space to create visual variety.
- Proofread the resumé carefully.

MODULE SUMMARY

- Your resumé should fill at least one page. Use two or more pages if you have extensive experience and activities.
- Make the resumé attractive and readable: use plenty of white space, bold headings, and revise and edit to perfection.
- Emphasize your key points:
  - Put them in headings
  - Use keywords
  - List them vertically
  - Provide details
- Emphasize information that is
  - Relevant to the job you want
  - Expressed in industry- and ad-related language
  - Specific about how you can contribute to the job

- Resumés use sentence fragments. Make items concise and parallel. Emphasize action verbs and gerunds.
- The **chronological** resumé summarizes your experiences and activities in a timeline, starting with the most recent events and going backward. It emphasizes degrees, dates, and job titles. Use a chronological resumé when your education and experience
  - Provide a logical preparation for the position
  - Show a steady progression leading to the present
- **Functional** and **skills** resumés emphasize your experiences and applied skills. Use a skills resumé when
  - Your education and experience are not the usual route to the position for which you are applying
  - You are changing fields

○ You want to highlight the extent of your experience from a combination of paid jobs and community and volunteer work

○ Your recent work history may create the wrong impression (has gaps, indicates a demotion, shows job-hopping, etc.)

- To create a scannable resumé, create a plain text using industry jargon, buzzwords, and acronyms.
- In a Web resumé, put your strongest qualification(s) first, and specify the position you want. Omit street addresses and phone numbers, consider having links to parts of the resumé, and proofread carefully.

ASSIGNMENTS FOR MODULE 25

Questions for Critical Thinking

25.1 How would you create a Skills Statement for Mohammed Shaffer's resumé (Figure 25.2)?

25.2 How would you quantify an important transferable skill you have developed? Choose one transferable skill you know would benefit any employer and describe it in measurable terms.

25.3 When would you consider creating a video resumé?

Exercises and Problems

25.4 Analyzing Job Postings

1. Find three job postings (print or electronic) for an entry-level position you are interested in.
2. For each job posting, identify the keyword descriptors, including those for interpersonal, intrapersonal, communication, technological, and technical skills.
3. Create a list of these keywords to use for your headings and information for Exercises 25.5 though 25.10.

25.5 Analyzing Your Accomplishments

1. List the 10 accomplishments that give you the most personal satisfaction—perhaps achievements that other people wouldn't notice. They can be accomplishments or things you did years ago.

   Use jot notes or clustering to answer the following questions for each accomplishment:
   a. What skills or knowledge did you use?
   b. What personal traits did you exhibit?
   c. What about this accomplishment makes it personally satisfying for you?
2. Find a print or Web ad for a company or industry that appeals to you.
3. Create skills statements about each of your accomplishments:
   a. Use the language of the advertised position and the industry.
   b. Start with your accomplishments that appear most relevant to the position.
   c. Quantify your accomplishments when possible.

As your instructor directs

a. Share your answers with a small group of students.
b. Summarize your answers in a memo to your instructor.
c. List the most significant of these on your resumé.

25.6 Remembering What You've Done

Use the following list to jog your memory about what you've done. For each, give three or four details as well as a general statement.

Describe a time when you

1. Used research to gain agreement on an important point
2. Made a presentation or a speech to a group
3. Identified a problem faced by a group or organization and developed a plan for solving the problem
4. Responded to criticism
5. Interested other people in something that was important to you and persuaded them to take the actions you wanted
6. Helped a group deal constructively with conflict
7. Demonstrated creativity

As your instructor directs

a. Identify which job(s) each detail is relevant for.
b. Identify which details would work well on a resumé.
c. Identify which details, further developed, would work well in a job letter.

25.7 Evaluating Career Objective Statements

None of the following career objective statements is effective. What is wrong with each as it stands? Which might be revised to be satisfactory? Which should be dropped?

1. To use my acquired knowledge of accounting to eventually own my own business
2. A progressively responsible position as a MARKETING MANAGER where education and ability would have valuable application and lead to advancement
3. To work with people responsibly and creatively, helping them develop personal and professional skills
4. A position in international marketing that makes use of my specialization in marketing and my knowledge of foreign markets
5. To design and maintain websites

25.8 Writing a Paper Resumé

Write a resumé on paper that you could mail to an employer or hand to an interviewer at an interview.

As your instructor directs

a. Write a resumé for the field in which you hope to find a job.
b. Write two different resumés for two different job paths you are interested in pursuing.
c. Adapt your resumé to a specific company you hope to work for.

25.9 Writing a Scannable Resumé

Create a scannable, electronic version of one of the resumés you created for Exercise 25.7. Post your resumé on three industry-specific websites.

25.10 Creating a Video Resumé

Create a video resumé.

As your instructor directs

a. Share your video with three peers and get feedback.
b. Reshoot your video based on peer feedback.
c. Upload your video and request class and viewer feedback.
d. Upload your final version.

POLISHING YOUR PROSE

Proofreading

Wait until the final draft is complete to edit and proofread. There is no point in proofreading words and passages that might change. (Some writers claim to proofread documents while they're composing; this practice is like trying to mow the lawn and trim the hedges at the same time.)

Editing includes checking for you-attitude and positive emphasis, fixing any sexist or biased language, and correcting grammatical errors.

Proofreading means making sure that the document is free from typos. Check each of the following aspects:

- **Spelling:** Scan for misspelled or misused words that spell checkers don't catch: *not* instead of *now*, *you* instead of *your*, *its* instead of *it's*, *their* instead of *there* or *they're*, *one* instead of *won*, and so forth.
- **Consistency:** Check abbreviations and special terms.
- **Names:** Double-check the reader's name.
- **Punctuation:** Make sure that parentheses and quotation marks come in pairs. Be on the lookout for missing or extra commas and periods.
- **Format:** Look for errors in spacing, margins, and document design, especially if you compose your document on one computer and print it out at another. Use the correct format for citations—MLA, APA, *Chicago Manual of Style*, and so on.
- **Numbers and dates:** Double-check all numbers to make sure they add up. Make sure page numbers appear where they should and are sequential. Do the same for tables of contents or appendices. Check dates.

Proofreading is as individual as writing style. Try these methods or invent your own:

- *Read the document from the last word to the first* to catch spelling errors.
- *Read the document in stages*—first page, second page, third page—with plenty of "rest" in between so you are fresh for each page.
- *Read pages out of sequence* so you can concentrate on the characters on the page rather than the meaning.
- *Read the document aloud*, listening for awkward or incorrect phrasing.
- *Ask a friend to read the document aloud*, with punctuation, while you follow along with the original.

Whatever your approach, build time into the composing process for proofreading. If possible, finish the document a day or two before it's due to allow enough time. (If the document is a 100-page report, allow even more time.) If you're in a hurry, use a spell checker, proof the document yourself, and ask a friend or colleague to proof it as well.

Exercises

Proofread the following passages:

1. Ours are a company worth doing business with. Your can count on our promiss to provide not only the best service but, also the finest in materials, fit, and, finish. All of are products our made to exacting specifications meaning that you received the best product for the best prices. If you aren't satisfied for any reason, simply call the toll-free hotline at 1-800-555-1212 to get a promp refund. Or you can right us at: The John Doe Company, 123 Main Street Anytown Canada M6V 2B4. Remember; our moto is "the customers is always's right?

2. Resumee for Kathy Jones
   332 West Long Strt.
   Moncton, New Brunswick E4Z 1Z8
   614-555-8188

Objection

A management position in fullfilament services where my skills, expereince can be best be used to help your company acheeve it's goals.

Relevent Experience:

2010 to Present Day: Ass. Manager for high-end sports equipment distributor. Responsible for checking new customers out.

2005–2010: Owned and Operated Jones, Inc., a telephone order procesing company for lady's apparel.

2008: Received a plague for Must Promising Executive of the Year" from *Monthly* Magazine.

2010: Delivery address to local high school seniors on why accuracy is important in business.

Special Skills
Type 7 or more words per minute
Studied English all my life. Fluent in French.
Shot at local gun club.

Check your answers to the odd-numbered exercises in the Polishing Your Prose Answer Key.

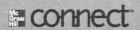

Creating Persuasive Application Letters

Learning Objectives

After reading and applying the information in Module 26, you'll be able to demonstrate

Knowledge of

LO1 The two types of application letter formats

Skills to

LO2 Organize the solicited application letter

LO3 Organize the prospecting application letter

LO4 Catch the reader's interest even when the company isn't planning to hire

LO5 Show that you have the qualifications for the job

LO6 Persuade the employer that you're in the very top group of applicants

LO7 Use information about the company effectively in your letter

Employability Skills 2000+ Checklist

Module content builds these Conference Board of Canada Employability Skills 2000+

Communicate

Manage Information

Think and Solve Problems

Participate in Projects and Tasks

Demonstrate Positive Attitudes and Behaviours

A well-written application letter captures the recruiter's interest, ensuring he or she will read your resumé. The letter is also your first step in showing a specific company what you have to offer.

The best application letters are customized for their audiences. Use the cover letter to provide a brief preview of your resumé, focusing on

- Key requirements of the job for which you're applying, using the language in the job posting
- Skills and knowledge that differentiate you from other applicants
- Language and information that demonstrates your knowledge of the organization and the industry
- Experiences expressed in transferable, marketable skills

Note that the advice in this book applies to job-hunting in Canada. Conventions, expectations, and criteria differ from culture to culture: different norms apply in different countries. Even within Canada, different discourse communities (Module 2) may have different preferences. Whether you're seeking employment in your home province, nationally, or internationally, however, PAIBOC analysis (see Figure 26.1) is vital to your success.

FIGURE 26.1   **PAIBOC Questions for Analysis**

P	What are your **purposes** in writing? As usual, you have several: to attract and hold attention, to stand out favourably from other candidates, to demonstrate you have researched the organization and the position, and to preview your resumé.
A	Who is your **audience**? What audience characteristics are relevant to this particular message? What does your audience want to know? How much time will your audience give your message? What can you do to influence your audience favourably to continue reading?
I	What **information** must your message include? In a cover letter, highlight 1) the superiority of your skills, and 2) the fit between the organization's needs and your qualifications.
B	What reasons or reader **benefits** can you use to support your position? Use the application letter to summarize briefly the qualifications you bring to the position and their value to the organization.
O	What **objections** can you expect your readers to have? What elements of your message will your audience perceive as negative? How can you write to overcome audience objections or de-emphasize negative elements?
C	How will the **context** affect reader response? Consider your relationship to the reader, the reader's values and expectations, recent organizational history and current morale, the economy, the time of year, and any special circumstances surrounding the message exchange. *Here is the overriding cultural context: recruiters want to interview only those prospects whose application letter and resumé demonstrate their value to the organization.*

LO5 Every employer wants businesslike employees who understand professionalism. Follow these guidelines to make your application letter professional:

- Create your letter on a computer. Use the same font style and size as in your resumé.
- Whenever possible, address your letter to a specific person; if you do not know the person's name, address your letter to Human Resources.
- Use the language of the organization and the industry.
- Use contact or employee names if the reader knows them and thinks well of them, if they think well of you and will say good things about you, and if you have permission to use their names.
- Always connect an experience (course work, co-op placement, community involvement) with a resultant skill that you know the prospective employer wants.
- Unless you're applying for a creative job, use business stationery and a conservative style: few contractions, and no sentence fragments, clichés, or slang.
- Edit the letter carefully and proof it several times to make sure it's perfect.

What Kind of Letter Should I Use?

It depends on whether or not the company has asked for applications.

Two different hiring situations call for two different kinds of application letters. Write a **solicited letter** when you know that the company is hiring:

- You've seen an ad
- You've been advised to apply by a professor or friend
- You've read online or in a trade publication that the company is expanding

Sometimes, however, the advertised positions may not be what you want, or you may want to work for an organization that has not announced that it has openings in your area. Then the situation calls for an **unsolicited** or **prospecting letter**.

A prospecting letter will help you tap into the hidden job market (Module 24). In some cases, your prospecting letter may arrive at a company that has decided to hire but has not yet announced the job. In other cases, companies create positions to get a good person who is on the market.

How Are the Two Letters Different?

They begin and end differently.

When you know the company is hiring, organize your letter in this way:

1. State that you're applying for the job (phrase the job title as your source phrased it). Tell where you learned about the job (Web, referral, ad). Briefly show that you have the major qualifications required by the ad: a degree, professional certification, job experience, and so forth. Summarize your other qualifications briefly in the same order in which you plan to discuss them in the letter. This **summary sentence** or **paragraph** covers everything you will talk about and serves as an organizing device for your letter.

> I have a good background in standard accounting principles and procedures, and a working knowledge of some of the special accounting practices of the oil industry. This knowledge is based on practical experience in the oil fields: I've pumped, tailed rods, and worked as a roustabout.
>
> Let me put my oil industry experience and accounting knowledge to work for Standard Oil.

2. Develop your major qualifications in detail. Be specific about what you've done; relate your achievements to the work you'd be doing in this new job. This is not the place for modesty!

3. Develop your other qualifications, even if the ad doesn't ask for them. (If the position description states numerous qualifications, pick the most important three or four.) Show what separates you from the other prospects who will also apply. Demonstrate your knowledge of the organization.
4. Ask for an interview; tell when you'll be available to be interviewed. End on a positive note.

Figures 26.2 and 26.3 are examples of solicited letters.

FIGURE 26.2 **A Solicited Letter (1)**

210 Steeles Avenue West   Phone: 905.555.3828
Brampton, ON L6Y 2K3   Email: mshafe@bell.live

February 1, 2013

Region of Peel
1126 Fewster Drive
Mississauga, ON L4W 2A4

Open punctuation →

Attention Human Resources

Subject: Job/95423-134317
           HHW Facility Operator (Co-op)

As a second-year Chemical Engineering Technology Co-op student at Sheridan Institute, I have the skills and knowledge to contribute to the operation of your Hazardous Waste facility. Through practical application, I understand the Occupational Health and Safety Act WHMIS. Furthermore, in my summer jobs I learned how to handle and store hazardous materials.

Letter uses short sentences, clear language and language of the industry and job posting throughout →

At Sheridan I have also developed excellent written and oral communication skills which enable me to communicate information about hazardous waste and depot services to the public clearly and helpfully.

I have my Class G driver's license, a clean driving record, and my own vehicle. I am very flexible and am able to work rotating shifts and weekends. I am used to hard physical shift work. For the past two summers, I worked rotating shifts at an auto parts factory to pay my college tuition. You can count on me to be at work on time and complete tasks to the best of my ability. I take initiative and work well in a team environment.

My Grade Point Average of 3.96 (out of 4.0) illustrates that I am diligent and a quick learner. I will quickly adapt to the Region of Peel's system of receiving, categorizing, storing, and co-coordinating waste shipment.

Letter asks for the interview →

Please contact me to arrange an interview to further discuss how I can contribute to your organization.

Sincerely

Mohammed Shafer

Mohammed Shafer

Encl.

FIGURE 26.3   **A Solicited Letter (2)**

638 Changery Court
Lethbridge, AB T1J 2A5
May 21, 2012

Shelley Aquina
Human Resources Manager
Home Outfitters
425 18 Avenue Northwest
Calgary, AB T2N 2G6

Dear Shelley Aquina:
RE: File # 7664566-F

Please consider me for the position of sales manager, advertised in the *Calgary Sun*, Saturday, May 20. I possess the educational background, work experience, and exceptional organizational and communication skills for which you have advertised.

In June I will graduate with a business administration diploma from Mount Royal University, Calgary, Alberta. Throughout my college career I worked with peers on a variety of projects, including sales proposals, formal reports, and sales presentations. In my third year I was chosen team captain for our marketing project, a year-long analysis, and oral and written report of possible marketing initiatives for a Calgary client, MediaWaves. My responsibilities included identifying time lines, delegating tasks, negotiating conflicts among group members, reporting to the client and our Marketing professor, and revising and editing the final 30-page report. Our team project not only secured the top grade in the class, but the client also accepted our recommendations, resulting in an immediate 10 percent sales increase for MediaWaves.

Since Grade 11, I have worked part-time and summers at Canadian Tire in Lethbridge, Alberta. Starting as a stock clerk, I worked my way up to sales associate. My supervisor has commented on my excellent sales skills, particularly my product knowledge and ability to up-sell. During my employment with Canadian Tire—a high-energy, fast-paced environment—I learned to focus calmly on clients' concerns and to communicate confidently. As a result of my performance, I was promoted to assistant manager. While working part-time, attending school, and participating in varsity basketball, I learned to juggle multiple priorities, to manage my time, and to problem-solve.

Please see my resumé for further details.

The market for home decorations and furnishings has become increasingly competitive, and with the entry of American big-box stores like Heritage Homes, it promises to become even more so. I would welcome an opportunity to apply my skills to increase your market share. Please call me at 403-555-4339 to arrange an interview time and date at your convenience.

Sincerely,

Carlos DeLeon

Carlos DeLeon
ENC: Resumé

Margin annotations (left):
- Addresses reader as ad indicates
- Repeats words of the ad
- Specifics directly connect the experience with the resultant skill
- Demonstrates research and industry awareness

Margin annotations (right):
- Quotes file number as ad requests
- Thesis or controlling paragraph tells the reader what's going to be proven in the letter
- Jargon of the marketing industry
- Skills would have been identified in the ad as necessary for the position
- Asks for the interview

L03 Prospecting Letters

When you don't have any evidence that the company is hiring, organize your letter this way:

1. Catch the reader's interest.
2. Create a **bridge** between the attention-getter and your qualifications. Focus on what you know and can do. Since the employer is not planning to hire, he or she won't be impressed

with the fact that you're graduating. Summarize your qualifications briefly in the same order in which you plan to discuss them in the letter.

3. Develop your strong points in detail. Be specific. Relate what you've done in the past to what you could do for this company. Show that you know something about the company. Identify the niche you want to fill.

4. Ask for an interview and tell when you'll be available for interviews. (Don't tell when you can begin work.) End on a positive, forward-looking note.

Figure 26.4 shows an example of a prospecting letter.

FIGURE 26.4   **A Prospecting Letter**

Kristine Manalili
2 Inverary Court
Porters Lake, Nova Scotia B3E 1M8
902-555-6488 kmanalili@hotmail.com

Kristine creates a boxed "letterhead"

2012-06-25

Mr. John Harrobin
HealthRhab Inc.
2653 Dublin Street
Halifax, NS B3K 3J7

Dear Mr. Harrobin:

Providing an athlete with physiotherapy can assist with a debilitating injury in the short term. However, treatment alone does not provide the long-term product and therapy information necessary for complete recovery. It can be a real challenge finding employees who are conversant with the latest injury-management modalities, who are familiar with the most current injury-management support equipment, and who also work well with rehabilitating clients. However, you will see from my enclosed resumé that I have this useful combination of skills.

In an unsolicited or prospecting letter, open with a sentence that creates reader interest and provides a natural bridge to talking about yourself

Refers to her enclosed resumé

Rita Haralabidis tells me that HealthRhab needs people to identify injury-management therapy and equipment for your clients. My education and work experience have provided me with the injury evaluation and product knowledge that you require. While studying in Nunavut Arctic College's Sports Injury Management program, for example, I provided more than 200 hours of successful client care at the college clinic.

Refers to mutual acquaintance

Shows knowledge of the company

Moreover, I was able to apply the most current therapy modalities and learn about sophisticated sports injury products and equipment while serving my four-month co-op term at Wu's Sports Clinic in Victoria, British Columbia. Wu's Clinic is renowned for its progressive therapy options. My co-op placement provided me with practical experience in injury prevention and treatment. Equally important, I learned about the latest equipment, products, and techniques available to maximize client rehabilitation and recovery.

Demonstrates knowledge and skills she promised in first paragraph

Relates what she's done to what she could do for this company

My communication skills and product knowledge would enable me to adapt immediately to clients' specific needs and to develop programs for your clients. I am flexible, a quick study, and committed to proactive health care. I will call you next week to arrange a mutually convenient time when we can discuss putting my talents to work for HealthRhab.

Promises action

Sincerely,

Kristine Manalili
Enclosed: Resumé

LO2 The First Paragraph of a Solicited Letter

When you know that the firm is hiring, refer to the specific position in your first sentence. Your letter can then be routed to the appropriate person, thus speeding up consideration of your application. Identify where you learned about the job: "the position of junior accountant announced in Sunday's *Vancouver Sun*," "Kadji Kado, our placement director, told me that you are looking for…"

Note how the following paragraph picks up several of the characteristics of the ad:

> **Ad:**   Business Education Instructor at University of New Brunswick. Candidate must possess a bachelor's degree in Business Education. Will be responsible for providing in-house training to business and government leaders… Candidate should have at least six months' office experience. Prior teaching experience not required.
>
> **Letter:**   Please consider me for the position of **Business Education Instructor**, advertised on Workopolis.com. My Business Education degree, knowledge of adult education principles, and previous office experience make me the ideal candidate for the position.

LO6 Good word choices can help set your letter apart from the hundreds of letters the company is likely to get in response to an ad. The following first paragraph of a letter in response to an ad by Allstate Insurance Company shows knowledge of the firm's advertising slogan and sets itself apart from the dozens of letters that start with "I would like to apply for…"

> The Allstate Insurance Company is famous for its "Good Hands" policy. I would like to lend a helping hand to Allstate as a financial analyst, as advertised in yesterday's *National Post*. I have an Accounting Co-op diploma from Georgian College and I have worked with figures, computers, and people.

Note that the last sentence forecasts the organization of the letter, preparing for paragraphs about the student's academic background and (in this order) experience with "figures, computers, and people."

LO4 First Paragraphs of Prospecting Letters

Ex. 26.5

In a prospecting letter, asking for a job in the first paragraph is dangerous; unless the company plans to hire but has not yet announced openings, the reader is likely to throw the letter away. Instead, catch the reader's interest. Then in the second paragraph shift the focus to your skills and experience, showing how they can be useful to the employer.

Here are effective first and second paragraphs of a letter applying to be a computer programmer for an insurance company:

> Computers alone aren't the answer to demands for higher productivity in the competitive insurance business. Merging a poorly written letter with a database of customers just sends out bad letters more quickly. But you know how hard it is to find people who can both program computers and write well.
>
> My education and training have given me this useful combination of skills. I'd like to put my degree in computer technology and my business writing experience to work in Sun Canada's service approach to insurance.

Last Paragraphs

In the last paragraph, indicate when you'd be available for an interview. If you're free any time, say so. But it's likely that you have responsibilities in class and work. If you'd have to go out of town for an interview, there may be only certain days of the week or certain weeks that you could leave town for several days. Use a sentence that fits your situation.

> I could come to Thunder Bay for an interview anytime between March 17 and 21.
>
> Please call me at 519-555-4229 for an interview time and date at your convenience.

Should you wait for the employer to call you, or should you call the employer to request an interview? In a solicited letter, you may want to wait to be contacted: you know the employer wants to hire someone, and if your letter and resume show that you're one of the top applicants, you'll get an interview.

In a prospecting letter, definitely call the employer. Because the employer is not planning to hire, you'll get a higher percentage of interviews if you're assertive. When you do call, be polite to the person who answers the phone.

If you're writing a prospecting letter to a firm that's more than a few hours away by car, say that you'll be in the area the week of such-and-such and could stop by for an interview. Some companies pay for follow-up visits, but not for first interviews. A company may be reluctant to ask you to make an expensive trip when it isn't yet sure it wants to hire you.

End the letter on a positive note that suggests you look forward to the interview and that you see yourself as a person who has something to contribute, not as someone who just needs a job.

> On Wednesday, April 25, I will call you between 9:00 and 9:30 a.m. to schedule a time when we can discuss how my skills can contribute to ISM Canada's continued growth.

LO2 LO3 What Parts of the Two Letters Are the Same?

The body paragraphs discussing your qualifications are the same.

In both solicited and prospecting letters, you should follow these guidelines:

- Address the letter to a specific person.
- Indicate the specific position for which you're applying.
- Be specific about your qualifications.
- Show what separates you from other applicants.
- Demonstrate knowledge of the company and the position.
- Refer to your resume (which you would enclose with the letter).
- Ask for an interview.

LO4 Showing Knowledge of the Position and the Company

Employability Skills

If you can substitute another inside address and salutation, and send out the letter without any further changes, it isn't specific enough. Use your knowledge of the position and the company to choose relevant evidence from what you've done to support your claims that you could help the company.

One or two specific details are usually enough to demonstrate your knowledge. Be sure to use the knowledge, not just repeat it. Never present the information as though it will be news to the reader. After all, the reader works for the company and presumably knows much more about it than you do.

Separating Yourself from Other Applicants

Your knowledge of the company separates you from other applicants. You can also use course work, an understanding of the field, and experience in jobs and extracurricular events to show that you're unique.

This student uses summer jobs and course work to set herself apart from other applicants:

> A company as diverse as Desjardins Credit Union requires extensive record keeping as well as numerous internal and external communications. Both my summer jobs and my course work have prepared me for these responsibilities. As office manager for Safety Express Limited, I was in charge of most of the bookkeeping and letter writing for the company. I kept accurate records for each workday, and I often entered more than 100 transactions in a single day. In business and technical writing courses, I learned how to write persuasive letters and memos and how to present extensive data in clear and concise reports.

How Long Should My Letter Be?

Highlight the fit between the position and your qualifications clearly and concisely.

Your cover letter and resumé may be one of hundreds under review. The more readable your application letter, the more likely you will attract the favourable attention of those responsible for deciding whom to interview. Keep your letter as concise and clear as possible. Try to keep it to one page.

Without eliminating content, make each sentence concise to be sure that you're using space as efficiently as possible. If your letter is still slightly over a page, use smaller margins, a type size that's one point smaller, or justified proportional type to get more on the page.

If you really need more than one page, though, use it. The extra space gives you room to be more specific about what you've done and to add details about your experience that separate you from other applicants. Employers don't want longer letters, but they will read them *if* the letter is well written and *if* you establish early in the letter that you have the credentials and skills the company needs.

How Do I Create the Right Tone?

Ex. 26.6

Use you-attitude and positive emphasis.

You-attitude and positive emphasis help you sound assertive without being arrogant.

You-Attitude

Unsupported claims may sound overconfident, selfish, or arrogant. Create you-attitude (Module 13) by describing exactly what you have done and showing how that relates to what you could do for this employer.

Lacks you-attitude:	An inventive and improvising individual like me is a necessity in your business.
You-attitude:	Building a summer house-painting business gave me the opportunity to find creative solutions to challenges.

422   UNIT 6   Job Hunting

Remember that the word *you* refers to your reader. Using *you* when you really mean yourself or "all people" can insult your reader by implying that he or she still has a lot to learn about business.

Since you're talking about yourself, you'll use *I* in your letter. Do so sparingly. Reduce the number of *I*'s by revising some sentences to use *me* or *my*.

> Under my presidency, the Agronomy Club...
>
> Courses in media and advertising management gave me a chance to...
>
> My responsibilities as a co-op student included...

In particular, avoid beginning every paragraph with *I*. Begin sentences with adverbs (*presently*, *currently*), prepositional phrases, or introductory clauses.

LO7 EXPANDING A CRITICAL SKILL

Targeting a Specific Company in Your Letter

If your combination of skills is in high demand, a one-size-fits-all letter may get you an interview. But when you must compete against dozens—perhaps hundreds or even thousands—of applicants for an interview slot, you need to target your letter to the specific company. Targeting a specific company also helps you prepare for the job interview.

The Web makes it easy to find information about a company. The example below shows how applicants could use available information about Sleeman Breweries.

Check for Facts About the Company

Like most corporate websites, Sleeman offers dozens of facts about the company. A computer network administrator might talk about helping to keep the 3500 LANs working well. A Web weaver might talk about supporting a new investor relations site or about developing even more interactive content for both national and international customers. Someone in corporate communications, advertising, marketing, or multimedia programs might write a prospecting letter about Sleeman's recent media campaign. An interviewee with experience in international business might pitch the company on the expertise necessary to do business in Boston, Germany, and South Africa. And someone in human resources management might talk about the electronic processing of HR data benefits for the thousands of employees joining this expanding company, or about current recruitment and retention strategies for the company that CIBC World Markets Inc. calls "a well-managed, creative company."

Check News Releases and Speeches

Recent press releases have covered everything from the company's national expansion—across the Maritimes, into Quebec, and Western Canada—to its international partnerships with U.S., German, and South African breweries. Anyone in international business might talk about helping Sleeman expand its base into China—and beyond.

In May 2009, in recognition of its "commitment to the environment and its sustainable packaging practices," the company received a Certificate of Environmental Sustainability from corrugated container supplier Atlantic Packaging Products Ltd. Students about to complete environmental studies, marketing, finance, and management programs might demonstrate how their course work and experience prepare them to expand community-focused programs, or students might offer technical or managerial expertise on the best way for Sleeman Breweries to adopt e-business strategies to support its continuing growth.

Check the Corporate Culture

In his interviews, Chair and CEO John Sleeman emphasizes that his family-owned business produces a quality product based on his great-great-grandfather's recipe. The company's website material also refers to the family beer-making tradition and the site's design reinforces this commitment to traditional values. These promotional strategies appeal to the mature consumers who buy Sleeman beers. Yet Sleeman's partnership arrangements and media advertisements indicate the company's enthusiasm for creativity and flexibility. Prospective job applicants would do well to stress their creative abilities and their support of community arts activities.

Sources: Ontario Brewing Awards Winners List, (2011, May 10) retrieved from http://www.canadianbeernews.com/2011/05/10/ontario-brewing-awards-2011-winners-list/; Cheers to Sleeman, (2009, June 12) *Canadian Packaging*, retrieved from http://www.canadianmanufacturing.com/packaging/sustainability/cheers-to-sleeman-2465; 2009 CBS Interactive Inc., Sleeman Breweries Ltd., *BNET Industries*, retrieved from http://resources.bnet.com/topic/sleeman+breweries+ltd.html; Michael Van Aelst, quoted in Oliver Bertin (2001, June 20), Sleeman brew balance of risk and caution, *Globe and Mail*, M1.

Positive Emphasis

Be positive. Don't plead ("Please give me a chance") or hedge ("I cannot promise that I am substantially different from everyone else").

Avoid word choices with negative connotations (Module 12). Note how the following revisions make the writer sound more confident.

Negative: I have learned an excessive amount about writing through courses in journalism and advertising.

Excessive suggests that you think the courses covered too much—hardly an opinion likely to endear you to an employer.

Positive: Courses in journalism and advertising have taught me to recognize and to write good copy. My profile of a professor was published in the campus newspaper; I earned an A on my direct mail campaign for the Canadian Dental Association to persuade young adults to see their dentists more often.

How Should I Write an Email Application?

Compose a document using a word-processing program. Then attach it to a courteous email message.

Employability Skills

When you submit an email letter (see Figure 26.5) with an attached resumé, you need to

- Use a plain, professional-sounding email address, such as your own name (Module 25).
- Tell in what word-processing program your scannable resumé is saved.

FIGURE 26.5   **An Email Application Letter**

To: r_h_catanga@ibm.com
From: Tracey McKenna <mckenna.74@rogers.ca>
Subject: Application for jof17747
Cc:
Bcc:
Attached: D:\Jobhunt\resume.scan;

Attach your scannable resumé.

Omit salutation.

Put job number in the subject line and the first paragraph.

Attached is a scannable resumé in WordPerfect for the accounting position announced on IBM's website (jof17747). I will receive a B.Sc. in accountancy from McMaster University in Hamilton, ON this August and plan to take the CPA exam in December.

Tell what program it's in.

Choose details that use words from job ad and interest reader.

As a result of my studies, I've learned to identify the best measures for fixed assets and property controls, and to figure inter-company/ intra-company and travel expenses. I can analyze expenditures and compare them to past statements to identify trends and recommend ways to reduce costs.

Furthermore, I can use Excel to create computer graphics to provide the clear, reliable accounting data that IBM needs to continue growing each year. Please visit my Web page to see the report I wrote on choosing the best method to accelerate depreciation.

My three years of experience at Allstate have given me the opportunity to take leadership and show responsibility. I developed a procedure for making out arbitration reports that saved so much time I was asked to teach it to the other employees in my department.

At your convenience, I could come to Toronto for an interview any Tuesday or Thursday afternoon.

Repeat name and email address at the end.

Tracey McKenna
mckenna.74@rogers.ca
http://www.mcmaster/business/students/mckenna/report.htm

If you have a Web page, list it to show that you're technologically savvy. Keeping the "http://" in the URL creates a hotlink in many email programs.

- Put the job number or title for which you're applying in your subject line and in the first paragraph.
- Prepare your letter in a word-processing program with a spell checker to make it easier to edit and proof the document.
- Don't send anything in all capital letters.
- Don't use smiley faces or other emoticons.
- Put your name and email address at the end of the message. Most email programs send along the "sender" information on the screen, but a few don't, and you want the employer to know whose letter this is!

MODULE SUMMARY

- When you know the company is hiring, send a solicited application letter. When self-recruiting, send a prospecting or unsolicited cover letter.
- Organize your solicited letter this way:
  - State that you are applying for the job, and tell where you learned about the job (ad, referral, etc). Briefly show that you have the major qualifications for the position. In your opening paragraph, summarize your qualifications in the order in which you discuss them in the letter.
  - Develop your major qualifications in detail.
  - Develop your other qualifications. Show what separates you from the other candidates who will apply.
  - Demonstrate your knowledge of the organization.
  - Ask for an interview; say when you are available to be interviewed and to begin work. End on a positive note.
- Organize your prospecting letter this way:
  - Catch the reader's interest.
  - Create a bridge between the opening and your qualifications. Summarize your qualifications in the order in which you discuss them in the letter.
  - Develop your strong points in detail. Relate what you've done in the past to what you could do for this company. Demonstrate your knowledge of

the company. Identify the specific position you are interested in.
  - Ask for an interview and state when you are available for interviews. End on a positive note.
- In both letters
  - Address the letter to a specific person.
  - Indicate the specific position for which you are applying.
  - Be specific about your qualifications.
  - Show what separates you from the other applicants.
  - Demonstrate your knowledge about the company and the position.
  - Refer to your resumé (which you enclose or send with the letter).
  - Ask for an interview.
  - Use your knowledge of the company, your course work, your understanding of the field, and your experience in jobs and extracurricular activities to show that you're unique.
  - Use you-attitude by providing specific details and by relating what you have done with the knowledge or experience the employer needs. Use positive emphasis to sound confident.

ASSIGNMENTS FOR MODULE 26

Questions for Critical Thinking

26.1 How could you write a cover letter that differentiates you positively from other applicants?

26.2 What techniques can you use in the first paragraph to catch the reader's positive interest immediately?

26.3 Identify four methods you can use to create you-attitude throughout your letter.

26.4 When you submit your application letter and resumé by email, what should you write in the email itself?

Exercises and Problems

26.5 Analyzing First Paragraphs of Prospecting Letters

The following are first paragraphs in prospecting letters written by new graduates. Evaluate the paragraphs on these criteria:

- Is the paragraph likely to interest the reader and motivate him or her to read the rest of the letter?
- Does the paragraph have some content that the student can use to create a transition to talking about his or her qualifications?
- Does the paragraph avoid asking for a job?

1. Ann Gibbs suggested that I contact you.

2. Each year, the holiday shopping rush makes more work for everyone at the Bay, especially for the Credit Department. While working for the Bays' Credit Department for three holiday seasons and summer vacations, I became aware of many credit situations.

3. Whether to plate a five-centimetre eyebolt with cadmium for a tough, brilliant shine or with zinc for a rust-resistant, less-expensive finish is a tough question. But your salespeople must answer similar questions daily. With my experience in the electroplating industry, I can contribute greatly to your customer growth.

4. Prudential Insurance Company did much to help my university career, as the sponsor of my National Merit Scholarship. Now I think I can give something back to Prudential. I'd like to put my education, including a degree in finance from university, to work in your investment department.

5. Since the beginning of Delta Electric Construction Co. in 1997, the size and profits have grown steadily. My father, who is a stockholder and vice-president, often discusses company dealings with me. Although the company has prospered, I understand there have been a few problems of mismanagement. I feel with my present and future qualifications, I could help ease these problems.

26.6 Improving You-Attitude and Positive Emphasis in Job Letters

Revise each of these sentences to improve you-attitude and positive emphasis. You may need to add information.

1. I understand that your company has had problems due to the mistranslation of documents for international ad campaigns.
2. Included in my resumé are the courses in finance that earned me a fairly attractive grade average.
3. I am looking for a position that gives me a chance to advance quickly.

4. Although short on experience, I am long on effort and enthusiasm.
5. I have been with the company from its beginning to its present unfortunate state of bankruptcy.

26.7 Writing a Solicited Letter

Write a letter of application in response to an announced opening for a full-time job that a new graduate could hold.

Turn in a copy of the listing. If you use option (a), (b), or (d) below, your listing will be a copy of an actual listing. If you choose option (c), you will write the listing and can design your ideal job.

a. Respond to an ad that you find in a newspaper, in a professional journal, in the placement office, or on the Web. Use an ad that specifies the company, not a blind ad. Be sure that you are fully qualified for the job.
b. Find a job description and assume that it represents a current opening. Use a directory to get the name of the person to whom the letter should be addressed.
c. If you have already worked somewhere, assume that your employer is asking you to apply for full-time work after graduation. Be sure to write a fully persuasive letter.
d. Respond to one of the listings below. Use a directory or the Web to get the name and address of the person to whom you should write.

1. Cotts Beverages is hiring an **assistant auditor**. Minimum 12 years of accounting experience. Work includes analysis and evaluation of operating and financial controls and requires contact with many levels of company management. Extensive travel (50 percent of job hours) required through the Canadian West, along with some international work. Effective written and oral communication skills a must, along with sound decision-making abilities. Locations: Edmonton, Toronto, Halifax, New York, Los Angeles, Dallas, Atlanta, Philadelphia, Denver, Chicago. Refer to job FA-2534.

2. Roxy Systems (Roxy.com) seeks **Internet marketing coordinators** to analyze online campaigns and put together detailed reports, covering ad impressions and click-through rates. Must have basic understanding of marketing; be organized, creative, and detail-oriented; know Microsoft Excel; have excellent communication skills; and be familiar with the Internet. Send letter and resumé to mike@roxy.com.

3. Bose Corporation seeks **public relations/communications administrative associate** (Job Code 117BD). Write, edit, and produce the in-house newsletter using desktop publishing software. Represent the company

to external contacts (including the press). Provide administrative support to the manager of PR by scheduling meetings, preparing presentations, tabulating and analyzing surveys, and processing financial requests. Excellent organizational, interpersonal, and communication skills (both written and oral) required. Must be proficient in MS Office and FileMaker Pro.

4. The Gap is hiring **executive development program trainees**. After completing 10-week training programs, trainees will become assistant buyers. Prefer people with strong interest and experience in retailing. Apply directly to the store for which you want to work.

5. A local non-profit seeks a **coordinator of volunteer services**. Responsibilities for this full-time position include coordinating volunteer schedules, recruiting and training new volunteers, and evaluating existing programs. Excellent listening and communication skills required.

26.8 Writing a Prospecting Letter

1. Look in the business sections of your local and national newspapers for stories that suggest an organization is expanding and may be hiring for positions in various areas. Identify an area or department (accounting, finance, human resources, information technology, marketing, publicity and promotion, research and development, etc.) in which you would like to work.

2. Apply for a specific position. The position can be one that already exists, or one that you would create, if you could, to match your unique blend of talents. Be sure that you are fully qualified for the job.

3. Use the Web or directories to get the name and address of the person with the power to create a job for you.

POLISHING YOUR PROSE

Using *You* and *I*

You-attitude (Module 13) means that you'll use lots of *yous* in business messages. However, use *you* only when it refers to your reader. When you mean "people in general," use another term.

Incorrect:	When I visited your office, I learned that you need to find a way to manage your email.
Correct:	When I visited your office, I saw the importance of managing one's email.
Incorrect:	Older customers may not like it if you call them by their first names.
Correct:	Older customers may prefer being called by courtesy titles and their last names.

Omit *you* when it criticizes or attacks the reader.

| Not you-attitude: | You didn't turn your expense report in by the deadline. |
| You-attitude: | Expense reports are due by the fifth of each month. We have no record of receiving your report. |

When you talk about what you've done, use *I*.

| Correct: | In the past month, I have completed three audits. |

In general, keep *I*'s to a minimum. They make you sound less confident and more self-centred.

Weak:	I think that we would save money if we bought a copier instead of leasing it.
Better:	We would save money by buying a copier instead of leasing it.
Weak:	I want to be sure that I understand how I will be affected by this project.
Better:	How will this project affect our unit?

When you write a document that focuses on you (such as a progress report or a job application letter), vary sentence structure so that you don't begin every sentence with *I*.

Correct:	This job gave me the opportunity to…
Correct:	As an intern, I…
Correct:	Working with a team, I…

When you use a first-person pronoun as part of a compound subject or object, put the first-person pronoun last.

| Correct: | She asked you and me to make the presentation. |
| Correct: | You, Mohammed, and I will have a chance to talk to members of the audience before the dinner. |

Be sure to use the right case. For the above two examples, you might omit the other part(s) of the compound to see the case you should use, as follows:

She asked me…

I will have a chance…

These are grammatically correct, so you would use the same form when you restore the other words.

Exercises

Revise the following sentences to eliminate errors and improve the use of *you* and *I*.

1. I worked with a team to create a class website. I was responsible for much of the initial design and some of the HTML coding. I also tested the page with three people to see how easily they could navigate it. I and the other team members presented the page to a committee of local businesspeople.
2. I have taken a lot of time and trouble to get a copy of *Using Excel* for each of you.
3. If you offend someone in the team, you need to resolve the conflict you have created.
4. Please return the draft to me and Mehtap.
5. I think that it would be a good idea for us to distribute an agenda before the meeting.
6. I have asked each department head if he or she had information to announce at the meeting, collated the responses, and arranged the topics to cover in an agenda. I have indicated how much time each topic will take. I am herewith distributing the agenda for Friday's meeting.
7. You haven't made the website accessible to users with impaired vision.
8. My last job showed me that you have to be able to solve problems quickly.
9. I observed department meetings during my co-op. I also sat in on client meetings. I designed PowerPoint slides for client presentations. I participated in strategy sessions. Finally, I drafted brochures.
10. The client asked me and my supervisor to explain our strategy more fully.

Check your answers to the odd-numbered exercises in the Polishing Your Prose Answer Key.

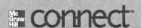

MODULE 27

Managing the Interview Process

Learning Objectives

After reading and applying the information in Module 27, you'll be able to demonstrate

Knowledge of

LO1 Job interview best practices

LO2 The attitudes and behaviours employers seek

Skills to

LO3 Be your best self at a job interview

LO4 Plan and practise for the interview

LO5 Answer traditional interview questions

LO6 Prepare for behavioural and situational interviews

LO7 Participate in phone or video interviews

LO8 Make a good impression in follow-up letters and emails

Managing the Interview Process   **MODULE 27**   **429**

Employability Skills 2000+ Checklist

Module content builds these Conference Board of Canada Employability Skills 2000+

Communicate

Manage Information

Think and Solve Problems

Demonstrate Positive Attitudes and Behaviours

Be Adaptable

Learn Continuously

Work with Others

Participate in Projects and Tasks

Today many employers expect job candidates to

Successful job applicants prepare an interview strategy tailored to their audience.

- Follow instructions to the letter. The owner of a delivery company tells candidates to phone at a precise hour. Failing to do so means that the person can't be trusted to deliver packages on time.[1]
- Participate in many interviews, including a panel or group interview. In these interview situations, several people in the organization are present throughout the interview. Each person is assigned a question to ask the candidate, and the whole team assesses the applicant's interview performance.
- Have one or more interviews by phone, computer, or video.
- Take one or more tests, including psychological/personality assessments, aptitude tests, computer simulations, and essay exams where you're asked to explain what you'd do in a specific situation.
- Be approved by the team you'll be joining. In companies with self-managed work teams, the team has a say in who is hired.
- Provide—at the interview or right after it—a sample of the work you're applying to do. You may be asked to write a memo or a proposal, calculate a budget on a spreadsheet, make a presentation, or do a mini-teach.

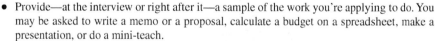 What's the Best Interview Strategy?

Prepare so that you get what you want.

Develop an overall strategy based on your answers to these three questions:

1. *What do you want the interviewer to know about you?* Pick two to five points that represent your strengths for that particular job. These facts may be achievements, positive character traits (such as enthusiasm, attention to detail, creativity), and experiences that qualify you for the job and separate you from other applicants.

   Identify and write down a specific action or accomplishment to support each strength (Module 25). For example, be ready to give an example to prove that you're "hardworking." Show how you have saved money, served customers better, or led the team in other organizations where you've worked.

In Nelvana's creative environment, employees are hired because they possess both the skills to do the job and the creativity to imagine original ideas. Applicants' portfolios are expected to contain evidence of both.

At the interview, listen to every question to see how you can make one of your key points part of your answer. If the questions don't allow you to make your points, bring them up at the end of the interview.

2. *What disadvantages or weaknesses do you need to minimize?* Expect to be asked to explain apparent weaknesses in your record: lack of experience, so-so grades, or gaps in your record.

3. *What do you need to know about the job and the organization to decide whether to accept this job if it is offered to you?* Do research to ensure the organization is the right fit for you. Analyze the company website: its language, colours, and navigation can tell you plenty about organizational values. Read blogs, bulletins, and associated industry journals.

Network. Use information interviews (Module 24) as opportunities to scope out the reception area, the way visitors are greeted and treated, congruence between mission statement and morale. Talk to as many employees and friends of employees as you can.

Keep a list of topics you want to research further. Before the interview, prioritize these, and reframe them as questions to ask during the interview.

Checkpoint

Interview Strategy

Plan an interview strategy based on these three questions:

1. What two to five facts about yourself do you want the interviewer to know?
2. What disadvantages or weaknesses do you need to overcome or minimize?
3. What do you need to know about the job and the organization to decide whether or not you want to accept this job if it is offered to you?

LO3 LO4 What Details Should I Think About?

Decide what you'll wear, how to get there, and what you'll take with you.

What to Wear

Your interview clothing should be at least as formal as the clothing of the person likely to interview you. When the interview is scheduled, ask the person who invites you whether the company has a dress policy. Even if the dress is "casual," wear a dressy shirt and a good-quality skirt or pants, not jeans.

If you're interviewing for a management or office job, wear a business suit in a conservative colour (black, grey, or navy) and a season-appropriate fabric. If you have good taste and a good eye for colour, follow your instincts.

If fashion isn't your strong point, thumb through newspapers and magazines for ideas, or visit stores, noting details—the exact shade of blue in a suit, the number of buttons on the sleeve, the placement of pockets, the width of lapels. You can find quality clothes at bargain prices in second-hand and vintage clothing shops in your town or city.

If you're interviewing for a position that involves working, visiting, or supervising muddy or dirty sites, wear sturdy clothes that suggest you're willing to get dirty.[2] In this case, looking "good" is less important than looking businesslike.

Consider the corporate culture. A woman interviewing for a job at Gap wore a matching linen skirt and blouse that were similar to Gap clothing. Her clothing was evidence that she'd researched the job.[3]

Choose comfortable shoes. The last thing you want to be thinking about during an important interview is how much your feet hurt! You may also do a fair amount of walking during the office visit or plant trip.

Take care of all the details. Check your heels to make sure they aren't run-down; make sure your shoes are shined. Have your hair cut or styled conservatively. Keep jewellery and makeup understated. Personal hygiene must be impeccable. If you wear cologne or perfume, keep it to a minimum. More and more workplaces have "scent-free" policies to accommodate people with allergies.

How to Get There

If you're going to a place you haven't been to before, do a practice run at the same time of day your interview is scheduled for. Check out bus transfers or parking fees. On the day of the interview, leave early enough so that you'll get to the interview 15 minutes early.

Use the extra time to check your appearance in the restroom mirror and to look through the company publications in the waiting room. If an accident does delay you, call to say you'll be late.

What to Take to the Interview

Take extra copies of your resumé. If your campus placement office has already given the interviewer a data sheet, present the resumé at the beginning of the interview: "I thought you might like a little more information about me."

Bring something to write on, something to write with, and a typed list of the questions you want to ask.

Bring copies of your work or a portfolio: an engineering design, a copy of a report you wrote on a job or in a business writing class, an article you wrote for the campus paper. You don't need to present these unless the interview calls for them, but they can be very effective.

Bring the names, addresses, and phone numbers of your references if you haven't already provided them.

Bring complete details about your work history and education, including dates and street addresses, in case you're asked to fill out an application form.

If you can afford it, buy a briefcase to carry these items. An inexpensive briefcase is fine.

What Notes to Take

During or immediately after the interview, write down the details:

- The name of the interviewer, or all the people you talked to, if it's a group interview or an office visit. (The easiest way to get the interviewer's name is to ask for his or her card.)
- The traits/facts the interviewer seemed to like best about you.
- Any negative points or concerns that came up that you need to counter in your follow-up letter or phone calls.
- Answers to your questions about the company.
- The date you'll hear from the company.
- Details you'll want to include in your follow-up thank-you letter.

[LO3 LO4] What Should I Practise Before the Interview?

Practise everything, and often; practice builds confidence.

Your interviewing skills will improve with practice. Rehearse everything you can: put on the clothes you'll wear and practise entering a room, shaking hands, sitting down, and answering questions. Ask a friend to interview you, and video record the interview. Saying answers aloud is surprisingly harder than saying them in your head. Recording is more valuable if you can do it at least twice, so you can modify your behaviour the second time and check to see if the modification works.

How to Act

Should you "be yourself"? There's no point in assuming a radically different persona. If you do, you run the risk of getting into a job that you'll hate (though the persona you assumed might have loved it). On the other hand, we all have several selves: we can be lazy, insensitive, bored, slow-witted, and tongue-tied, but we can also be energetic, perceptive, interested, intelligent, and articulate. Be your best self at the interview.

To increase your confidence, review your positive personality traits and accomplishments—the things you're especially proud of having done—in writing (Module 25). You'll make a better impression if you have a firm sense of your own self-worth.

Every interviewer repeats the advice that parents often give: Sit up straight, don't mumble, and look at people when you talk. It's good advice for interviews. Be aware that many people respond negatively to smoking.

Office visits that involve meals and semi-social occasions call for sensible choices. When you order, choose something that's easy and not messy to eat. Watch your table manners. Eat a light lunch, with no alcohol, so that you'll be alert during the afternoon. At dinner or an evening party, decline alcohol if you don't drink or are underage. If you do drink, accept just one drink: you're still being evaluated. Be aware that some people respond negatively to applicants who drink hard liquor.

Parts of the Interview

Every interview has an opening, a body, and a close.

In the **opening** (two to five minutes), good interviewers will try to put you at ease. Some interviewers will open with easy questions about your major or interests. Others open by telling you about the job or the company. If this happens, listen so you can answer later questions to show that you can do the job and contribute to the company that's being described.

The **body** of the interview (10 minutes to an hour) is an all-too-brief time for you to highlight your qualifications and find out what you need to know to decide if you want to accept a second interview. Expect questions that allow you to highlight your strong points, and questions that probe any weaknesses evident from your resumé. (You were neither in school nor working last fall. What were you doing?) Normally the interviewer will also try to sell you on the company and give you an opportunity to ask questions.

Be aware of time so that you can make sure to get to your key points and questions: "We haven't covered it yet, but I want you to know that I…" "I'm aware that it's almost 10:30. I do have some more questions that I'd like to ask about the company."

In the **close** of the interview (two to five minutes), the interviewer will usually tell you what happens next: "We'll be bringing our top candidates to the office in February. You should hear from us in three weeks." One interviewer reports that he gives applicants his card and tells them to call him. "It's a test to see if they are committed, how long it takes for them to call, and whether they even call at all."[4]

Close with an assertive statement. Depending on the circumstances, you could say, "I've enjoyed learning more about ITracks; I'd really like to see the new system you talked about." Or, "This job seems to be a good match with my qualifications and expertise."

 Cultural FOCUS

In many cultures, smoking is acceptable and normal; in Canada, smoking is becoming less acceptable. If you are a smoker, try not to smoke at all before the interview. Tobacco smoke clings to fabric and a non-smoker will be able to smell it. If you do need to smoke before the interview, try not to smoke for at least 30 minutes before the interview. Never smoke as soon as you leave the interview. Wait until you are away from the property, as you never know who may be watching you leave.

LO2 LO5 How Should I Answer Traditional Interview Questions?

Choose answers that fit your qualifications and your interview strategy.

As Table 27.1 shows, successful applicants use different communication behaviours than do unsuccessful applicants. Successful applicants are more likely to

- Use the company name during the interview
- Support their claims with specific details
- Ask specific questions about the company and the industry

In addition to practising the content of questions, try to incorporate tactics recommended in column three of Table 27.1.

TABLE 27.1   The Communication Behaviours of Successful Interviewees

Behaviour	Unsuccessful Interviewees	Successful Interviewees
Statements about the position	Had only vague ideas of what they wanted to do; changed "ideal job" up to six times during the interview.	Were specific and consistent about the position they wanted; were able to tell why they wanted the position.
Use of company name	Rarely used the company name.	Referred to the company by name four times as often as unsuccessful interviewees.
Knowledge about company and position	Made it clear that they were using the interview to learn about the company and what it offered.	Made it clear that they had researched the company; referred to specific brochures, journals, or people who had given them information.
Level of interest, enthusiasm	Responded neutrally to interviewer's statements: "OK," "I see." Indicated reservations about company or location.	Expressed approval of information verbally and non-verbally; explicitly indicated desire to work for this particular company.
Non-verbal behaviour	Made little eye contact; smiled infrequently.	Made eye contact often; smiled.
Picking up on interviewer's cues	Gave vague or negative answers even when a positive answer was clearly desired ("How are your math skills?").	Answered positively and confidently—and backed up the claim with a specific example of "problem solving" or "toughness."
Response to topic shift by interviewer	Resisted topic shift.	Accepted topic shift.
Use of industry terms and technical jargon	Used almost no technical jargon.	Used technical jargon: "point of purchase display," "NCR charge," "two-column approach," "direct mail," "big pharma."
Use of specifics in answers	Gave short answers—10 words or fewer, sometimes only one word; did not elaborate. Gave general responses: "fairly well."	Supported claims with specific personal experiences, comparisons, statistics, statements of teachers and employers.
Questions asked by interviewee	Asked a small number of general questions.	Asked specific questions based on knowledge of the industry and the company. Personalized questions: "What would my duties be?"
Control of time and topics	Interviewee talked 37 percent of the interview time; initiated 36 percent of the comments.	Interviewee talked 55 percent of the total time, initiated subjects 56 percent of the time.

Source: Based on research reported by Lois J. Einhorn (1981, July), An inner view of the job interview: An investigation of successful communicative behaviors, *Communication Education*, 30, 217–28; Robert W. Elder and Michael M. Harris, Eds. (1999), *The employment interview handbook* (Thousand Oaks, CA: Sage): 300, 303, 327–28.

Checkpoint

Successful Interviewees

- Know what they want to do
- Have researched the company in advance
- Use the company name in the interview
- Support skills and knowledge claims with specifics
- Use industry language
- Ask specific questions
- Talk more of the time

Interviewers frequently ask the following questions during interviews. Prepare on paper before the interview so that you'll be able to come up with answers that are responsive, honest, and paint a positive picture of you.

Employability Skills

Choose answers that fit your qualifications and your interview strategy.

1. *Tell me about yourself.*

   Don't launch into an autobiography. Instead, talk about your achievements as they relate to the organization's culture and goals. Give specific examples to prove each of your strengths.

2. *What makes you think you're qualified to work for this company? Or: I'm interviewing 120 people for two jobs. Why should I hire you?*

   This question might feel like an attack. Use it as an opportunity to state your strong points: your qualifications for the job, the skills, knowledge, and character traits that separate you from other applicants.

3. *What two or three accomplishments have given you the greatest satisfaction?*

   Pick accomplishments that you're proud of, that create the image you want to project, and that enable you to share one of the things you want the interviewer to know about you (Module 25, Exercise 25.4). Focus not just on the desired result, but also on the transferable skills—teamwork, problem solving, and critical thinking—that made the achievement possible.

4. *Why do you want to work for us? What is your ideal job?*

   Even if you're interviewing just for practice, make sure you have a good answer—preferably two or three reasons you'd like to work for that company. Do your homework; know everything possible about the company and the job. If you don't seem to be taking the interview seriously, the interviewer won't take you seriously, and you won't even get good practice.

5. *What college or university courses did you like best and least? Why?*

   This question may be an icebreaker; it may be designed to discover the kind of applicant the organization is looking for. If your favourite class was something outside your program, prepare an answer that shows that you have qualities that can help you in the job you're applying for: "My favourite class was Canadian Literature. We got a chance to think on our own, rather than just regurgitate facts; we made presentations to the class every week. I found I really like sharing my ideas with other people and presenting reasons for my conclusions about something."

6. *Why are your grades so low?*

   If possible, show that the cause of low grades has now been solved or isn't relevant to the job you're applying for: "My father almost died last year, and my schoolwork really suffered."

"When I started, I didn't have any firm goals. Since I discovered the program that is right for me, my grades have all been B's or better." "I'm not good at multiple-choice tests. But you need someone who can work with people, not someone who can take tests."

7. *What have you read recently? What movies have you seen recently?*

These questions may be icebreakers; they may be designed to probe your intellectual depth. Be prepared: read at least one book or magazine (regularly) and see at least one movie that you could discuss at an interview.

8. *Show me some samples of your writing.*

The year you're interviewing, go through your old papers and select the best ones, editing and reformatting them, if necessary, so that you'll have samples if you're asked for them. Show interviewers essays, reports, or business documents, not poetry or song lyrics.

If you don't have samples at the interview, mail them to the interviewer immediately after the interview.

9. *Where do you see yourself in five years?*

Employers ask this question to find out if you are a self-starter or if you passively respond to what happens. You may want to have several scenarios for five years from now to use in different kinds of interviews. Or you may want to say, "Well, my goals may change as opportunities arise. But right now, I want to…"

10. *What are your interests outside of work? What campus or community activities have you been involved in?*

Although it's desirable to be well rounded, naming 10 interests might work against you: the interviewer might wonder when you'll have time to work. If you mention your fiancé(e), spouse, or children in response to this question ("Well, my fiancé and I like to go sailing"), it is perfectly legal for the interviewer to ask follow-up questions ("What would you do if your spouse got a job offer in another town?"), even though the same question would be illegal if the interviewer brought up the subject first.

11. *What have you done to learn about this company?*

An employer may ask this to see what you already know about the company (if you've read the recruiting literature, the interviewer doesn't need to repeat it). This question may also be used to see how active a role you're taking in the job search and how interested you are in this job.

12. *What adjectives would you use to describe yourself?*

Use only positive ones. Be ready to illustrate each with a specific example of something you've done.

13. *What is your greatest strength?*

Employers ask this question to give you a chance to sell yourself and to learn something about your values. Pick a strength related to work, school, or activities: "I'm good at working with people." "I can really sell things." "I'm good at solving problems." "I learn quickly." "I'm reliable. When I say I'll do something, I do it." Be ready to illustrate each with a specific example of something you've done.

14. *What is your greatest weakness?*

Employers ask this question to get a sense of your values and self-awareness. Use a work-related negative, and emphasize what you're doing about it. Interviewers won't let you get away with a "weakness" like being a workaholic or just not having any experience yet. Instead, use one of the following three strategies:

a. Discuss a weakness that is not related to the job you're being considered for, and that will not be needed even when you're promoted. End your answer with a positive related to the job:

For a creative job in advertising: I don't like accounting. I know it's important, but I don't like it. I even hire someone to do my taxes. I'm much more interested in being creative and working with people, which is why I find this position interesting.

For a job in administration: I don't like selling products. I hated selling cookies when I was a Girl Guide. I'd much rather work with ideas—and I really like selling the ideas that I believe in.

b. Discuss a weakness that you are working to improve:

In the past, I wasn't a strong writer. But last term I took a course in business writing that taught me how to organize my ideas and how to revise. Now I'm a lot more confident that I can write effective reports and memos.

c. Discuss a work-related weakness:

Sometimes I procrastinate. Fortunately, I work well under pressure, but a couple of times I've really put myself in a bind.

15. *Why are you looking for another job?*

Stress what you're looking for in a new job, not why you want to get away from your old one.

If you were fired, say so. There are four acceptable ways to explain why you were fired:

a. You lost your job, along with many others, when the company downsized for economic reasons.
b. It wasn't a good match. Add what you now know you need in a job, and ask what the employer can offer in this area.
c. You and your supervisor had a personality conflict. Make sure you show that this was an isolated incident and that you normally get along well with people.
d. You made mistakes, but you've learned from them and are now ready to work well. Be ready to offer a specific anecdote proving that you have indeed changed.

16. *What questions do you have?*

Employability Skills

This gives you a chance to cover things the interviewer hasn't brought up; it also gives the interviewer a sense of your priorities and values. Don't focus on salary or fringe benefits. Instead, prepare a typed list of specific questions such as

- What would I be doing on a day-to-day basis?
- What kind of training programs do you have? If, as I'm rotating among departments, I find that I prefer one area, can I specialize in it when the training program is over?
- How do you evaluate employees? How often do you review them? Where would you expect a new trainee (banker, staff accountant, salesperson) to be three years from now?
- What happened to the last person who had this job?
- How are interest rates (a new product from competitors, imports, demographic trends, government regulation, etc.) affecting your company?
- How would you describe the company's culture?

- This sounds like a great job. What are the drawbacks?

Increasingly, candidates are asking about work–life balance and about the control they'll have over their own work:

- Do people who work for you have a life off the job?
- If my job requires too much travel, can I change jobs without doing serious damage to my career?
- Do you offer flextime?
- How much pressure do you have to achieve your projects? How much freedom is there to extend a deadline?[5]

You won't be able to anticipate every question you may get. (One interviewer asked applicants, "What vegetable would you like to be?" Another asked, "If you were a cookie, what kind of cookie would you be?")[6] Check with other people who have interviewed recently to find out what questions are being asked in your field.

LO6 How Can I Prepare for Behavioural and Situational Interviews?

Think about skills you've used that could transfer to other jobs. Learn as much as you can about the culture of the company you hope to join.

Many companies are now using behavioural or situational interviews. **Behavioural interviews** ask the applicant to describe actual behaviours, rather than plans or general principles. Thus, instead of asking, "How would you motivate people?" the interviewer might ask, "Tell me what happened the last time you wanted to get other people to do something." Follow-up questions might include, "What exactly did you do to handle the situation? How did you feel about the results? How did the other people feel? How did your superior feel about the results?"

In your answer

- Describe the situation
- Tell what you did
- Describe the outcome
- Show that you understand the implications of what you did and suggest how you might modify your behaviour in other situations

For example, if you did the extra work yourself when a team member didn't do his or her share, does that fact suggest that you do not handle conflict well or prefer to work alone? You might go on to demonstrate that doing the extra work was appropriate in that situation, but that you could respond differently in other situations.

Since behavioural questions require applicants to tell what they actually did—rather than to say what ought to be done—interviewers feel they offer better insight into how someone will actually function as an employee. Figure 27.1 lists common behavioural questions.

Situational interviews put you in a situation that allows the interviewer to see whether you have the qualities the company is seeking.

Situational interviews may also be conducted using traditional questions but evaluating behaviours other than the answers. For its customer assistance centre, Greyhound hired applicants who made eye contact with the interviewer and smiled at least five times during a 15-minute interview.[7]

Increasingly common is the situational interview that asks you to do—on the spot—the kind of thing the job would require. An interviewer for a sales job handed applicants a ballpoint pen and said, "Sell me this pen." (It's OK to ask who the target market is and whether this is a repeat or a new customer.)

FIGURE 27.1 **Behavioural Interview Questions**

Describe a situation in which you

1. Created an opportunity for yourself in a job or volunteer position.
2. Used writing to achieve your goal.
3. Went beyond the call of duty to get a job done.
4. Communicated successfully with someone you disliked.
5. Had to make a decision quickly.
6. Overcame a major obstacle.
7. Took a project from start to finish.
8. Were unable to complete a project on time.
9. Used good judgment and logic in solving a problem.
10. Worked under a tight deadline.
11. Worked with a tough boss.
12. Handled a difficult situation with a co-worker.
13. Made an unpopular decision.
14. Gave a presentation.
15. Worked with someone who wasn't doing his or her share of the work.

Candidates who make it through the first two rounds of interviews for sales jobs at Dataflex are invited to participate in a week's worth of sales meetings, which start at 7 a.m. four times a week. The people who participate—not merely attend—are the people who get hired.[8] Other interview requests include asking applicants to participate in role-plays, to make presentations, or to lead meetings.

LO7 How Can I Prepare for Phone or Skype Interviews?

Practise short answers. Practise until you feel comfortable.

Try to schedule phone interviews for home, not work, and for a time when things will be quiet. If a company wants to interview you on the spot, accept only if the timing is good. If it isn't, say so: "We just sat down to dinner. Could you call back in 30 minutes?" Then get your information about the company, ask your roommates to be quiet, and get your thoughts in order. Use a landline, not a cell phone, to ensure good reception.

Three strategies are important when preparing for a phone interview:

- Research the company information, and identify in writing how your qualifications can contribute.
- Record yourself so you can make any adjustments in pronunciation and voice qualities.
- Practise short answers to questions. After giving a short answer in the interview, say, "Would you like more information?" Without a visual channel, you can't see the body language that tells you someone else wants to speak.

During the interview, listen closely to the questions; speak slowly; do the interview standing up: "an erect and confident poise will help you come across more confidently."[9]

For Skype interviews, use the same guidelines as for a phone interview.

As technology changes, many companies are altering their interview practices. If the company sends a list of questions, asking you to pre-record the responses

- Practise your answers.
- Record the interview as many times as necessary to present yourself at your best.
- Be specific. Since the employer can't ask follow-up questions, you need to be detailed about how your credentials could help the employer.

For phone, Skype, or pre-recorded interviews, smile when you talk to put more energy into your voice.

LO8 How Should I Follow Up the Interview?

Send a letter that reinforces positives and overcomes any negatives. Use PAIBOC analysis to clarify your message content.

Following up after the interview is a multi-step process. Immediately after the interview, make notes on any questions and ideas that impressed you. These notes can help focus your first letter.

Then, based on your PAIBOC analysis, send an email or hard copy letter to reinforce positives from the first interview, to overcome any negatives, and to get information you can use to persuade the interviewer to hire you (see Figure 27.2).

FIGURE 27.2 **PAIBOC Questions for Analysis**

P	What are your **purposes** in writing? You have several: to demonstrate your emotional intelligence, to emphasize your interest in the job, to reinforce the fit between the organization and you, and to influence the recruiter's opinion positively.
A	Who is your **audience**? What do they value? What do they need? How can you further demonstrate to your audiences that you have the qualifications and interpersonal skills they seek?
I	What **information** must your message include? What information—about the company and the position—did the interviewers emphasize? What further information can you provide to impress your readers favourably?
B	What reasons or reader **benefits** can you use to support your position?
O	What **objections** can you expect your readers to have? What negative elements of your message must you de-emphasize or overcome?
C	How will the **context** affect the reader's response? Think about your relationship to the reader, the economy, the goals of the organization, the time of year, and any special circumstances.

Career coach Kate Weldon suggests asking the following questions in a follow-up phone call:

- "What additional information can I give you?"
- "I've been giving a lot of thought to your project and have some new ideas. Can we meet to go over them?"
- "Where do I stand? How does my work compare with the work others presented?"[10]

A letter (whether a hard copy or an email attachment) is a more formal follow-up message than an email. Base your decision on which to send on your audience analysis. A letter thanking your hosts is essential, however, when your interview includes an office visit or other forms of

Take notes during and immediately after the interview: they're the source of your follow-up letters.

hospitality. A well-written letter can be the deciding factor that gets you the job.[11] In your letter, be sure to do the following:

- Thank the interviewer for his or her time and hospitality.
- Reinforce the interviewer's positive impressions.
- Counter any negative impressions that may have come up at the interview.
- Use the language of the company, and refer to specific things you learned during your interview or saw during your visit.
- Be enthusiastic.
- Refer to the next step: whether you'll wait to hear from the employer or you will call to learn about the status of your application.

Be sure that the letter is well written and error-free. One employer reports

> I often interviewed people whom I liked…but their follow-up letters were filled with misspelled words and names, and other inaccuracies. They blew their chance with the follow-up letter.[12]

Career coaches and recruiters concur. Sending poorly written emails, using shorthand language and/or emoticons, texting: all can reflect sloppy work habits and poor judgment.[13]

Figures 27.3 and 27.4 offer examples of follow-up messages.

FIGURE 27.3 **A Follow-Up Email**

From:	Ahmed Dhanray <adhanray@address.ca>
To:	dland@notime.ca
Sent:	Monday, August 11, 2013, 5:45 PM
Subject:	Thank you

Dear Delmarie Land:

Acknowledges hospitality and reinforces interest in the position →

Thank you for your hospitality during my interview last Thursday. After visiting Notime International and speaking with you and your team, I am convinced that a career in logistics is the right choice for me.

Seeing Kelly, Gene, and Leah work together to coordinate an international client's shipment gave me a sense of the deadlines you have to meet and of the collaboration required for customer service success. As we discussed, I learned to meet deadlines and work collaboratively during my summer co-op placement with Crowley Logistics. As I mentioned during the interview, my team at Crowley suggested a computerized warehouse system that saved the company more than $30 000 in its first year of implementation. I welcome the opportunity to make a similar contribution at Notime.

← *Reminds the reader of strengths*

Follow-up makes it easy for the reader →

Please call me at 416-555-4567 if you have additional questions, or if I can provide you with more information.

Sincerely,
Ahmed Dhanray

FIGURE 27.4 A Follow-Up Letter

Refers to important items he saw and heard during the interview

Provides positive confirmation of interest in the position

71 Autumn Ridge Road
Kitchener, ON N2P 2J6

March 23, 2013

Mr. Gino Focasio
Human Resources Department
Perlmutter Canada
8069 Lawson Road
Milton, ON L9T 5C4

Dear Mr. Focasio:

Thank you for interviewing me for the industrial engineering technician position, available in your Milton plant. I appreciate the time that Ms. Rossiter, Mr. Alverez, Mr. Storino, and you gave me.

My expertise in jig and fixture design, and in AutoCAD software, would contribute to your commitment to continuous improvement, as described by Mr. Storino during the interview. Seeing your machining and assembly processes assured me that I would be able to apply my CNC programming experience to benefit the company.

Again, thank you for your time and for the plant tour. I am very excited at the prospect of working with Perlmutter Canada. Please call me at 519-555-5912, or email me at zhang@address.com if you have any additional questions.

Sincerely,

Zhang Huang

Zhang Huang

Reminds interviewer of his strong points

Makes it easy for the reader to respond

As part of the process, some career coaches suggest writing additional letters developing a discussion, or answering a question that came up in the interview. These notes indicate your interest in the job, and keep you uppermost in the minds of the interviewers.[14]

Checkpoint

Follow-Up Letters

A letter after an office visit should

- Remind the interviewer of what he or she liked about you
- Counter any negative impressions
- Use the jargon of the company and refer to specifics from the visit
- Be enthusiastic
- Refer to the next move

442   **UNIT 6**   Job Hunting

The skilled trades continue to be underemployed, despite their multiple attractions: excellent remuneration, numerous opportunities, and work flexibility. York Region's Apprenticeship project, supported by the Ontario Youth Apprenticeship Program, offers high school students a semester of technical apprenticeship, under the tutelage of skilled co-op teachers. Licensed skilled trades workers, including plumbers, electricians, and construction workers, can make over $100,000 annually. Yet a recent Manpower Inc. survey found that "according to employers [skilled trades] still are the most difficult-to-fill roles in Canada and the U.S." (Manpower Group (2012). 2012 talent shortage survey research results. Retrieved from http://www.manpowergroup.us/campaigns/talent-shortage-2012/pdf/2012_Talent_Shortage_Survey_Results_US_FINALFINAL.pdf)

What If My First Offer Isn't for the Job I Most Want?

Phone your first-choice employer to find out where you are on that list.

Some employers offer jobs at the end of the office visit. In other cases, you may wait for weeks or even months to hear. Employers usually offer jobs orally. You must say something in response immediately, so plan some strategies.

If your first offer is not from your first choice, express your pleasure at being offered the job, but do not accept it on the phone. "That's great! May I let you know?" Most firms will give you a week to decide.

Then call the other companies you're interested in. Explain, "I've just gotten a job offer, but I'd rather work for you. Can you tell me what the status of my application is?" Nobody will put that information in writing, but almost everyone will tell you over the phone. With this information, you're in a better position to decide whether to accept the original offer.

Make your acceptance contingent on a written job offer confirming the terms. That letter should spell out not only salary but also fringe benefits and any special provisions you have negotiated. If something is missing, call the interviewer for clarification: "We agreed that I'd be reviewed for a promotion and higher salary in six months, but I don't see that in the letter." You have more power to resolve misunderstandings now than you will after six months or a year on the job.

When you've accepted one job, let the other places you visited know that you're no longer interested. Then they can go to their second choices. If you're second on someone else's list, you'll appreciate other candidates' removing themselves so the way is clear for you. Because the world is a small place, because everyone is the customer, and because you may someday want to work for the company you're currently turning down, follow the *KISS* formula: *Keep it short and simple.*

Dear Jackson Phillips:

Thank you for offering me the sales position in your electronics division.

Since Allied Signal enjoys an international reputation for innovative quality products, I'm pleased to be considered as part of the Allied team.

After a great deal of thought, however, I have decided to look for employment opportunities closer to home while investigating courses for an advanced degree. I must, therefore, decline your offer.

Again, thank you for your consideration.

Sincerely,

EXPANDING A CRITICAL SKILL

Projecting Professional Attitude

As more Canadians use clothing to reflect their personalities and/or ethnicities, organizations are adopting more flexible dress codes.

Even on dress-down or casual Fridays, however, organizations still expect employees to take care of business. Attention to detail, organization, accuracy, economy, and courtesy are the norm. According to Max Messruer, chair of Accountemps and author of the best-selling *Job Hunting for Dummies®* (IDG Books Worldwide), what you wear determines others' perceptions of you and directly affects your career advancement.

On casual days, wear clothes in good condition that are one or two "notches" below what you'd wear on other days. If suits are the norm, choose blazers and slacks or skirts. If blazers and slacks or skirts are the norm, choose sweaters or knit sport shirts; khakis, simple skirts, or dressier jeans; or simple dresses. Wear good shoes and always be well groomed. Avoid anything that's ill fitting or revealing.

Other symbols also convey professionalism. Your work area, for instance, says a lot about you. If your organization allows employees to personalize their desks or offices with photographs, knickknacks, and posters, don't display so much that you seem frivolous. And never display offensive photos or slogans, even in an attempt to be funny. The same caution goes for screen savers and radio stations.

It isn't professional to play a morning "shock jock" who uses coarse language and offensive stereotypes.

If your organization allows employees to listen to music, keep the volume at a reasonable level. If your organization allows, consider wearing headphones.

Avoid playing computer games, surfing the Web inappropriately, or ordering personal items on company time. These activities are fine on your own clock, but unethical, and in some cases illegal, on the organization's clock. You can be fired for browsing for inappropriate material online.

Keep your voicemail messages succinct and professional—find out what co-workers say in theirs.

Keep your desk organized. File papers; keep stacks to a minimum. Throw away anything you don't need. Don't store food in your office. Clean periodically. Water your plants.

The volume of your voice can also disturb others. Although most people wouldn't shout across an office, many of us don't realize how loud our voices can be when we're excited or happy. Keep personal conversations to a minimum, in person and on the phone.

Learn the culture of your organization and fit into it as much as you can. When in doubt, model your dress and behaviour on someone the organization respects.

MODULE SUMMARY

- To be your best self at the interview,
  - Develop an overall interview management strategy based on your answers to these three questions:
    1. What two to five personal or professional characteristics do you want the interviewer to know about you?
    2. What disadvantages or weaknesses do you want to overcome or minimize?
    3. What do you need to know about the organization and the job to decide whether you want to accept this job if it is offered to you?
  - Plan the interview logistics—what to wear, how to get there, what to bring—so that you can concentrate on rehearsing a confident interview session.

  1. Wear clothes appropriate for the position.
  2. Bring an extra copy of your resumé, something to write on and with, copies of your best work, and a list of typed questions you want to ask.
  - Rehearse: ask a friend to interview you; watch a recording of yourself so that you can evaluate and modify your behaviour.
  - During and immediately after the interview, note the name of the interviewer, positives and negatives, answers to your questions, and the date you will hear from the company.
- Successful applicants are prepared; they
  - Know what they want to do
  - Use the company name throughout the interview

○ Demonstrate that they have researched the company

○ Support claims with specific examples and stories

○ Use industry and company jargon

○ Ask specific questions

○ Talk more of the time

- In behavioural interviews, recruiters ask applicants to describe actual behaviours and outcomes.

  ○ To answer a behavioural question, describe the situation, tell what you did, describe the outcome, show that you understand the implications of your behaviour, and describe how you might modify your behaviour in other situations.

- Situational interviews put you in a position that allows the interviewer to see if you have the qualities the company is seeking.

- For a phone interview, ensure you have no distractions, do the interview standing up, and listen carefully to each question before giving concise answers.

- If you make a recording, make sure to re-record to show your best self.

- Use follow-up phone calls to reinforce positives from the first interview, to overcome any negatives, and to get information you can use to persuade the interviewer to hire you.

- Use a follow-up letter to

  ○ Remind the reviewer of your qualities

  ○ Counter any negative impressions

  ○ Use the language of the industry and company to refer to specifics that came up in the interview, or that you saw in your visit

  ○ Be enthusiastic

  ○ Refer to next steps

ASSIGNMENTS FOR MODULE 27

Questions for Critical Thinking

27.1 How can you demonstrate your greatest strengths during an interview?

27.2 How can you deal with your weaknesses if they come up during an interview?

27.3 What are your options if you are asked what you believe is an illegal interview question? Which option seems best to you? Why?

27.4 Why is "mirroring" an interviewer's communication style a good interview tactic?

Exercises and Problems

27.5 Interviewing Job Hunters

Talk to students at your school who are interviewing for jobs this term. Possible questions to ask them include the following:

- What field are you in? How good is the job market in that field this year?

- What questions have you been asked at job interviews? Were you asked any illegal or sexist questions? Any really oddball questions?

- What answers seemed to go over well? What answers bombed?

- Were you asked to take any tests (skills, physical, drugs)?

- How long did you have to wait after a first interview to learn whether you were being invited for an office visit? How long after an office visit did it take to learn whether you were being offered a job? How much time did the company give you to decide?

- What advice would you have for someone who will be interviewing next term or next year?

As your instructor directs

  a. Summarize your findings in a memo to your instructor.

  b. Report your findings orally to the class.

  c. Join a group of two or three other students to write a blog describing the results of your survey.

27.6 Interviewing an Interviewer

Talk to someone who regularly interviews candidates for entry-level jobs. Possible questions to ask are

- How long have you been interviewing for your organization? Does everyone on the management ladder at your company do some interviewing, or do people specialize in it?

- Do you follow a set structure for interviews? What are some of the standard questions you ask?

- What are you looking for? How important are 1) good grades, 2) leadership roles in extracurricular groups, or 3) relevant work experience? What advice would you give to someone who doesn't have one or more of these?

- What behaviours do students exhibit that create a poor impression? Think about the worst candidate you've interviewed. What did he or she do (or not do) to create such a negative impression?
- What behaviours make a good impression? Recall the best student you've ever interviewed. Why did he or she impress you so much?
- How does your employer evaluate and reward your success as an interviewer?
- What advice would you give to someone who still has a year or so before the job hunt begins?

As your instructor directs

a. Summarize your findings in a memo to your instructor.
b. Report your findings orally to the class.
c. Team up with a small group of students to write a group report describing the results of your survey.
d. Write to the interviewer thanking him or her for taking the time to talk to you.

27.7 Preparing an Interview Strategy

Based on your analysis for Problems 27.5 and 27.6, prepare an interview strategy.

1. List two to five things about yourself that you want the interviewer to know before you leave the interview.
2. Identify any weaknesses or apparent weaknesses in your record and plan ways to explain them or minimize them.
3. List the points you need to learn about an employer to decide whether to accept an office visit or plant trip.

As your instructor directs

a. Share your strategy with a small group of students.
b. Describe your strategy in a memo to your instructor.
c. Present your strategy orally to the class.

27.8 Preparing Answers to Behavioural Interview Questions

Think about

1. A conflict you have been part of and your role in resolving it
2. A team you have worked on and the role you played
3. A time you were asked to behave in a way you thought was unethical
4. A time you were unable to complete a project by the due date

5. A time you handled a difficult situation with a co-worker
6. A time you overcame a major obstacle
7. A time you adapted to a difficult situation

As your instructor directs

a. Share your answers with a small group of students.
b. Present your answers in a memo to your instructor, and explain why you've chosen the examples you describe.
c. Present your answers orally to the class.

27.9 Preparing Questions to Ask Employers

Prepare a list of questions to ask at job interviews.

1. Prepare a list of three to five general questions that apply to most employers in your field.
2. Prepare two to five specific questions for each of the three companies you are most interested in.

As your instructor directs

a. Share the questions with a small group of students.
b. List the questions in a memo to your instructor.
c. Present your questions orally to the class.

27.10 Writing a Follow-Up Letter After an Office Visit or Plant Trip

Write a follow-up email message or letter after an office visit or plant trip. Thank your hosts for their hospitality, relate your strong points to things you learned about the company during the visit, overcome any negatives that may remain, be enthusiastic about the company, and submit receipts for your expenses so you can be reimbursed, if the company has indicated they will do so.

27.11 Clarifying the Terms of a Job Offer

Last week, you got a job offer from your first-choice company, and you accepted it over the phone. Today, the written confirmation arrived. The letter specifies the starting salary and fringe benefits you had negotiated. However, during the office visit, you were promised a 5 percent raise after six months on the job. The job offer says nothing about the raise. You do want the job, but you want it on the terms you thought you had negotiated.

Write to your contact at the company, Damon Winters.

POLISHING YOUR PROSE

Matters on Which Experts Disagree

Any living language changes. New usages appear first in speaking. Here are five issues on which experts currently disagree:

1. Plural pronouns to refer to *everybody*, *everyone*, and *each*. Standard grammar says these words require singular pronouns: *his* or *her* rather than *their*.
2. Split infinitives. An infinitive is the form of a verb that contains *to*: to understand. An infinitive is "split" when another word separates the *to* from the rest of an infinitive: *to easily understand, to boldly go*. The most recent edition of the *Oxford English Dictionary* allows split infinitives.
3. *Hopefully* to mean *I hope that. Hopefully* means "in a hopeful manner." However, a speaker who says, "Hopefully, the rain will stop" is talking about the speaker's hope, not the rain's.
4. *Verbal* to mean *oral. Verbal* means "using words." Therefore, both writing and speaking are verbal communication. Non-verbal communication (e.g., body language) does not use words.
5. Comma before *and* (the serial or series comma). In a series of three or more items, some experts require a comma after the next to last item (the item before the *and*); others don't. This book uses serial commas.

Ask your instructor and your boss if they are willing to accept the less formal usage. When you write to someone you don't know, use standard grammar and usage.

Exercises

Each of the following sentences illustrates informal usage. (a) Which would your instructor or your boss accept? (b) Rewrite each of the sentences using standard grammar and usage.

1. Everyone should bring their laptops to the sales meeting.
2. The schedule includes new product information, role-plays with common selling situations, and awards to the top salespeople.
3. To really take advantage of the meeting, you need to bring all of your new product info.
4. Prepare to make a brief verbal report on a challenging sales situation.
5. Think of a time when it was hard to even get in the door to see a potential customer.
6. Hopefully, we will have time to work through many of these situations in our role-plays.
7. Awards include best rookie sales representative, the most improved region, everyone who beat their quota, and sales representative of the year.
8. We'll feature verbal quotes from customers in our radio ads.
9. Our website will let people listen to each customer summarizing verbally what they like best about our products.
10. Hopefully, the website will be live so that we can access it during the meeting.

Check your answers to the odd-numbered exercises in the Polishing Your Prose Answer Key.

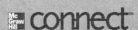

Synthesizing and Documenting Information

Learning Objectives

After reading and applying the information in Module 15, you'll be able to demonstrate

Knowledge of

LO1 How to summarize and paraphrase information

LO2 How to create good notes

LO3 Why researchers document their sources of information

LO4 How to cite and document sources correctly

Skills to

LO5 Begin to write summaries and précis

LO6 Begin to take useful notes

LO7 Document sources legally, ethically, and correctly

Employability Skills 2000+ Checklist

Module content builds these Conference Board of Canada Employability Skills 2000+

Communicate

Manage Information

Think and Solve Problems

Be Adaptable

Learn Continuously

Participate in Projects and Tasks

This module describes how to note and synthesize information, how to use in-text citations for business reports, and how to document sources using APA and MLA styles. Throughout this module, APA style in-text citations credit both primary and secondary sources.

LO1 LO5 How Do I Summarize Information?

Read and listen for meaning, then write a synopsis, paraphrase, or précis.

We process information by sorting it into meaningful patterns. This pattern-making includes summarizing and paraphrasing. When you **summarize**, you condense the data you're hearing or reading. You omit all details except those that capture and compress the meaning.

Summarizing Documents

To summarize text, use active reading strategies

- Pre-read, skim and scan the article, document, or visual (Module 14).
- Identify and analyze the context; use PAIBOC analysis to answer:
  - What's the medium? Research report? Scholarly journal? Newspaper? Magazine? Blog? University Web page? Intranet page? Social network page? The medium frames the meaning: every discourse community (Module 2) has its own language rules, dependent on purpose and audience. Academic writing, for example, is often longer, denser, and more formal than business writing. Scientific and technical report writers often use the passive voice (see the Revising and Editing Resources) to meet audience expectations.
  - What's the purpose of the document, and who is the intended audience?
  - Who wrote it? What are the author's credentials? What's the evidence of expertise?
  - How does the writer develop the argument or thesis? What is the pattern of organization? Comparison/contrast? Problem/solution? Elimination of alternatives? (Module 17)
  - When was it published? How current is it?
  - What's the language level?
- Find the thesis, or main idea in the abstract or in the introduction.
- Read the concluding paragraph: Does it sum up the information? What does it suggest the reader think or do?

- Find the topic sentences that control each paragraph. How are they related to the thesis?
- Look for proof. How does the author support his or her thesis? What's the evidence? Examples? Statistics? Studies? Experiments? Personal experience? Interviews?
- Set the text aside, and jot down or cluster (Module 4) an overview of the material: note (1) the main idea, (2) the medium, (3) the author's name, (4) an example or proof, (5) your questions about the material. Figure 15.1 illustrates a cluster summary of these points.
- Reread the document to ensure your summary information is accurate.
- Find the answers to your questions. If it suits your purpose, add them to your summary.
- Record all biographic data if you are using the summary in your report or presentation.
- Ask a peer or friend to check your summary against the original text.
- Add anything relevant.

Table 15.2 lists additional Internet information resources you can research and summarize.

FIGURE 15.1   **Clustering Information**

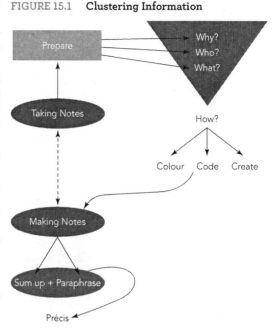

LO1 LO5 Summarizing Oral Communications

To summarize a lecture, presentation, interview, or speech,

- Listen for understanding; identify and analyze the context (Module 20):
  - Whenever possible, pre-read on the topic.
  - Listen for an overview. Use PAIBOC analysis: What? Why? Who? When? Where?
  - Identify the speaker's purpose. Note it.
  - Identify the speaker's expectations of his or her audience. Note them.
  - Listen for the thesis. Note it.
  - Identify and analyze the organizational pattern. How does the speaker develop the argument, or thesis (Module 21)?
  - Listen for the proof. Note examples, statistics, evidence.
  - Listen for points of emphasis. Note them.
  - Listen for the close: How does the speaker sum up? What does the speaker want the audience to think, or do? Note that.
  - Read the handouts or supplementary material if provided.
  - Note your questions. What is unclear? What else do you need to know to understand?
  - Ask your questions, if appropriate to the situation
- Jot down or cluster (Figure 15.1) an overview of the material: (1) the thesis or main idea, (2) the speaker's name, if relevant to your purpose, (3) evidence and examples, (4) points of emphasis, (5) the conclusion.
- Check your summary for accuracy.
  - If possible, ask the speaker to confirm that you have heard and understood all relevant information.
  - Read related documents.
  - If possible, compare your summary with that of another audience member.
- Add any relevant information.

Paraphrasing

Ex.
15.5
15.7–
15.9

When you **paraphrase**, you put information you're recording or reporting *into your own words* while maintaining the meaning.

You write a **précis** when you both paraphrase and summarize information. A précis interprets, summarizes, and translates information
- while listening actively (Module 20) during a presentation, lecture or interview
- while listening actively to provide feedback
- when reading material you want to learn
- when translating research data to incorporate the ideas into your reports

When you paraphrase or précis another person's words to include them in your oral and written reports, you don't use quotation marks because the ideas are now in your own words. However, you must credit the original source of the information with in-text citation or footnotes and in your references.

TABLE 15.1　Sources for Web Research, Analysis, and Synthesis

Canadian Government Information

Statistics Canada
http://www.statcan.ca

Most recent five years of data, constantly updated
http://www40.statcan.ca/ol/esto1

Profile of Canadian communities, tables for more than 5000 Canadian communities from most recent census, with the ability to create local base maps
www12.statcan.ca/english/census01/home/index.cfm

Canada Business Service Centres
www.cbsc.org

Canada's Business and Consumer Site
www.strategis.ic.gc.ca

Environment Canada
www.ec.gc.ca

Subject Matter Directories

AccountingNet
www.acountingnet.com

The Computer User High Tech Dictionary
www.computeruser.com/resources/dictionary/Dictionary.html

Education Index
www.educationindex.com

International Business Kiosk
www.calintel.org/kiosk

Management and Entrepreneurship
www.lib.lsu.edu/bus/management/html

The WWW Virtual Library: Marketing
www.knowthis.com

Reference Collections

Britannica Online
www.eb.com

CEO Express
www.ceoexpress.com

Your library offers billions of bytes of information.

Hoover's Online (information on more than 13 000 public and private companies worldwide)
www.hoovers.com/free

Reference Desk
www.refdesk.com

Interactive Atlas of Canada
http://atlas.nrcan.gc.ca/site/english/maps/topo/map

News Sites

Most Popular Business Websites EBizMBA
www.ebizmba.com/articles/business-sites

CBC News
www.cbc.ca/news

CBC Radio
http://cbc.ca/programguide

Business Week **Online**
www.businessweek.com

Canadian Business Online
www.canadianbusiness.com

The *Globe and Mail* **Online**
www.globeandmail.com

Maclean's **Online**
www.macleans.ca

The *National Post* **Online**
www.nationalpost.com

The *New York Times* **on the Web**
www.nyt.com

The *Wall Street Journal* **Interactive Edition**
www.wsj.com

Language FOCUS

Paraphrasing means that you are condensing the information you have and putting it *all* in your own words. You cannot just use synonyms for a few words and call it a précis or paraphrase. A paraphrase is also shorter than the original piece, so you leave out examples and illustrations that the original writer or speaker used.

When you paraphrase information, you are still using another person's ideas; therefore, you must always identify your source: who wrote it, what is the title and date of information, and where did it come from?

LO1 LO5 How Do I Use My Research Effectively?

Use sources strategically; integrate them seamlessly; credit them correctly.

Seeking information to clarify, verify, or develop your ideas, to find expert advice or inspiration, or to suggest topics for further development is part of the research process. Equally important parts of the process are to integrate the information smoothly into your document or presentation, and document your sources correctly.

Citation means attributing an idea or fact to its source in the body of the report:

"According to the 2012 Census..."

"Jane Bryant Quinn argues that..."

Documentation means providing the biographic information (in an APA References page or a MLA Works Cited page) your readers need to find the original source.

Whether you choose to paraphrase the information or quote others' work directly, incorporate the material seamlessly, and give your source credit.

Ex.
15.5
15.7–
15.9

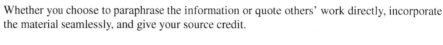

EXPANDING A CRITICAL SKILL

LO2 LO6 Taking Great Notes

Note-taking is not duplicating information verbatim, but translating and recording information in a way *that informs you*. The best notes encode and encapsulate meaning.

This interpreting and synthesizing process uses both critical and creative thinking skills. First, you have to know *why* you are recording the information; then you have to focus on, filter, analyze, organize, and interpret the information to understand *what* you should record (Module 14).

You use your creative thinking skills to note the information in a way that is both meaningful and memorable for you.

Once you have identified your purpose, the context, and the content you want to record, experiment to find the most efficient note-taking system for you. Try the following strategies:

- Test all available tools: don't assume that creating e-notes is the best method for you. Try
  - ○ Taking notes in longhand
  - ○ Recording information on small note cards—one idea, quotation, summary, or paraphrase, with bibliographic information, per card; you can then organize your report information by rearranging the cards
  - ○ Creating doodle notes, jot-dots, clusters

- Use an alphabetic shorthand: spell words phonetically; omit capitals, punctuation, and all unnecessary letters (Grossman, 1976, pp. 1–13; Jensen, 2003, p. 119). For example, you might write "You cite your sources even when you use your own words" as

u cte yr srcs evn whn u uz yr wn wrds

Use common symbols: use symbols that let you "write rapidly and interpret easily" (Jensen, 2003, p. 119):

TABLE 15.2 **Note-Taking Symbols**

>	greater than	(+)	positive, good
<	less than	(-)	negative, against
=	the same, equals	w/o	without
≠	different	↓	down, under, decreasing
X	times, cross	↑	above, up, increasing
→	toward, going	w/	with
←	from	$	dollars, money
∴	therefore, because	Q	question
∞	infinity		

- Create your own code. Make your own symbols to summarize, organize, and emphasize information.
  - ○ Use mind mapping (Module 4) to note patterns, sequences, hierarchies, and relationships.
  - ○ Use spacing, different-size fonts, and different colours to highlight information you want to emphasize.
  - ○ Keep a separate section to note what you want to follow up: questions, unclear information, and additional resources.

Creating purposeful notes is an acquired skill that depends on your understanding of both content and context. Learning to take great notes is easier when you practise daily, read widely and frequently, and have an extensive vocabulary. Competent note-takers use PAIBOC to analyze purpose and audience, and to understand the pattern the writer or speaker is using to organize the information.

Language FOCUS

When taking notes, it is best to record them in the language they are given in. If the lecturer is using English, record your notes in English. Do not try to translate into your own language while taking notes, as this might lead to mistakes later when you are studying or writing a report. For example, if you have incorrectly translated a word during a lecture or in a meeting, it will affect the accuracy of your report when you are writing it later and not able to double-check on your translation accuracy.

Using Précis

When you paraphrase and summarize other's ideas or words, make sure that your précis

- fits seamlessly into the sentence,
- demonstrates, reinforces or proves the point you are making, and
- gives credit to the originator (St. Francis Xavier University, 2012a)

Using Quotations

When you quote words and phrases, "integrate them [into your text] as smoothly as possible" to ensure consistency (St. Francis Xavier University, 2012b).

Introduce a full sentence quote with a colon:

> Journalist and professor Leslie Butler is adamant about the ethical ramifications of plagiarism: "It's a personal violation" (L. Butler, July 8, 2012).

Introduce a word or phrase with a comma:

> Plagiarism, as journalist and professor Leslie Butler insists, "is a personal violation" (L. Butler, July 8, 2012).

Indent long quotations on the left and right to set them off from your text. Indented quotations do not need quotation marks; the indentation shows the reader that the passage is a quotation. Since many readers skip quotations, always summarize the main point of the quotation in a single sentence before the quotation. If the last sentence before the quotation is a complete sentence, end the sentence with a colon, not a period, since it introduces the quotation.

> Create an **RSS** Feed for the most current information available. **Really Simple Syndication** sends subscribers up-to-date news articles:
>
> > RSS (Rich Site Summary) is a format for delivering regularly changing web content. Many news-related sites, weblogs and other online publishers syndicate their content as an RSS Feed to whoever wants it. (http://www. whatisrss.com/)

You can also interrupt a quotation to analyze, clarify, or question it. When you add or change words to clarify the quotation, or to make the quotation fit the grammar of your sentence, use square brackets [ ] around the new or changed words. Omit any words in the original source that are not essential for your purposes. Use an ellipsis (…) to indicate omissions.

Why Must I Document My Sources?

Citing your sources of information protects you from charges of plagiarism, demonstrates your honesty, and enhances your credibility.

Copyright laws protect people's creative output: "Copyright applies to all original literary, dramatic, musical and artistic works" (Industry Canada, 2011). Ideas can't be owned, but the expression of those ideas can be. For example: "There have been many movies about Pirates, but only one Jack Sparrow" (Click & Copyright, 2012).

Legally, therefore, researchers are required to identify the source of information that they do not originate. **You must credit the source even when you put that information into your own words, or recreate a visual with your own software.** Not doing so—intentionally or unintentionally—means you are plagiarizing. Stealing someone else's work has serious legal, academic, and personal consequences (PlagiarismdotOrg, 2012). Academic penalties can include a grade failure or expulsion. In business, you can be sued for damages and lost revenue.

Furthermore, since our laws express our social values (L. Butler, personal communication, July 8, 2012), you are also **ethically responsible for crediting the ideas, facts, figures, symbols, and words of others.** Using someone else's work without giving him or her credit violates the individual's personal and professional rights. Doing so, even unintentionally, can damage your reputation.

Correctly documenting your sources also **makes you look good.** Investigating and citing a wide range of sources on your topic demonstrate your competence and your analytical and critical thinking skills. Using a variety of authoritative sources can suggest alternative points of view that lead to new insights and provide you with the evidence you need to develop and prove your thesis. Documenting this research ethically proves your professionalism.

How Should I Document My Sources?

Use APA or MLA format.

The two most widely used formats for endnotes and bibliographies are those of the **American Psychological Association** (APA) and the **Modern Language Association** (MLA). (This module uses APA in-text citations.) Figure 15.2 shows both APA and MLA models.

Formatting styles, like language itself, constantly evolve; you can find MLA (www.mla.org) and APA (www.apa.org) updates on their respective home pages. Moreover, you can use free APA and MLA formatting software such as RefWorks or Son of Citation to create your documentation material.

 Cultural FOCUS

In some cultures, perhaps your own, repeating word for word what a scholar has said is considered the best way to show you have understood and agree with certain points. It is also considered the best way to show respect for that scholar. However, for documents to be acceptable in North America (and many other Western cultures), you have to cite the source and also integrate the points into your own writing. This is how respect for the original writer or thinker is shown; it also demonstrates your own understanding of the ideas. By following the expected rules here, you are showing respect for and understanding of the cultural norms, just as you would expect others to show the same respect while working in your culture.

Although citation software, like all technology, is always evolving, it still cannot think for itself. Be aware that the software creates errors (like not capitalizing proper names); if you use it, be prepared to edit thoroughly.

APA style is used to cite and document sources in business, technology, and social sciences. APA in-text citations give authors' last names and the date of the work in parentheses in the text. Put an ampersand for two authors (Paiz & Angeli, 2012) or commas and an ampersand for multiple authors (Paiz, Angeli, Wagner, Lawrick, Moore, & Anderson, 2012), then a comma and the date. If there are more than six authors, use the name of the first author followed by the abbreviation et al., which means and others (Paiz et al., 2012) Only give the page number for a direct quotation (Paiz et al., p. 74). If you use the author's name(s) in the sentence, give only the date in parentheses. The **References** page provides the full bibliographic citations, arranged alphabetically by the first author's last name.

FIGURE 15.2A   APA Format for Documenting Sources

References

American Psychological Association. (2012). *APA style.* Retrieved from www.apastyle.org

British Science Association. (n.d.). Welcome to the honesty lab. *Dishonestylab.com.* Retrieved from www.britishscienceassociation.org/web

Click & Copyright (2012). Copyright infringement. Retrieved from www.clickandcopyright.com/copyright-resources/copyright-infringement.aspx

Grossman, J. (1976). *Quickhand™.* New York: John Wiley & Sons, Inc.

Industry Canada (2011). A guide to copyrights. Ottawa: Canadian Intellectual Property Office. Retrieved from www.cipo.ic.gc.ca/eic/site/cipointernet-internetopic.nsf/eng/wr02394.html

Industry Canada. (2012). The copyright modernization act. Ottawa: Canadian Intellectual Property Office. Retrieved from http://balancedcopyright.gc.ca/eic/site/crp-prda.nsf/eng/home

iParadigms. (2012). What is plagiarism? Retrieved from www.plagiarism.org/learning_center/what_is_plagiarism.html

Jensen, E. (2003). *Student success secrets.* New York: Barron's Educational Series, Inc.

Mind Tools Ltd. (1995–2009). Mind maps, a powerful approach to note taking. Retrieved from www.mindtools.com/pages/article/newISS_01.htm

Modern Language Association of America. (2009). *MLA handbook for writers of research papers.* (7th ed.). New York: The Modern Language Association of America.

Paiz, J. M., Angeli, E., Wagner, J., Lawrick, E., Moore, K., Anderson, M., Soderlund, L., Brizee, A., and Keck, R. (2012a). Reference list: Electronic sources (web publications). *Purdue Online Writing Lab.* Retrieved from http://owl.english.purdue.edu/owl/resource/560/10/

Paiz, J. M., Angeli, E., Wagner, J., Lawrick, E., Moore, K., Anderson, M., Soderlund, L., Brizee, A., and Keck, R. (2012b). APA general format. *Purdue Online Writing Lab.* Retrieved from http://owl.english.purdue.edu/owl/resource/560/01/

PlagiarismdotOrg. (2009) What is plagiarism? Retrieved from http://plagiarism.org/

RefWorks (2009) Home page. Retrieved from www.refworks.com

St. Francis Xavier University. (2012a). Plagiarism. Angus L. Macdonald Library. Retrieved from http://library.stfx.ca/help/plagiarism.php

St. Francis Xavier University. (2012b). Quoting and paraphrasing. The Writing Centre. Retrieved from http://sites.stfx.ca/writingcentre/Quoting_and_Paraphrasing

University of Ottawa. (2012). Study skills—Note taking. *Student Academic Success Service.* Retrieved from www.sass.uottawa.ca/mentoring/undergraduate/note-taking.php

What is RSS? RSS explained. (n.d.). Retrieved from www.whatisrss.com

York University. (2009, Nov. 4). Note taking at university. *Learning Skills Services.* Retrieved from www.yorku.ca/cds/lss/skillbuilding/notetaking.html

Note: Emails and interviews by researcher are not listed in References. Identify emails and your interviews in the text as personal communications. Give name of author or interviewee and as specific a date as possible. Example: (L. Butler, personal communication, July 8, 2012).

FIGURE 15.2B   **MLA Format for Documenting Sources**

Works Cited

American Psychological Association. "APA Style." 2012. Web. 20 Aug. 2012.

British Science Association. "Welcome to the Honesty Lab." *Dishonestylab.com*. n.d. Web. 20 Aug. 2012.

Butler, Lorraine. Personal Communication, 8 July 2012.

Click & Copyright. "Copyright Infringement." Web. 10 Oct. 2012

Grossman, Jeremy. *Quickhand™*. New York: John Wiley & Sons, Inc., 1976. Print.

Industry Canada. Canadian Intellectual Property Office. "A Guide to Copyrights." 6 Dec. 2011. Web. 20 Aug. 2012.

---. Canadian Intellectual Property Office. *The Copyright Modernization Act.*" 18 July 2012. Web. 20 Aug. 2012.

iParadigms. "What is Plagiarism?" 2012. Web. 20 Aug. 2012.

Jensen, Eric. *Student Success Secrets*. New York: Barron's Educational Series, Inc., 2003. Print.

Mind Tools Ltd. "Mind Maps, a Powerful Approach to Note Taking." *Mind Tools™*, 1996–2012. Web. 20 Aug. 2012.

Modern Language Association of America. *MLA Handbook for Writers of Research Papers*. 7th ed. New York: The Modern Language Association of America, 2009. Print.

PlagiarismdotOrg. "What Is Plagiarism?" 2009. Web. 20 Aug. 2012.

Paiz, J. M., Angeli, E., Wagner, J., Lawrick, E., Moore, K., Anderson, M., Soderlund, L., Brizee, A., and Keck, R. "APA General Format." *Purdue Online Writing Lab*. 2012. Web. 20 Aug. 2012.

---. "Reference List: Electronic Sources (Web Publications)." *Purdue Online Writing Lab*. 2012. Web. 20 Aug. 2012.

RefWorks. Home Page. 2009. Web. 20 Aug. 2012.

St. Francis Xavier University. "Plagiarism." Angus L. Macdonald Library. 2012. Web. 20 Aug. 2012.

---. "Quoting and paraphrasing." The Writing Centre. 2012. Web. 20 Aug. 2012.

University of Ottawa. "Study Skills—Note Taking." *Student Academic Success Service*. 2012. Web. 20 Aug. 2012.

"What Is RSS? RSS Explained." n.d. Web. 20 Aug. 2012.

York University. "Note Taking at University" *Learning Skills Services*, 4 Nov. 2009. Web. 20 Aug. 2012.

"MLA…style is most commonly used to write papers and cite sources within the liberal arts and humanities" (Paiz et al., 2012b). MLA in-text citations give the author's last name and page number in parentheses in the text. Example: (Paiz and Angeli 74). If you use the author's name in the sentence, give only the page number (74). The **Works Cited** provides the full bibliographic citation, arranged alphabetically by author's last name.

MODULE SUMMARY

- To summarize and/or paraphrase information effectively,
  - Prepare: Identify your purposes; pre-read; clarify the context.
  - Listen or read for a broad overview. Look for meaning.
  - Make sure you understand the material; if you don't, keep reading, read other sources, and ask questions until you do.
  - Create your own memorable and meaningful notes.
- To summarize and/or paraphrase information legitimately, ethically, and professionally, document your sources.
- Identifying your sources of information demonstrates your honesty, enhances your credibility, and protects you from charges of **plagiarism**—the conscious or unconscious theft of others' work.
- **Copyright laws** protect people's creative output; you are legally responsible for attributing intellectual property to its owner.

- Using someone else's work without giving credit is also unethical, since it violates the author's personal and professional rights.
- Academic penalties can include a grade failure or expulsion; in business, you can be sued for damages and revenue.
- As you research, document your sources immediately; this habit will save you hours of time and labour when composing your final copy.
- **Citation** means providing the source in the body of the report. When citing sources,
  - Pay attention to the order of the words and the punctuation. When you use a short quotation that is part of the main body of the text, the sentence period goes after the in-text citation. In a long indented quotation (about 30 words or more), the page number, in parentheses, follows the period at the end of the sentence. For example, for a short

quote, RefWorks is "an online research management, writing and collaboration tool" (RefWorks, 2009). And for a long, indented quote:

> RefWorks an online research management, writing and collaboration tool is designed to help researchers easily gather, manage, store and share all types of information, as well as generate citations and bibliographies. (RefWorks, 2009)

- **Documentation** means giving the bibliographic information readers need to find the original source.
  - ○ **APA** and **MLA** are the most commonly used formats for documenting references and endnotes.
  - ○ Free online software automatically formats your bibliographic information.

ASSIGNMENTS FOR MODULE 15

Questions for Critical Thinking

15.1 What kind of information would you find most difficult to summarize or paraphrase? Why?

15.2 What is unintentional plagiarism? What three strategies can you use to avoid it?

15.3 During a casual lunch conversation, a person at your table makes a comment that gives you a brilliant idea you can use in your report. Should you credit the person? Why or why not?

15.4 How can a researcher using only secondary sources come up with original material?

Exercises and Problems

15.5 Researching Plagiarism

Got to www.plagiarism.org and assess the site. What is the purpose of the site, and who are the audiences for the information?

Choose a research area from one of the six topic headings (What is plagiarism? Education tips on plagiarism prevention, Types of plagiarism, Plagiarism FAQ, How do I cite sources? What is citation?), or the Solutions topics on the right-hand side of the page. Read about and make notes on your topic.

As your instructor directs,

a. Discuss your findings and your notes with two or three peers who chose the same research area as you. What information did you find surprising? What did you already know? What did your team members all agree was the most important information?

b. Together with your two peers, use the most important information to create

  1. A three-minute slide presentation on your topic for your instructor and the class

  2. A ten-question quiz on your topic for your instructor and the class

15.6 Participating in an International Ethics Assessment

Together with the Brunel University Law School, the British Science Association (www.britishscienceassociation.org) has initiated a global "study to explore public concepts of honesty" (www.honestylab.com).

Go to www.honestylab.com, open the tab "More about dishonesty," and click on the link "Take the Honesty Test today" near the end of the text to participate in the study. Watch the videos, answer the questions, and participate in the activities. Create whatever notes you will need to summarize your responses and reactions to the questions and activities.

As your instructor directs,

a. Together with two peers, discuss the experience: What surprised you? How similar were your answers? Where were the differences? How do you and your peers account for these differences?

b. Together with your two peers, draft an email memo to your instructor and the class. In your memo

  1. Sum up some of the similarities and differences in responses among the members of your triad.

  2. Offer explanations for the differences.

  3. In your final paragraph, summarize your team members' individual reactions to the honesty study, and the questions and activities. Do you think the study will provide relevant, reliable data? Why or why not?

15.7 Creating Notes on a Document Resource

Create notes on any of the following resources:

www.sass.uottawa.ca/mentoring/undergraduate/note-taking.php

www.academicintegrity.uoguelph.ca/plagiarism_avoiding.cfm

www.cipo.ic.gc.ca/eic/site/cipointernet-internetopic.nsf/
eng/wr02394.html

www.alysion.org/handy/althandwriting.htm

http://owl.english.purdue.edu/owl/resource/619/1/

www.bridgewater.edu/WritingCenter/Workshops/summariztips.
htm

www.ic.gc.ca/eic/site/ippd-dppi.nsf/eng/home

http://lifehacker.com/software/note-taking/a-beginners-
guide-to-mind-mapping-meetings-288763.php

www.writingcentre.uottawa.ca/hypergrammar/grammar.html

www.socialresearchmethods.net/kb/ethics.php

www.utoronto.ca/ucwriting/paraphrase.html

www.yorku.ca/cds/lss/skillbuilding/notetaking.html

Before you begin, be sure to

1. Know your purpose: You are making notes to *write a précis* of the information (see Exercise 15.8).
2. Know your audiences: You are creating notes *for your peers, your instructor, and yourself.*
3. *Read all these directions* and all of the document material *before* making your notes.
4. *Pre-read the document.* Skim and scan for context and meaning: skim the material; scan headings, subheadings, and visuals; note white space, bold, italics, and underlining.
5. *Read the document again* as you make your notes.

Identify and note the most important information:

- The author, his or her credentials, evidence of expertise
- The purpose of and audiences for the document
- The organizational pattern: How does the author develop the argument: Direct or indirect pattern? Chronological? Problem/solution? Functional? Spatial? Elimination of alternatives? (Module 17)
- The controlling idea or thesis of the document
- Three different ways the author proves or demonstrates his or her argument
- The level of difficulty: Is the document easy to understand? Moderately easy? Difficult? Impossible? Note why you think so.
- The most significant idea you learned by reading the document
- One way you will apply what you learned
- Your questions or information you want to follow up

Now create notes, manually or digitally, on any one of the resources.

As your instructor directs,

a. Use APA or MLA style to credit the source you chose.
b. Exchange notes with at least one peer (more is better) who has created notes on a different source. Read his or her notes. Provide feedback: 1) Do you understand the information based on reading the notes? What information is unclear? Why? 2) What note-taking strategies strike you as unusual, innovative, or

particularly useful? Why? Then listen to the other person's feedback about your notes.

c. Reread and revise your notes based on the feedback, if necessary.
d. If you created electronic notes, send these as an email attachment to your instructor and the rest of the class. Be sure to include your APA or MLA documentation.
e. If you created handwritten notes, scan and send these as an email attachment to your instructor and the rest of the class. Be sure to include your APA or MLA documentation.

15.8 Writing a Précis on a Document

Précis the original document you chose in Exercise 15.7, using only the notes you created and revised.

- Use a word processor to draft a summary of the text in your own words.
- Summarize in sentences and paragraphs.
- Rewrite the summary until it is one-third the length of the original material.

As your instructor directs,

a. Use APA or MLA style to credit the source.
b. Exchange your précis with at least one peer (more is better) who has made a précis of a different source. Read his or her précis. Read the original source. Provide feedback: 1) How clear is the précis? Does the précis capture the meaning of the original? What information is missing? Does the précis writer use his or her own words? If not, what words or phrases would have to be put in quotations? Why? 2) How concise is the précis? Is it a third of the original? If not, does the précis writer have good reasons for the length? What are the reasons? Now listen to the other person's feedback on your précis.
c. Reread and revise your précis based on the feedback, if necessary.
d. Send your précis as an email attachment to your instructor and the rest of the class. Be sure to include your APA or MLA documentation.
e. In the email itself, describe what you found most difficult about writing the précis. Identify one specific way you can apply précis writing.

15.9 Creating Notes and a Précis on a Multimedia Source

Find a multimedia or interactive Web tutorial on any of the topics mentioned in Modules 14 and 15. (Possibilities include copyright; the legal, ethical, or professional implications of research; academic versus business research; and how to add in-text citations, choose a document style, paraphrase, avoid plagiarism, use quotations, write a précis, take notes, write summaries, or synopsize.)

1. Prepare to take handwritten or digital notes on the material.
2. Watch, listen to, and read the resource at least three times. Take notes.
3. Using only your notes, précis the material for the class, your instructor, and yourself.

As your instructor directs,

a. Use APA or MLA style to credit the source.

b. Send your précis as an email attachment to your instructor and the rest of the class. Be sure to include your APA or MLA documentation.

c. In the email itself, write a paragraph describing any differences between writing a précis of a written document and writing a précis of a multimedia source. How was it different? Was the difference due to content? To the medium? To your experience of having already done summaries and paraphrases? Explain.

POLISHING YOUR PROSE

Using APA and MLA Style

For examples of APA and MLA style, see Figure 15.2. Quick reference tips are available online at www.apastyle.org/faqs.html (APA) and http://owl.english.purdue.edu/owl/resource/557/01/ (MLA).

Identify and correct the errors in APA format in the following Reference items:

1. Trivers, Robert, The Folly of Fools, New York: Basic Books. 2011.
2. Altered States Self-experiments in chemistry. Oliver Sacks August 27, 2012, p. 40 -- 48. Retrieved August 24, 2012, from http://www.newyorker.com/reporting/2012/08/27/120827fa_fact_sacks#ixzz24Txi9fvC
3. Flavelle, Dana. Toronto Star, Canadian debt loads getting heavier, Friday, August 24, 2012, SECTION B, p. BE-2.
4. Study: Economic downturn and educational attainment, 2008 to 2011. Stats Can, The Daily, Thursday, June 21, 2012, retrieved June 26, 2012, from http://www.statcan.gc.ca/daily-quotidien/120621/dq120621c-eng.htm
5. John Loomis, telephone conversation with author, June 20, 2012.
6. Four dramatic ways retirement has changed since '08, By Kevin Press, BrighterLife.ca. Retrieved from http://brighterlife.ca/2012/08/13/four-dramatic-ways-retirement-has-changed-since-08/

Identify and correct the errors in MLA format in the following Works Cited items:

1. Trivers, Robert, The Folly of Fools, New York: Basic Books. 2011.
2. Altered States Self-experiments in chemistry. Oliver Sacks August 27, 2012, p. 40 -- 48. Retrieved August 24, 2012, from http://www.newyorker.com/reporting/2012/08/27/120827fa_fact_sacks#ixzz24Txi9fvC
3. Flavelle, Dana. Toronto Star, Canadian debt loads getting heavier, Friday, August 24, 2012, SECTION B, p. B1-2.
4. Study: Economic downturn and educational attainment, 2008 to 2011. Stats Can, The Daily, Thursday, June 21, 2012, retrieved June 26, 2012, from http://www.statcan.gc.ca/daily-quotidien/120621/dq120621c-eng.htm
5. John Loomis, telephone conversation with author, June 20, 2012.
6. Four dramatic ways retirement has changed since '08, By Kevin Press, BrighterLife.ca. Retrieved from http://brighterlife.ca/2012/08/13/four-dramatic-ways-retirement-has-changed-since-08/

Check your answers to the odd-numbered exercises in the Polishing Your Prose Answer Key.

connect

Practise and learn online with Connect. Connect allows you to practise important skills at your own pace and on your own schedule, with 24/7 online access to an eBook, practise quizzes, interactives, videos, study tools, and additional resources.

MODULE 16

Writing Information Reports

Learning Objectives

After reading and applying the information in Module 16, you'll be able to demonstrate

Knowledge of

LO1 Types of reports

LO2 Specific kinds of information reports

LO3 The importance of writing good purpose statements

LO4 Informal report writing style

Skills to

LO5 Begin to write purpose statements

LO6 Compose information reports

LO7 Begin to develop a good writing style

Employability Skills 2000+ Checklist

Module content builds these Conference Board of Canada Employability Skills 2000+

Communicate	**Be Adaptable**
Manage Information	**Learn Continuously**
Think and Solve Problems	**Participate in Projects and Tasks**

Reports provide the information that people in organizations need to record information, and to plan, make decisions, and solve problems. Usually, reports are written *up* in an organization: supervisors and managers assign report topics and timelines to subordinates.

Your workplace may have report templates. However, these templates may include audience-inappropriate language and redundant sections.[1] Whenever you can, use clear language and a report style format that meets the needs of your audiences and achieves the report's purposes. Whether you follow a template or create your own, being able to write effective reports gets rewards: recognition for your competence, promotions, and pay increases.[2]

What Is a Report?

Many different kinds of documents can be reports.

In some organizations, one- and two-page memos are called *reports*. In other organizations, a report is a long document with illustrations and numerical data. Still other companies produce PowerPoint slides as a report. **Informal reports** may be letters and memos, slide presentations, website summaries, business cases, or even computer printouts of production or sales figures. **Formal reports** contain formal elements such as a title page, a letter or memo transmittal page, a table of contents, and a list of illustrations (see Module 18). Reports can provide information, provide information and analyze it, and/or provide information and analysis to support a recommendation (see Table 16.1).

Writers decide on the type of report, its format, organizational pattern, and information, its length, language, level of formality, and channel of distribution based on PAIBOC analysis, and of the expectations of their organization and intended audiences (Module 2).

Ex.
16.1–
16.3

What Do Reports Have in Common?

To orient readers, reports usually contain an **introduction**, **body**, and **conclusion**:

- The *introduction* section puts the report in context for readers; it includes
  - ✔ A lead-in sentence: "This report describes…"
  - ✔ A purpose statement: "The purpose of this report is to…"
  - ✔ The scope of the report: "In this report, I explain the need for the program, and its structure and costs."
  - ✔ A summary of findings or results: "Employee feedback for the program was overwhelmingly positive."

LO1   TABLE 16.1   **Types of Reports**

Reports Can Provide:

Information only

- **Progress, conference, trip, and periodic reports** provide information and summaries.
- **Incident reports** describe health and safety transgressions.
- **Sales reports** give sales figures for the week or month.
- **Quarterly reports** show productivity and profits for the quarter.

Information plus analysis

- **Annual reports** detail financial data and an organization's accomplishments over the past year.
- **Audit reports** interpret facts revealed during an audit.
- **Make-good or payback reports** calculate the point at which a new capital investment will pay for itself.
- **Technical reports** describe scientific/technical processes.
- **Business plans** describe and analyze business, market, and financial projections.

Information plus analysis plus a recommendation

- **Feasibility and yardstick reports** analyze and evaluate possibilities, and recommend what the organization should do.
- **Justification reports** justify the need for a purchase, an investment, a new personnel line, or a change in procedure.
- **Problem-solving reports** identify the causes of an organizational problem and recommend a solution.
- **Proposals** analyze a need and recommend a solution.

FIGURE 16.1   **PAIBOC Questions for Analysis**

P	Why are you writing the report? What is the report's **purpose**? What is the situation? What results do you want? Are you updating your supervisor on your progress? Introducing a new initiative? Reporting a health and safety issue? Asking for time and money to attend a conference? Justifying buying an expensive piece of equipment? Analyzing the feasibility of an idea?
A	Who is your **audience**? What are your audience's expectations? Does your audience want/need updates? Information? Analysis? Justification? What does your audience value? What is important to your audience? What evidence will convince them?
I	What **information** must your message include? What does your audience already know? What do they need to know? What kind of information will your audience find most persuasive?
B	What reasons or reader **benefits** can you use to support your position? If your solution will cost the reader (in time or money), what benefits—to the organization, the audience, your colleagues—can you use to rationalize or outweigh those costs?
O	What **objections** can you expect your readers to have? What negative elements of your message must you de-emphasize or overcome? *One important objection is time*: how long will it take your audience to read your report? To overcome that objection, revise your report for clarity and conciseness, edit it for correctness, and use a reader (a friend, colleague, or family member) to proof it.
C	How will the **context** affect the reader's response? Think about your relationship to the reader, the organizational culture and morale, the current economic situation, the time of year, and any special circumstances.

- The *body* section presents specifics (facts, figures, statistics, examples, visuals) the audience needs to understand a situation, and, in some cases, to make a decision.
- The *conclusion* section summarizes the most important information covered in the body, and can include
  - ✔ Recommendations, if the report's purpose is to effect change or solve a problem
  - ✔ Supplementary material the audience may want (appendices, questionnaires)
  - ✔ References, when the report uses secondary sources of information (Modules 14 and 15)

What Should I Do Before I Write Any Report?

Do your research. Define the situation. Draft a purpose statement.

Creating a report includes

- Defining the situation
- Gathering and analyzing the necessary information
- Organizing the information
- Drafting the report
- Revising and editing the report
- Submitting the report

Before you begin to draft your report, you'll need to analyze your purposes and audiences. You also need to complete part of your research, in order to define the situation your report will discuss, and to identify the topics you will cover.

Your supervisor's direction and your analysis will help you to define the situation or problem. However, you may need to narrow your focus. For example, the topic "using social media to improve business" is far too broad. Instead, use the following example to narrow the perspective and find your purpose:

- Choose one type of social media.
- Identify the specific situation or problem: what do you want the report to accomplish?
- Identify the specific audience with a stake in the situation, or with the power to support or implement your suggestions.

Your purpose statement might then be "Our company can use Twitter to build business." Your audience might be your boss, colleagues, or aspiring entrepreneurs.

Remember that *how you define the problem shapes the solutions you find*. For example, suppose that a manufacturer of frozen foods isn't making money. If the researcher defines the situation as a marketing problem, he or she may analyze the product's price, image, advertising, and position in the market. But perhaps the real problem is that overhead costs are too high due to poor inventory management, or that an inadequate distribution system does not get the product to its target market. Defining the problem accurately is essential to finding an effective solution.

LO3 LO5 Writing Purpose Statements

Once you've defined your problem or situation, you're ready to write a purpose statement. The purpose statement goes in the introduction, and is the organizing principle of every report. A good **purpose statement** makes three things clear:

- The situation or problem
- The specific information that must be explored, or questions that must be answered, to resolve the situation or solve the problem
- The rhetorical purpose (to explain, to inform, to recommend, to propose, to request) the report is to achieve

The following purpose statements have all three elements.

Scope:
Information
report
explores

> Current management methods keep the elk population within the carrying capacity of the habitat but require frequent human intervention. Both wildlife conservation specialists and the public would prefer methods that controlled the elk population naturally.
> This report will compare the current short-term management techniques (hunting, trapping and transporting, and winter feeding) with two long-term management techniques, habitat modification and the reintroduction of predators. The purpose of this report is to recommend which techniques or combination of techniques would best satisfy the needs of conservationists, hunters, and the public.

Report Audience: Parks Canada Agency, responsible for Alberta's Elk Island National Park

— Situation or problem

— Organization pattern, method of development

— Purpose: To recommend

> When banner ads on Web pages first appeared in 1994, the initial response, or "click-through" rate, was about 10%. However, as ads have increased on Web pages, the click-through rate has dropped sharply. Rather than assuming that any banner ad will be successful, we need to ask, "What characteristics do successful banner ads share? Are ads for certain kinds of products and services, or for certain kinds of audiences, more likely to be successful on the Web?" The purpose of this report is to summarize the available research and anecdotal evidence and to recommend what Leo Burnett should tell its clients about whether and how to use banner ads.

Report Audience: Leo Burnett Advertising Agency

— Situation

Questions report examines and answers

— Purpose: To summarize research and make recommendation(s)

Situation and
purpose:
Proposal
written in
response to a
request

> Your request for a communications audit proposal reflects the City of Fredericton's commitment to its employees. A recent article in *The Globe and Mail* ("What Employees Care About," February 27, 2010, p. C1) details how poor communications cost organizations time and money. Good communication practices, however, have a proven 100 percent return on investment—in employee and customer satisfaction, employee retention, and improved productivity. My colleagues and I welcome the opportunity to work with you in identifying, developing, and implementing your communications' best-practices tools.

Report Audience: City of Fredericton HR Director

Focus of proposal:
Vendor's proposal
describes what vendor
will do

To write a good purpose statement, you have to understand the basic situation, or problem, and have some idea of the questions that your report will answer. You can (and should) write a working purpose statement (Module 14) to help focus your research; expect to change your purpose statement as a result of your research findings.

LO2 LO6 What Types of Short Reports Will I Write?

You will write summary reports, documenting information.

Supervisors expect employees to report information using short, informal documents. These internal reports summarize work, conferences, and sales trips, and describe work progress and health and safety incidents, using memo format (Modules 6 and 7).

Information and Closure Reports

An **information report** summarizes your work or research to date. Similarly, a **closure report** summarizes a project and assesses the results.

Information and closure reports include

- An *introduction paragraph*, summarizing the report topic, purposes, and most important outcomes, from the reader's perspective
- A *chronological account* (Module 17) of problem identification, actions, and results
- A *concluding paragraph* assessing the success of the project or work

Depending on the writer's mandate, the conclusion might include suggestions for further action.

See Figures 16.2 and 16.3 for examples of these two types of reports.

FIGURE 16.2   Information Report, Memo Format

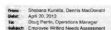

From:	Shobana Kunella, Dennis MacDonald
Date:	April 20, 2013
To:	Doug Perlin, Operations Manager
Subject:	Employee Writing Needs Assessment

Hi Doug,

Over the last month, Dennis and I collected and assessed the information you requested about employees' writing concerns. We created a two-page, online survey and sent it to all employees. We held eight interdepartmental focus groups and interviewed managers of five departments: Accounting, Engineering, Human Resources, Sales and Marketing, and Research and Development. Altogether, we spoke to 76 people and received 383 surveys.

In this report, I summarize the findings and suggest next steps.

What We Write

The survey results and interviews indicate that every employee writes emails.

Additionally, employees write any or all of

- Letters
- Reports, including project and final project reports, proposals, RFPs, technical descriptions, feasibility, audits, studies, and formal technical reports
- Contracts
- Research papers
- Articles
- Manuals
- Meeting minutes

What We Want

People were consistent in their concerns. Everyone wanted support in grammar, proofreading, editing, and tone. Additionally, employees said they wanted help with

- Formatting, consistency, and unity
- Writing concisely
- Writing clearly
- Organizing information
- Using appropriate language

Employees had very different opinions about how to learn these skills. The majority liked the idea of onsite training. Others would prefer to take a course or get individual coaching.

We need more information to make a decision. Dennis and I need to research the costs for people's preferences. Please let me if we should go ahead and when you would like the information.

FIGURE 16.3   **Closure Report, Memo Format, Email Attachment**

Date: March 15, 2012

To: Rob Dhillon, Human Resource Director

From: Irene Kaushansky, Staff Training and Development

Subject: Coaching Elisa Roberts

During our meeting of January 11, Elisa, you, and I agreed that Elisa would receive training in how to make successful accounts receivable calls. We agreed to hire a professional coach to help Elisa with the skills she needed to be successful in her new role. Further, we agreed that Elisa would identify the coach she felt she could work well with, and begin the training as soon as possible.

The purpose of this report is to describe the coaching program, and assess the results so far.

Coaching Elisa in Accounts Receivable Calls

In the week of January 18, Elisa and I interviewed three consultants about the coaching. We agreed that Mara Brady, of Brady and Associates, would be the right person to work with Elisa. Mara offered suggestions, and together she and Elisa decided on the program.

Coaching Parameters

Elisa, Mara, and I agreed on the training objectives:

1. To build Elisa's competence in AR calling
2. To identify AR calling best practices so that Elisa can train two other employees in successful AR calls

Mara recommended three coaching sessions of three hours each, a week apart, to begin January 25. In the first session, Elisa and Mara agreed to

- Analyze the current AR calling process
- Identify Elisa's telephone communication strengths
- Create SMART goals to build on those strengths

Coaching Methods

Mara suggested she observe Elisa making AR calls, and note (in writing) communication strengths and challenges. Together they would identify strategies (including active listening and negotiating techniques) to increase AR calling productivity, measured in

- Elisa's increased confidence
- Increased collection rate; amount to be determined after initial session
- Tips and techniques sheet

Further, they agreed that Elisa would keep a journal reflecting her learning experiences.

At the end of each session, Elisa and Mara would create a list of strategies for a best practices tip sheet. At the end of the three sessions, Elisa would evaluate the coaching experience and decide if she needed additional training.

Coaching Results

By the end of the second coaching session, I saw noticeable improvement in Elisa's AR calls. A week after the third session, I sat with Elisa during her AR calls and saw that she could

- Identify which clients would be motivated by AR calls
- Script a variety of calls
- Be courteous, calm, and confident throughout the call
- Listen to get results
- Control the tone and time of the call
- Ask for a commitment
- Produce written results, including suggestions for follow-up

Elisa has increased her collection rate by 30 percent and is developing the tip sheet and a coaching program for Janine and Armand. She feels she doesn't need more coaching sessions right now, but would like the option of calling Mara in for a follow-up session in a few months.

The cost of the coaching sessions was $1,800 plus HST. Based on Elisa's feedback and her increased productivity, we are very pleased with the results.

Conference and Trip Reports

Conference reports update your supervisor on industry trends, and justify the organizational expenditure (in your time and travel costs) by explaining the benefits to the audience. If your organization does not use templates, put the most significant information (for the audience) up front, and try to keep your report to a page or less. An example of a conference report appears in Figure 16.4.

Managers may accompany novice salespeople on client calls and record their observations about the representative's performance. These follow-up **trip reports** are kept in the rep's file for reference and may be copied to sales directors. Figure 16.5 shows an example of a trip report.

FIGURE 16.4   **Sample Conference Report, Email Attachment**

Conference Report: Fuel Cell Seminar and Exposition

Vancouver, B.C., November 16 to 19, 2013

This conference focused on high-temperature fuel cell research and development, and fuel processing and hydrogen development. Approximately 1,500 people attended, with international participants from Ireland, Denmark, Korea, Japan, and Germany.

The exhibition ran for four days, and was very well attended; ten fuel cell cars were available for test drives. After the plenary session and short technical presentations on Monday, participants could choose any of six parallel sessions, both mornings and afternoons, over the next three days.

The conference provided me with client networking opportunities and industry updates. I will be making use of both during client visits over the next month.

Highlights

Despite the recession, fuel cell shipments have increased globally, with greatest demand in Denmark, Europe, the Middle East, and Southeast Asia.

- Fuel cell power is now a recognized alternative energy source with universal applications.
- Greenhouse gas emission reductions are significant (up to 65% in large vehicles).
- The U.S., British, German, Korean, and Danish governments are committed to investing a billion dollars in funding for hydrogen and fuel cell R&D over the next two years.
- Canadian government support has increased since last year; the federal government has promised $3 million in R&D investment over the next five years.
- Hydrogen fuelling stations continue to be built in the United States—eight were built in 2012 alone. The American presenter said that poor infrastructure continues to plague the industry and suggested that governments and the private sector needed to be encouraged to understand the importance of hydrogen as the alternative energy source.
- One session examined alternative hydrogen sources production. Denmark is leading the world in biomass experimentation in this field.
- Cost reduction remains the priority: two sessions were devoted to panel discussions on possibilities. Since last year's conference, the emphasis has shifted from reducing material costs to improving manufacturing processes.

Approximately 110 more Canadian representatives attended than last year. Canada was also a significant presence in the exhibition. Perhaps the renewed enthusiasm is a result of the government's growing recognition of the importance of fuel cell technology.

FIGURE 16.5   **Sample Trip Report, Email Attachment**

Hi Lewis,

This email is long overdue; in future, I'll get my follow-up email to you in a timelier manner!

I had a great two days calling with you. You have made a very positive impact on your clients in such a short time.

I notice that you are very prompt with follow-up emails. This is excellent—it's one of the ways you can make yourself stand out as a sales rep. And you are making a good effort to meet as many people as possible when you are on campus, which is also great, especially at your travel schools.

As we discussed on Wednesday, one way to determine how important service is to instructors is to ask, "What do you look for in a sales rep?" It's another great question to set you apart. I am impressed that you are incorporating this line of questioning in your calls.

You were very strong in the presentation: you hit all the points you wanted to get across, and you took control of the room. You checked for questions, interest, and understanding, with challenges like "How do you see yourself using this in your course?" Your questions made the presentation very engaging. I know you were a little nervous leading up to it, but I suspect that as you get more practice, you'll feel more confident. And as always, the more you prep, the more confident you'll feel.

I'd like to see you continue to dig in your departments and get into areas where you haven't yet spent a lot of time. You'll pick up many units with a lot less work than in those big committee situations. Working both big and small will ensure you have a solid year. Push yourself out of your comfort zone, and you'll increase your sales.

I'd also like to see you get really comfortable questioning around technology and demonstrating on the fly. Let's talk after Closers to see where your comfort level is with the technologies for B&E and HSSL, and make plans accordingly.

I hope you found Closers helpful in developing strategies in all the different disciplines. Since you are the lead HSSL/B&E rep, I am going to arrange some extra product training for you. Let me know the areas where you would like more help.

Thanks again, Lewis. It's great to know I have such a strong rep in place in Man/Sask!

Incident Report

To protect employees, and themselves, most Canadian organizations comply with federal and provincial health and safety regulations. These regulations include WHMIS training and incident reporting. Usually, your organization will have a template you follow for an **incident report**. When you record an incident, use bullets or brief sentences to describe exactly what happened. Put the information in chronological order, note only observable behaviours, and do not record your inferences, assumptions, or feelings. See Figure 16.6 for an example.

Language FOCUS

WHMIS stands for **Workplace Hazardous Materials Information System**. WHMIS is a Canadian standard that companies must follow for the use, storage, handling, and disposing of controlled substances and hazardous materials, such as cancer-causing chemicals. See www.hc-sc.gc.ca/ewh-semt/occup-travail/whmis-simdut/index-eng.php for more information.

FIGURE 16.6   **Incident Report**

MediGroup Centre
945 Bradshaw Place
Prince Albert, SK S6V 2P5
306.566.5555

Accident/Incident Report

Date of Incident: *Mar. 13, 2012* Time: *2:13* AM/(PM)

Name of Injured Person: *Delphanie Hess*

Male: ___ Female: *✓*

Date of Birth: *November 19, 1985*

Address: *22 Longboat Ave., Prince Albert, ON*

Contact Phone Number: *416.232.1093*

Type of injury: *Verbal abuse*

Describe Incident: *Patient F. Baum arrived for app't 37 mins. late. When I explained he had missed his app't, he began yelling and swearing at me. He leaned over reception desk and said he would "punch" me. I apologized and asked "May I give you another app't?" Client turned and walked out door, still yelling. Slammed door.*

Required physician/hospital?   Yes___ No *✓*

Name of physician/hospital: *N/A*

Address: *N/A*

Physician/hospital phone number: *N/A*

Follow-up: *Written incident report; reported to Dr. Phillips*

Signature of injured person/parent/guardian: *D. Hess*   Date: *March 13, 2012*

Witness's signature: *Joanne Tuebot*   *(patient)*   Date: *March 13, 2012*

Reporter's signature: *D. Hess*   Date: *March 13, 2012*

Progress Reports

In **progress reports**, you report on what you've done, why it's important, and what you will do next.

When you're assigned to a single project that will take a month or more, you may be asked to file one or more progress reports. A progress report assures the employer or funding agency that you're making progress, and allows you and the employer or agency to resolve problems as they arise.

Different readers may have different concerns. An instructor may want to know whether you'll have your report in by the due date. A client may be more interested in what you're learning about the problem. Adapt your progress report to meet the needs of the audience.

You can use progress reports to do more than just report progress:

- *Suggest alternatives.* Explain, "I could continue to do X (what you approved); I could do Y instead (what I'd like to do now)." The detail in the progress report can help back up your claim. Even if the idea is rejected, you don't lose face because you haven't made a separate issue of the alternative.
- *Minimize potential problems.* As you do the work, you may find that implementing your recommendations will be difficult. In your regular progress reports, you can alert your boss or the funding agency to the challenges, preparing your audience psychologically to act on your recommendations.

A study of the progress reports in a large research and development organization found that less successful writers tended to focus on what they had done and said very little about the value of their work. Good writers, in contrast, spent less space writing about the details of what they'd done but much more space explaining the value of their work for the organization.[3]

Subject lines for progress reports are straightforward. Specify the project on which you are reporting your progress.

Subject: Progress on Developing a Marketing Plan for Compact Hybrids

Subject: Progress on Organizing IABC Toronto Chapter Annual Conference

If you are submitting weekly or monthly progress reports on a long project, number your progress reports, or include the time period in your subject line. Include dates for the work completed since the last report, and the work to be completed before the next report.

Report as positively as you honestly can. You build a better image of yourself when you show that you can take minor problems in stride, and that you're confident of your own abilities.

Negative: I have not deviated markedly from my schedule, and I feel that I will have very little trouble completing this report by the due date.

Positive: I am back on schedule and expect to complete my report by the due date.

Progress reports can be organized in three ways: by chronology, by task, and by supporting a recommendation.

Chronological Progress Reports

Chronological progress reports focus on what the writer has done and what work remains. Organize the report this way:

1. *Summarize your progress in terms of your goals and your original schedule.* Use measurable statements.

   Poor: My progress has been slow.

   Better: The research for my report is about one-third complete.

2. *Under the heading "Work Completed," describe what you have already done.* Be specific, both to support your claims in the first paragraph, and to allow the reader to appreciate your hard work. Acknowledge the people who have helped you. Describe any serious obstacles you've encountered and tell how you've dealt with them.

   Poor: I have found many articles about Procter & Gamble on the Web. I have had a few problems finding how the company keeps employees safe from chemical fumes.

   Better: On the Web, I found Procter & Gamble's home page, its annual report, and its mission statement. No one whom I interviewed could tell me about safety programs specifically at P&G. I have found seven articles about ways to protect workers against pollution in factories, but none mentions P&G.

3. *Under the heading "Work to Be Completed," or "Next Steps," describe the work that remains.* If you're more than three days late (for school projects) or two weeks late (for business proj-

ects), submit a new schedule, showing how you will be able to meet the original deadline. You may want to discuss "Observations" or "Preliminary Conclusions" if you want feedback before writing the final report or if your reader has asked for substantive interim reports.

4. *Either express your confidence that you'll have the report ready by the due date or request a conference to discuss extending the due date or limiting the project.* If you are behind your original schedule, show why you think you can still finish the project on time.

Figure 16.7 shows a chronological progress report.

Task Progress Reports

In a task progress report, organize information under the various tasks you have worked on during the period. For example, a task progress report for a group report project might use the following headings:

Finding Background Information on the Web and in Print

Analyzing Our Survey Data

Working on the Introduction of the Report and the Appendices

Under each heading, the group might discuss the tasks it has completed and those that remain.

FIGURE 16.7   **Sample Chronological Progress Report**

Date: November 2, 2012

To: Kathryn Hughes

From: Sheema Khan

Subject: Formal Report Progress

As you requested, this report summarizes the work I have completed on my formal report topic. I have found several excellent sources for current information on the status of women working in the building trades. Therefore, I have met the timelines stated in my proposal and anticipate submitting the report on the required due date.

Work Completed

Because I was able to access so many sound resources, I finished writing the first draft of the body of the report yesterday. A *Toronto Star* article about the lack of women in the trades helped focus my topic. This article provides information on Canada's current labour shortage, on apprentices and journeymen, and on the many construction jobs available that are not "in the field." The article includes a self-assessment quiz to help people recognize if they might want to work in construction trades. All of this information proved invaluable in drafting the text.

Through Internet research, I found the National Association of Women in Construction (NAWIC) and StatsCan, with relevant data on jobs and women's representation in the skilled trades.

By far the most important resource, however, has been my sister Maria, who graduated in engineering but now works as a superintendent for Schell Construction Canada. Through interviewing Maria, I learned about the barriers women face in the construction industry, and about the roles education, legislation, and restructuring can play in favourably transforming the industry.

Work in Progress

For the next six days, while revising the first draft, I will be inserting in-text citations and preparing the References page, using the *APA Formatting and Style Guide*. Then I will draft the Conclusions and Summary sections of the report.

Final Steps

By March 18, I will have drafted the first and last parts of the report. I have allotted another ten days for revising and editing. Maria will read the second draft to ensure my facts and citations are correct. And two friends have agreed to read this draft for unity and organization. All three will also be reading for correct grammar and punctuation. I intend finishing the final draft by March 31, for submission April 3.

All the information I have gathered while researching has proven to me that my topic is both personally and socially relevant. Thank you for providing this opportunity.

Recommendation Progress Reports

Recommendation progress reports recommend action: resourcing a new idea, increasing the funding for a project or changing its direction, cancelling a project that isn't working out. When the recommendation will be easy for the reader to accept, use the direct request pattern of organization from Module 8. If your recommendation is likely to meet strong resistance, the problem-solving pattern (Module 9) might be more effective.

LO4 LO7 EXPANDING A CRITICAL SKILL

Writing with Style

People's writing style conveys their attitudes about the subject and their audience. Good business writing is natural, polite, concise, and correct, indicating respect for readers. You develop your own writing style through knowledge and practice.

Make Your Writing Natural

Natural style is not spontaneous, but the result of critical thinking and revision.

- Use PAIBOC to analyze your purpose and your audience's expectations. In informal reports,
  - Use first person (*I*) and second person (*you*).
  - Put your readers in your sentences ("Thank you for…" "As you requested….")
  - Keep your paragraphs short.
  - Vary sentence structure and length. Remember, however, that the most readable sentences are between 14 and 20 words, and structured subject+verb+object.
  - Use active, action verbs (Writing and Editing Resources).
  - Use concrete nouns.
  - Avoid jargon and technical language.
  - Use parallel structure (Writing and Editing Resources).

Make Your Writing Polite

- Address your audience by name: people want to be recognized and treated as individuals.

- Research the names and preferred courtesy titles (Module 6) of the people whom you write to and for, and use them.
- Include the information your audience needs to know (purpose, scope, results) up front, in your introduction.
- Use neutral or positive language; avoid the negative.
- Rewrite as the reader: reader-centred writing uses an organization pattern, sentence structure, and language that meet the audience's needs for clarity and understanding (Module 13).

Make Your Writing Concise and Correct

- Compose drafts and sections of longer documents as soon you can; make notes on your research; summarize; paraphrase (Module 15).
- Save most of your time for revision; use proven revision strategies:
  - Apply WIRMI (What I Really Mean Is…) as you read your sentences and paragraphs.
  - Eliminate every unnecessary word.
  - Use readers: Ask colleagues or friends to read your writing; ask for specific feedback; revise.
- Edit for correct spelling, grammar, and punctuation.
- Ask a friend to proof your final copy.

MODULE SUMMARY

- Any kind of document or slide show can be a report. Usually, supervisors assign report topics and timelines to subordinates.
- **Information reports** collect data for the reader; **analytical reports** present and interpret data; **recommendation reports** recommend action or a solution.
- Creating a report includes
  - Defining the situation
  - Gathering and analyzing the necessary information
  - Organizing the information

  - Drafting the report
  - Revising and editing the report
  - Submitting the report
- Before you write any report,
  - Do your research
  - Define the situation
  - Draft a good purpose statement
- A good **purpose statement** frames your message for the reader. A good purpose statement clarifies
  - The organizational situation or problem

○ The specific questions that must be answered to resolve the situation or solve the problem

○ The rhetorical purposes (to describe, to explain, to request, to propose, to recommend) the report is written to achieve

• In information, closure, conference, and incident reports, provide the information chronologically.

• In progress reports, focus the reader on what you have done, and what work remains:

○ Summarize your progress in terms of your goals and original work schedule.

○ Use headings "Work Completed," "Next Steps"— describe what you have done and will do.

○ Express your confidence in meeting the due date, or request a meeting to discuss extending the due date or limiting the project.

• Use **positive emphasis** in progress reports to demonstrate confidence and competence.

• Good business writing style is natural, polite, concise, and correct. You develop your own style through knowledge and practice.

ASSIGNMENTS FOR MODULE 16

Questions for Critical Thinking

16.1 What do you have to know to identify the kind of report you are writing? Why?

16.2 How do you decide what kind of language—formal, informal, technical, jargon—to use when writing a report?

16.3 How can you create a reader-friendly report? Identify three ways you can make your report more readable for your audience(s).

Exercises and Problems

16.4 Writing a Summary and Evaluation Report

Find a new or recently established business social networking site. Write an information report describing the site to the director of your college/university Employment Placement Office. Evaluate the site based on the following criteria

• Appearance
• Navigability
• Accessibility
• Community
• Business support
• Job search support

As your instructor directs

Attach the completed report to an email. Send the email to

a. The Employment Placement Office director
b. Your instructor

16.5 Writing an Incident Report

Write an incident report to your supervisor describing a recent organizational or workplace accident, or health and safety transgression that you observed. If your organization has a template, use it; if not, create your own. For ideas, go to the McGill University Services Environmental Health and Safety site at www.mcgill.ca/ehs/forms/forms/accidentincidentreport.

As your instructor directs

Attach the completed report to an email. Send the email to

a. Your supervisor
b. Your instructor

16.6 Writing an Investigation Report

Write a short report on the co-op placement opportunities available for graduates in your field of study. Begin your research by interviewing students with co-op experience, alumni, recent program graduates, and your teachers. Visit your campus placement office and the library for suggestions on how to research and contact industries and companies that hire co-op students.

In your report, include feedback from co-op students and their salaries/wages, as well as ideas for organizations that your college/university could approach for co-op placements.

As your instructor directs

Write the report to

a. Your instructor and class members
b. Your campus placement/co-op office

16.7 Writing a Chronological Progress Report

Write a memo report summarizing your progress on a major report that you have to write.

In the introductory paragraph, summarize your progress in terms of your schedule and your goals. Under a heading titled "Work Completed," list what you have already done. (This is a chance to toot your own horn: if you have solved problems creatively, say so! You can also describe obstacles you've encountered that you have not yet solved.) Under "Work to Be Completed," list what you still have to do. If you are more than two days behind your original schedule, include a revised schedule, listing the completion dates for the activities that remain.

In your last paragraph, either indicate your confidence in completing the report by the due date or ask for a conference to resolve the problems you are encountering.

As your instructor directs

Send the email or paper progress report to

a. The other members of your group
b. Your instructor

16.8 Writing a Task Progress Report

Write a memo report summarizing your progress on your report in terms of its tasks.

As your instructor directs

Send the email or paper progress report to

a. The other members of your group
b. Your instructor

POLISHING YOUR PROSE

Who/Whom and I/Me

Even established writers sometimes get confused about when to use *who* versus *whom* and *I* versus *me*. These pronouns serve different functions in a sentence or part of a sentence.

Use *who* or *I* as the subject of a sentence or clause.

Correct: Who put the file on my desk?

(*Who* did the action, *put*.)

Correct: Keisha and I gave the presentation at our annual meeting.

(Both *Keisha* and *I* did the action, *gave*.)

Correct: Ai-Lan, who just received a PhD in management science, was promoted to vice-president.

(*Who* is the subject of the clause "who just received a PhD in management science.")

Use *whom* and *me* as the object of a verb or a preposition.

Correct: Whom did you write the report for?

(*Whom* is the object of the preposition *for*.)

Correct: She recommended Thuy and me for promotions.

(*Me* is an object of the verb *recommended*.)

Though some print sources may use *who* and *whom* interchangeably, stick to the rules until this practice becomes widely acceptable.

If you're not sure whether a pronoun is being used as a subject or object, try substituting *he* or *him*. If *he* would

work, the pronoun is a subject. If *him* sounds right, the pronoun is an object.

Correct: He wrote the report.

Correct: I wrote the report for him.

Exercises

Choose the correct word in each set of brackets.

1. Karen and [I/me] visited St. Francis Xavier University last week.
2. For [who/whom] is this letter intended?
3. Dr. Jacobsen, [who/whom] serves on the board of directors, is retiring.
4. Take it from Les and [I/me]: it pays to be prepared in business.
5. [Who/Whom] is the most experienced person on your staff?
6. There was only about an hour for Kelly, Maria, and [I/me] to get to the airport.
7. Between you and [I/me], my supervisor told me the committee will decide [who/whom] gets the promotion.
8. It is the customer for [who/whom] we make our product.
9. Three people at the firm [who/whom] can speak a second language are Van, Chang, and [I/me].
10. Trust [I/me]: it's not a good idea to begin a letter with "To [who/whom] it may concern," even if people frequently do.

Check your answers to the odd-numbered exercises in the Polishing Your Prose Answer Key.

connect

Writing Proposals and Analytical Reports

Learning Objectives

After reading and applying the information in Module 17, you'll be able to demonstrate

Knowledge of

LO1 How to compose more complex reports

LO2 How to organize report information

LO3 How to choose a pattern of organization

LO4 How to increase document readability

Skills to

LO5 Draft and revise analytical reports

LO6 Choose an appropriate organizing pattern

LO7 Increase document readability

Employability Skills 2000+ Checklist

Module content builds these Conference Board of Canada Employability Skills 2000+

Communicate

Manage Information

Think and Solve Problems

Be Adaptable

Learn Continuously

Participate in Projects and Tasks

Easy-to-read messages motivate people to do as you ask. When you write reports, organize the information to meet readers' expectations. Audiences usually want answers up front: Is the soil contaminated or not? Is the plan going to work? How and why? Should we expand or not?

Ex.
17.1–
17.8

LO5 As you revise, use PAIBOC analysis to 1) include only the information your reader needs, and 2) organize that information to influence your readers positively.

What Other Kinds of Reports Will I Be Asked to Write?

You'll be asked to write reports that analyze and justify information.

Analytical reports—including feasibility, yardstick, and justification reports, as well as proposals—organize and analyze information to persuade readers to accept the suggestions or recommendations of the writer.

These reports may be brief and use letter or memo format, depending on their purpose and audience expectations.

LO1 All reports, regardless of length, include an *introduction paragraph* stating the report's purpose and scope, and summarizing the problems or successes of the project (Module 16). And all reports *conclude* with a summary of the writer's key findings: this summary suggests next steps or *recommends* action, depending on the writer's purpose and audience expectations (Module 16).

LO1 LO2 Feasibility Reports

Feasibility or **yardstick reports** assess a plan or idea based on a set of criteria established by the organization or the writer. (Doing nothing or delaying action can be one of the conclusions of a feasibility report.) As an example, toy companies use feasibility studies to evaluate new toy designs, according to Peter Pook, Vice-President, Research and Development for Fisher-Price Toys.[1]

Ex.
17.4
17.7–
17.8

Feasibility and yardstick reports normally open by explaining the decision to be made, listing available alternatives, and explaining the criteria. In the body of the report, evaluate each alternative according to the criteria:

- Discuss each alternative separately when one alternative is clearly superior, when the criteria interact, and when each alternative is indivisible.
- Discuss each alternative under each criterion when the choice depends on the weight given to each criterion.

LO1
LO2 Business plans are developed in feasibility reports: the goal is to prove that the business idea is so sound that the audience—banks, angel investors, or venture capitalists—should invest in it (see Figure 17.1).

FIGURE 17.1   **Criteria Discussed in a New Business Venture Feasibility Study**

A. Business Description (Summary)

  The Company
- Mission Statement
- Vision
- Values
- Brand Personality
- Location
- The Market
- Strategic Positioning

B. Products and Services
- Products
- Services

C. Location
- Test Market
- Channels

D. Market Analysis
- Economic Factors
- Environmental Factors
- Political/Legal Factors
- Social/Cultural Factors
- Demographic Factors
- Primary Customers
- Secondary Customers

E. Competitive Analysis
- Direct Competitors
- Indirect Competitors

F. Financials

G. Conclusions
- Summary of Business, Market, and Potential Returns

H. Appendix

I. References

Whether recommendations should come at the beginning or the end of the report, or be repeated in both sections, depends on company culture and the reader's expectations. Most readers want the "bottom line" up front. However, if your proposed solution will cost time or money, you may want to provide all your evidence before giving the recommendation (Modules 9 and 10).

LO1
LO2 ## Justification Reports

Ex.
17.5

Justification reports recommend or justify a purchase, investment, hire, or change in policy. If your organization has a standard format for justification reports, follow that format. If you can choose your headings and organization, use the *direct, deductive,* or *good news* pattern (Module 8) when your recommendation is easy for your reader to accept:

1. *Indicate what you're asking for and why it's needed.* When the reader has not asked for the report, you must link your request to organizational goals.
2. *Briefly give the background of the problem or need.*
3. *Explain each of the possible solutions.* For each, give the cost, and the advantages and disadvantages.
4. *Summarize the action needed to implement your recommendation.* If several people will be involved, indicate who will do what and how long each step will take.
5. *Ask for the action you want.*
6. *Conclude with a short paragraph linking the recommended solution to a benefit outcome.*

Language FOCUS

Angel investors are people who are usually wealthy and invest in new companies, often in exchange for benefits from the company.

Venture capitalists are people who invest in new companies, or in companies that are experiencing financial difficulties but have potential to make great profits.

When the reader is reluctant to grant your request because action will cost time or money, use the *indirect, inductive,* or *bad news* variation of the problem-solving pattern described in Modules 9 and 10:

1. *Describe the organizational problem that your request will solve.* Provide specific examples (results) to demonstrate the seriousness of the problem.
2. *Prove that easier or less expensive solutions will not solve the problem.*
3. *Present your solution impersonally.*
4. *Show that the advantages of your solution outweigh the disadvantages.*
5. *Summarize the action needed to implement your recommendation.* If several people will be involved, indicate who will do what and how long each step will take.
6. *Ask for the action you want.*
7. *Conclude with a short paragraph linking the recommended solution to benefit outcomes.*

The amount of detail you need to give in a justification report depends on your reader's knowledge of and attitude toward your recommendation, and on the corporate culture. Many organizations expect justification reports to be short—only one or two pages. Other organizations may expect longer reports with much more detailed budgets and a full discussion of the problem and each possible solution.

Language FOCUS

A **mission statement** explains the purpose of the company or organization.

A **vision statement** describes the goals and objectives your company tries to meet or exceed.

Values are a written list of the goals and objectives your company tries to meet or exceed.

LO1 LO2 What Should Go into a Proposal?

What you're going to do, how and when you'll do it, and evidence that you'll do it well.

Proposals are reports that describe a method for finding information or solving a problem. Proposals have two goals: to get the project accepted, and to obtain support for the writer to do the job. *Proposals must stress reader benefits and provide specific supporting details.*

Employability Skills

Ex.
17.6
17.8

TABLE 17.1   **Relationships Between Situation, Proposal, and Final Report**

Company's Current Situation	The Proposal Offers To:	The Final Report Will Provide:
We don't know whether we should change	Assess whether change is a good idea	Insight, recommending whether change is desirable
We need to/want to change, but we don't know exactly what we need to do	Develop a plan to achieve the desired goal	A plan for achieving the desired change
We need to/want to change, and we know what to do, but we need help doing it	Implement the plan, increase (or decrease) measurable outcomes	A record of the implementation and evaluation process

Source: Adapted from Richard C. Freed, Shervin Freed, and Joseph D. Romano (1995), *Writing winning proposals: Your guide to landing the client, making the sale, persuading the boss* (New York: McGraw-Hill): 21.

FIGURE 17.2 **Proposal for Services (Indirect Pattern of Development, Modules 9 and 10)**

November 12, 2013
Sen Lee Chang, President
Tel-Direct Systems Inc.
1011 Bloor Street West
Oshawa, ON L1H 7K6

Dear Sen Lee Chang

Thank you for considering **communicore** for your training needs. Based on our conversation last Friday, I am pleased to propose this preliminary outline of the customer service workshop and to suggest ways to maximize your return on investment.

Workshop Overview

The two-day Customer Service Strategies workshop encourages participants to define and refine the criteria for superior customer service. During the workshop, participants will

- Begin with an ice-breaker, followed by self-assessment and goal-setting exercises
- Role-play active listening, questioning, and problem-solving strategies
- Analyze and identify excellent customer service attitudes and behaviours
- Identify and apply two conflict negotiating models
- Articulate best-practices behaviours as the organizational standard
- Set a goal for further development

Depending on participants' preference, we can begin at 8 or 8:30 a.m., and finish at 4 or 4:30 p.m. I've attached a proposed agenda for your approval.

Methods

Using a variety of interactive exercises—including case analysis, taped role-play, peer feedback, and peer and self-assessment—your employees will review, describe, and apply behaviours that build customer relationships.

Since customized content contributes to learning transfer, I would like to visit your locations for a few hours to observe your service representatives before the training dates. This complimentary needs assessment will allow me to gather information about current practices and to see your training facilities.

Resources

As we discussed, your employees will need uninterrupted time to review and practise customer service techniques. Because participants will be working together and moving around, they will need group seating, four to a table, and enough room to comfortably accommodate 16 people.

You mentioned that the room is equipped with a laptop, projector, and screen; participants will need writing materials, a USB key, and one flip chart per table. We will be bringing our own camera.

Qualifications

Our facilitators offer over 20 years' training experience, as well as expertise and accreditation in adult education principles, business, and interpersonal communications skills. As we agreed, I am attaching client reviews of our most recent training in customer service skills. Please visit our website: http://www.communicore.on.ca for more reviews.

Costs

The needs assessment is free. The cost for the training, including tailoring materials and exercises to participants' experiences, material printing and copying, two-day interactive facilitation, workshop evaluation sheet and summary, and written best-practices recommendations specific to your organization is $6 000, plus HST.

Again, thank you for your interest and consideration. At your convenience, please call or email me about your proposed employee training.

Sincerely

Kathryn Hughes

Kathryn Hughes
President

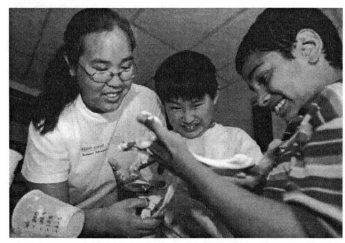

Psychology major Susan Ngo launched her successful business Bright Ideas Summer Adventure Camp with a $1,500 Ministry of Economic Development and Trade Grant, garnered through her winning business plan.

To write a good proposal, you need to have a clear view of the problem you hope to solve and the kind of research or other action needed to solve it. A proposal must answer the following questions convincingly:

- What problem are you going to solve?
- How are you going to solve it?
- What exactly will you provide?
- How can you deliver what you promise?
- What benefits can you offer?
- When will you complete the work?
- How much will you charge?

Figure 17.2 shows a sample proposal selling services.

LO1 LO2 Sales Proposals, Requests for Proposals (RFPs), and Grants

Decision makers routinely ask for proposals when purchasing expensive goods or services. For everything you offer, show the reader benefits (Module 11) using you-attitude (Module 13). Use content and language appropriate for your audience. Even if buyers want a state-of-the-art system, they may not appreciate or understand minute details or technical jargon.

Attention to details—including good visual impact and proofreading—helps establish your professional image and suggests that you'll give the same care to the project if your proposal is accepted (see Figures 17.2 and 17.3).

Provide a one-page cover letter with long proposals. Organize the cover letter this way:

1. Catch the reader's attention and summarize up to three major benefits you offer.
2. Discuss each of the major benefits in the order in which you mention them in the first paragraph.
3. Deal with any objections or concerns the reader may have.
4. Mention other benefits briefly.
5. Ask the reader to approve your proposal. Provide a reason for acting promptly.

Government agencies and companies issue **Requests for Proposals**, known as **RFPs**, when contracting out work. The RFP details the project and vendor requirements in "a formal document describing…how the contract companies should respond, how the proposals will be reviewed, and contact information."[2]

You follow the RFP exactly when you respond. Competitive proposals are often scored by giving points in each category. Evaluators look only under the headings specified in the RFP. If information isn't there, the proposal gets no points in that category.

Proposals for Funding

If you need money for a new or continuing public service project, you may want to submit a proposal for funding to a foundation, a corporation, a government agency, or a religious agency. In a proposal for funding, stress the needs your project will meet, and show how your project helps fulfill the goals of the organization you are asking to fund it. Every funding source has certain priorities; most post lists of the projects they have funded in the past.

FIGURE 17.3 **Proposal for Foundation Repair (Indirect Pattern, Modules 9 and 10)**

Contract/EST#: 7565

Bowen Foundation Repair Inc.
2486 Kingston Rd.; Scarborough, ON M1N 1V3
Tel: 555-866-0547 Fax: 555-866-1275 www.bfr.ca
LIC# B-19658

Date: November 19, 2013

Client Name: Judy Green   **Cell Phone No:** _____   **Home Phone No:** 555-321-5267
Work Phone No: _____   **Email:** _____
Jobsite: 24 Queen Mary Rd.
The undersigned proposes to furnish all materials and provide all material and labour necessary to complete all repairs described below.

Exterior Waterproofing Repair:

Trench 51' linear ft from 1' to 2' deep, sloping toward rear of property. Place filter-cloth in bottom of trenched area. Install 4" perforated weeping tile with nylon sock. Pour ¾" gravel over weeping tile system. Remove and dispose of all soil. Clean up work area. Remove and dump all debris. All material and labour included.

20-year transferable warranty against leakage in repaired area.
(Please retain this contract for warranty purposes.)

No deposit required. Payment due in full upon completion of work.

All of the above work to be completed in a good and workmanlike manner for the sum of:

_____ ($990.00) DOLLARS
GST# 85151766 RT0001 _____ ($128.70) HST

_____ **($1,118.70) TOTAL**

All changes in the work to be charged for same shall be made in writing.
   This estimate is made on the basis of current material and labour costs. This estimate is valid for 90 days from date above. Any delay in acceptance of this estimate beyond 90 days shall void this estimate, and a review of this estimate shall be performed before any agreement between the Client and Bowen Foundation Repair Inc. becomes binding.
   All warranties are based on normal weather conditions.
   BFR is not responsible for ground settlement.
   BFR is not responsible for leakage due to grade change and or acts of God, i.e., tornadoes, flooding, hurricane, and the like.

ACCEPTANCE

You are hereby authorized to furnish all materials and labour to complete the work mentioned in the above proposal, for which the undersigned agrees to pay the amount mentioned in said proposal, and according to the terms thereof.

Date: _____

Collen Bowen

_____   _____
INDIVIDUAL/COMPANY NAME   BOWEN FOUNDATION REPAIR INC.

Estimating the Budget

A good budget is crucial to making the winning bid. Ask for everything you need to do a quality job. Asking for too little may backfire, leading the decision maker to assume you don't understand the scope of the project.

Read the RFP to find out what is and isn't fundable. Talk to the program officer and read successful past proposals to find out three things:

- What size projects will the organization fund in theory?

- Does the funder prefer making a few big grants or many smaller grants?
- Does the funder expect you to provide in-kind or matching funds from other sources?

Think about exactly what will be done and who will do it. What will it cost to get that person? What supplies or materials will he or she need? Also, think about indirect costs for office space, retirement and health benefits and salaries, office supplies, administration, and infrastructure.

Detail the specifics of your estimates.

> **Weak:** 75 hours of transcribing interviews $1,500
>
> **Better:** 25 hours of interviews; a skilled transcriber can complete an hour of interviews in
>   3 hours; 75 hours @ $20/hour $1,500

Without inflating your costs, give yourself a cushion. For example, if the going rate for skilled transcribers is $20 an hour, but you think you might be able to train someone and pay only $17 an hour, use the higher figure. Then, even if your grant is cut, you'll still be able to do the project well.

Proposals for Class Reports

A proposal for a student report usually has the following sections:

1. **Purpose statement**: In your first paragraph (no heading), summarize in a sentence or two the topic and purpose(s) of your report.
2. **Problem**: What organizational problem exists? What is the situation? What needs to change? Why? What background or history is relevant?
3. **Feasibility**: Can a solution be found in the time available? How do you know?
4. **Audience**: Who in the organization has the power to implement your recommendation? What secondary audiences might be asked to evaluate your report? What audiences would be affected by your recommendation? Will anyone serve as a gatekeeper, determining whether your report is sent to decision makers? What watchdog audiences might read the report? (Module 2)
   For each of these audiences and for your initial audience (your instructor), give the person's name, job title, and business address, and answer the following questions:

   - What is the audience's major concern or priority?
   - What will the audience see as the advantages of your proposal?
   - What objections, if any, is the reader likely to have?
   - How interested is the audience in the topic of your report?
   - How much does the audience know about the topic of your report?
   - What terms, concepts, equations, or assumptions might one or more of your audiences need to have explained? Briefly identify ways in which your audiences may affect the content, organization, or style of the report.

5. **Topics to investigate**: List the questions and sub-questions you will answer in your report, the topics or concepts you will explain, and the aspects of the problem you will discuss. Indicate how deeply you will examine each aspect you plan to treat. Explain your rationale for choosing to discuss some aspects of the problem and not others.
6. **Methods/procedure**: How will you get answers to your questions? Whom will you interview or survey? What published sources will you use? What websites will you consult? (Module 14) Give the full bibliographic references (Module 15). Your methods section should clearly indicate where and how you will get the information you need to answer the questions in the Topics to Investigate section.
7. **Qualifications/facilities/resources**: What attitudes, knowledge, and skills qualify you to conduct this study? Do you work in the organization? Do you have a contact or source for information? What's your professional or personal interest? Do you have access to the resources you will need to conduct your research (computer, books, etc.)? Where will you turn for help if you hit an unexpected snag? You'll be more convincing if you have already scheduled an interview, checked out books, or identified online sources.

8. **Work schedule**: Create a timeline to plan your work. (See Figure 17.4 for an example.) List both the total time you plan to spend on each of the following activities, and the date when you expect to finish:

- Gathering information
- Analyzing information
- Preparing the progress report
- Organizing information
- Writing the draft
- Revising the draft
- Preparing the visuals
- Editing the draft
- Proofreading the report

Put your timeline into a work schedule either in a chart or on a calendar. A good schedule provides realistic estimates for each activity, allows time for unexpected problems, and indicates that you can manage a project and complete the work on time.

9. **Close/call to action**: In your final paragraph, indicate that you'd welcome any suggestions that your instructor may have for improving the research plan. Ask your instructor to approve your proposal so that you can begin work on your report. Provide a contact number or email address for confirmation.

Figure 17.5 shows a draft student proposal for writing a research report using primary and secondary sources.

FIGURE 17.4   **Create a Timeline to Plan Your Schedule**

Jan. 19	Feb. 9	Feb. 18	Mar. 1	Mar. 10	Mar. 15	Mar. 20	Mar. 23	Apr. 5	Apr. 17
Choose report topic; start research; draft proposal	Revise and submit proposal	Get approval; research	Begin first draft of body	Finish draft of body; draft conclusions	Have peer read; revise	Draft summary	Have peer read; revise	Edit and proof	Submit report

FIGURE 17.5   **Draft Proposal for a Student Report Using Primary and Secondary Sources (Direct Pattern, Module 8)**

Date: January 20, 2013

To: Professor Marcus Stawski

From: Teresa Amirud

Re: My Formal Report Topic

Costing is possibly the most vital aspect of the manufacturing process, since companies must use the most effective system in order to reduce costs and increase profits. In the manufacturing sector, different variations on costing systems can be tailored to suit the needs of any specific company. In my formal report, I plan to research the costing system used by EcoSound Inc. in its paint manufacturing process. I will research the strengths and weaknesses of the costing system used during the paint manufacturing process, up to the completion of each unit. Using this research, I will analyze the company's cost system to determine if this system is suitable for the product line.

Topic Rationale

In deciding what to research and analyze for my formal report, I tried to incorporate what I already know, what I would like to learn more about, and what interests me. I decided to focus on EcoSound operation paint production costing for two reasons:

- Having worked part-time at Rona in Milton for several years, I have the contacts needed to get primary information about the manufacturing of EcoSound's paint products.

FIGURE 17.5   **Draft Proposal for a Student Report Using Primary and Secondary Sources (Direct Pattern, Module 8), cont.**

- I mix and sell this paint to my customers daily; I thought it would be interesting to learn more about the manufacturing side of the products I am selling. Furthermore, the more knowledge I have about a product, the easier it is to sell the product and answer any questions customers have.

Operations costing also appeals to me as a formal report topic because the research and writing will help me with my Cost and Budgets course. Not only will I learn how to write a formal report, but I will also be applying a real world example to the Cost and Budgets curriculum. Learning more about the actual application of operation costing within a real company will increase my understanding of the concepts being discussed in Cost and Budgets.

Formal Report Focus

In my preliminary research, I was able to learn some of the basics of EcoSound paint production, which I will use to formulate research questions. In my report I will

- Examine where costs are added to the product, for example:
  - ○ Overhead costs added to each product based on the time spent at each work centre
  - ○ Labour costs added by working out the number of employees at each work centre and their salary to get a labour rate at each work centre
- Create a flow chart of the production process, listing the "work stations" that each unit goes through before completion
- Analyze why there is such a large retail profit margin (40–45%) on EcoSound name-brand paints
- Discuss whether EcoSound's costing system is effective

Through my research and analysis, I will determine the effectiveness and any weaknesses of the EcoSound system manufacturing process.

Research Sources

Primary Sources

- Josef Usdan—EcoSound sales representative
- Mario Eccles—EcoSound marketing representative
- Katrina Glausiusz—EcoSound accountant (Brampton plant)
- Myself
- Marian Feierabend—Cost and Budget instructor
- The knowledge I have gained about EcoSound paint products through my employment at Rona

Secondary Sources

- Internet—www.ecosound.ca; www.highbeam.com/doc/1G1-146498025.html; http://ezinearticles.com/?Activity-Based-Costing---Part-I&id=3984203
- *Managerial Accounting—Cost and Budget* textbook

Tentative Research and Writing Schedule

To remain on schedule in researching and writing my formal report, I have created a tentative work schedule:

- February 18   Get approval for my proposal; begin research
- March 1   Complete research; begin first draft of report body
- March 10   Finish draft of body; draft conclusions
- March 15   Have peer read drafts; make necessary changes
- March 20   Begin draft of summary
- March 23   Have peer read summary; make necessary changes
- April 5   Edit report
- April 10   Proofread report

As you can see, I have selected an appropriate formal report topic for which I will be able to find relevant information. Please let me know at tamirud@ryerson.ca if my plan meets with your approval.

How Should I Organize Reports?

You can organize information in any of seven patterns. Use PAIBOC analysis to determine the pattern that best achieves your purposes, and meets your audience's needs.

Any of these patterns can be used for all or part of a report:

1. General-to-particular or particular-to-general
2. Chronological
3. Comparison or contrast
4. Problem–solution
5. Elimination of alternatives
6. Geographic or spatial
7. Functional

1. General-to-Particular or Particular-to-General

General-to-particular starts with the situation as it affects the organization, or as it exists in general, and then moves to a discussion of the parts of the situation and solutions to each of these parts.

Particular-to-general starts with the problem as the audience defines it and moves to larger issues of which the problem is a part. Both are useful patterns when you need to redefine the reader's perception of the problem to solve it effectively.

For example, the directors of a student volunteer organization, Students Mentoring Students (SMS), have defined their problem as "not enough volunteers." After doing their research, the writers are convinced that poor training, an inadequate structure, and low campus awareness are responsible for both a high dropout rate and low recruitment rate. The general-to-particular pattern helps the audience see the problem in a new way:

> Why Students Helping Students (SMS) Needs More Volunteers
> Why Some SMS Volunteers Drop Out
>
> > Inadequate Training
> > Feeling that SMS Takes Too Much Time
> > Feeling that the Work is Too Emotionally Demanding
>
> Why Some Students Do Not Volunteer
>
> > Feeling that SMS Takes Too Much Time
> > Feeling that the Work is Too Emotionally Demanding
> > Preference for Volunteering with another Organization
> > Lack of Knowledge about SMS Operations
>
> How SMS Volunteers Are Trained
> Emotional Demands on SMS Volunteers
> Ways to Increase Volunteer Commitment and Motivation
>
> > Improving Training
> > Improving the Flexibility of Volunteer Hours
> > Providing Emotional Support to Volunteers
> > Providing More Information about Community Needs and SMS Services

2. Chronological

A chronological report records events in the order in which they happened or are planned to happen. Many information and progress reports use a chronological pattern:

Revisions Completed in October
Revisions Completed In November
Work Planned for December

3. Comparison or Contrast

Comparison or contrast examines each alternative in turn, discussing strengths and weaknesses. Feasibility studies and yardstick reports usually use this pattern.

A variation of the divided pattern is the **pro–con pattern**. In this pattern, under each specific heading, give the arguments for and against that alternative.

Whatever information comes second will carry more psychological weight. This pattern is least effective when you want to de-emphasize the disadvantages of a proposed solution, for it does not permit you to bury the disadvantages between neutral or positive material.

A report recommending new plantings for a garden over an expressway, for example, uses the pro–con pattern:

Advantages of Ornamental Grasses
    High Productivity
    Visual Symmetry
Disadvantages of Ornamental Grasses
    Investments and Replacement Costs
    Visual Monotony

4. Problem–Solution

Identify the problem; explain its background or history; discuss its extent and seriousness; identify its causes. Discuss the factors (criteria) that affect the decision. Analyze the advantages and disadvantages of possible solutions. Conclusions and recommendations can go either first or last, depending on the length of the report, and preferences of your reader. This pattern works well when the reader is neutral.

A report recommending ways to eliminate solidification of granular bleach during production, for example, uses the problem–solution pattern:

Reformulation for Alpha Bleach
Problems in Maintaining Alpha's Granular Structure

    Solidifying During Storage and Transportation
    Customer Complaints about "Blocks" of Alpha in Boxes
Why Alpha Bleach "Cakes"
    Alpha's Formula
    The Manufacturing Process
    The Chemical Process

Modifications Needed to Keep Alpha Flowing Freely

5. Elimination of Alternatives

After discussing the problem and its causes, discuss the *impractical* solutions first, showing why they will not work. End with the most practical solution. This pattern works well when the solutions the reader is likely to favour will not work, while the solution you recommend is likely to be perceived as expensive, intrusive, or radical.

A report on toy commercials, for example, eliminates the alternatives before concluding with the recommended solution:

> Effect of TV Ads on Children
> Camera Techniques Used in TV Advertisements
> Alternative Solutions to Problems in TV Toy Ads
> > Leave Ads Unchanged
> > Mandate Ad Blockers on All TV Production
> > Ask the Industry to Self-Regulate
> > Give CRTC Authority to Regulate TV Ads Directed at Children

6. Geographic or Spatial

In a geographic or spatial pattern, you discuss problems and solutions in units by their physical arrangement. Move from office to office, building to building, factory to factory, province to province, region to region, and so on.

Sales and market research reports, for example, may use a geographic pattern of organization:

> Sales Have Risen in the European Economic Community
> Sales Have Fallen Slightly in Asia
> Sales Have Fallen in North America

7. Functional

Functional patterns discuss the problems and solutions of each functional unit. For example, a report on a new plant might divide data into sections on the costs of land and building, on the availability of personnel, on the convenience of raw materials, and so on. A government report might divide data into the different functions an office performed, taking each in turn.

> PST Plant Move
> - Manufacturing
>   Equipment
>   Offices
> - Sales and Marketing
>   Furniture
>   Filing Cabinets
> - Executive Offices
>   Furniture
>   Filing Cabinets

LO4 LO7   EXPANDING A CRITICAL SKILL

Increasing Readability

Readers do not want to read every word in a business document. They want instantaneous meaning; they want to skim and scan for the information they need. They want business documents to be as eye-easy as the best Web writing.[3]

What Makes Documents Easy to Read?

Increase readability with blueprints, transitions, topic sentences, white space, and headings that "talk."

Blueprints forecast what you will discuss in a section or in the entire report. In an overview paragraph, blueprints tell the reader how many points there are and number them. This overview paragraph establishes **repetition for reinforcement**: the blueprint establishes a contract with readers, who now know what they are going to read and in what order:

Paragraph without blueprint

Employee Stock Ownership Programs (ESOPs) have several advantages. They provide tax benefits for the company. ESOPs also create tax benefits for employees and for lenders. They provide a defence against takeovers. In some organizations, productivity increases because workers now have a financial stake in the company's profits. ESOPs help the company hire and retain good employees.

Revised paragraph with blueprint

Employee Stock Ownership Programs (ESOPs) provide four benefits. First, ESOPs provide tax benefits for the company, its employees, and lenders to the plan. Second, ESOPs help create a defence against takeovers. Third, ESOPs may increase productivity by giving workers a stake in the company's profits. Fourth, as an attractive employee benefit, ESOPs help the company hire and retain good employees.

Transitions are words, phrases, and sentences that tell the reader the discussion is continuing on the same point or is shifting points.

There are economic benefits, too.

(Tells the reader that the discussion is still on advantages, and now moving to economic advantages.)

An alternative plan is...

(Tells the reader that a second option is coming up.)

These advantages, however, only apply in the case of short-term patients and not to those in long-term care.

(Prepares reader for a shift from short-term patients to those in long-term care.)

The **topic sentence** introduces or summarizes the main idea of a paragraph. Competent readers skim documents by searching for topic sentences at the beginning of paragraphs, because that's where competent writers put them.

Revised paragraph without summarizing topic sentence

Another main use of ice is to keep the fish fresh. Each of the seven different kinds of fish served at the restaurant requires almost 3.78 litres twice a day, for a total of 52.9 litres. An additional 22.7 litres a day are required for the salad bar.

Revised paragraph with summarizing topic sentence

Seventy-six litres of ice a day are needed to keep food fresh. Of this, the largest portion (52.9 litres) is used to keep the fish fresh. Each of the seven varieties requires almost four litres twice a day ($7 \times 7.56 = 52.9$ litres). The salad bar requires an additional 22.7 litres a day.

White space increases reading ease because it separates and emphasizes ideas (Modules 5 and 6). To create white space, use

- Headings and subheadings
- Short paragraphs
- Tabs or indents
- Lists—with numbers or bullets

Headings are signposts that divide your letter, memo, or report into sections. **Subheadings** signal a subsection: the writer is providing specifics within the section. The best headings and subheadings "talk" to the reader; they

- Are short and specific
- Use highlighting: bold or italics
- Are differentiated: subheadings use a smaller or different font

- Summarize what the reader is about to read
- Cover all the material until the next heading
- Are parallel (i.e., use the same grammatical structure)

The following suggestions can help employers avoid bias in job interviews:

1. Base questions on the job description.
2. Ask the same questions of all applicants.
3. Select and train interviewers carefully.

Revising for readability (using blueprints, transitions, topic sentences, white space, and "talking" headings and subheadings) creates a story line your readers can readily follow.

MODULE SUMMARY

- **Feasibility**, **yardstick**, and **justification** reports analyze and evaluate information readers need to make decisions.
- **Proposals** are reports that describe a method for finding information, or solving a problem.
- PAIBOC analysis will help you choose the **content** and **organizational pattern** that best meets your audience's needs and expectations, and serves your purpose(s). You can organize your information using any of seven patterns:
  - ○ **General-to-particular** or **particular-to-general**. **General-to-particular** begins with the situation as it affects the organization or manifests itself in general. Then the report discusses the parts of the problem and offers solutions to each of these parts. **Particular-to-general** starts with specifics and then discusses the larger implications for the organization.
  - ○ **Chronological** records events in the order in which they happened or are planned to happen.

- ○ **Comparison or contrast** examines each alternative in turn; the **pro–con pattern**, a variation of the pattern, gives the arguments for and against that alternative under each specific heading.
- ○ The **problem–solution** pattern identifies the situation, explains causes, and analyzes the advantages and disadvantages of possible solutions.
- ○ **Elimination of alternatives** identifies the situation, explains causes, and discusses the least practical solution first, ending with the solution the writer favours.
- ○ **Geographic or spatial** patterns discuss the problems and solutions by units.
- ○ **Functional pattern** examines the problems and solutions of each functional unit.
- Revising for readability (using blueprints, transitions, topic sentences, white space, and "talking" headings and subheadings) makes your writing reader-friendly.

ASSIGNMENTS FOR MODULE 17

Questions for Critical Thinking

17.1 When would you include visuals in your report?

17.2 How can you write headings in reports that are actually useful to readers?

17.3 How do you decide how to organize sections in your report?

Exercises and Problems

17.4 Writing a Yardstick Report

Write a two-page yardstick report to your instructor and peers suggesting how users can protect themselves from cyber-crime on social networking sites. Choose a specific site (Facebook, MySpace, etc.) and research specific exam- ples (fraud, identity theft, scams). Using primary and second- ary sources (your own observation and experience as well as expert advice), identify three possible solutions. Establish specific criteria by which to measure the solutions. Evaluate each based on your criteria. Conclude your report by identi- fying the best way users can protect themselves.

17.5 Writing a Justification Report

Write a two-page report to your supervisor justifying a change in policy, or a purchase, investment, or hire. Choose a topic that you can cover in two pages, and use an organizational pattern that your reader will find convincing. Possible topics include

- Introducing flex hours
- Extending breaks
- Funding a course you would like to take
- Purchasing a new coffee machine
- Bringing pets to work
- Hiring an new employee

17.6 Explaining "Best Practices"

Write a report describing the "best practices" of a unit or team of which you are a member. Convince your reader that other teams in your organization/college/university should adopt these practices.

17.7 Writing a Feasibility or Yardstick Report Recommending Action

Write a report identifying alternative actions your unit or organization could take, evaluating each solution, and recommending the best choice. Address your report to the person who has the power to approve your recommendation. Possibilities are

- Making your organization more eco-friendly
- Finding an additional worker for your department
- Making your organization more employee-friendly
- Making a change to improve efficiency
- Making changes to improve accessibility for customers or employees with disabilities

17.8 Writing a Proposal for a Student Report

Write a proposal to your instructor to do the research for a formal or informal report. The headings and questions in the section "Proposals for Class Reports" are your RFP; be sure to answer every question and to use the headings exactly as stated in the RFP.

Exception: Where alternative headings are given, combine them (Qualifications and Facilities) or use them as separate headings.

POLISHING YOUR PROSE

Writing Subject Lines and Headings

Subject lines are the title of a letter, memo, or email message. Headings within a document tell the reader what information you will discuss in that section. Good subject lines are specific, concise, and appropriate for your purposes and the response you expect from the reader. Subject lines are required in memos, optional in letters.

- Put in good news if you have it.
- If information is neutral, summarize it.
- Use negative subject lines if the reader may not read the message or needs the information to act, or if the negative is your error.
- In a request that is easy for the reader to grant, put the subject of that request, or a direct question, in the subject line.
- When you must persuade a reluctant reader, use a common ground, a reader benefit, or a directed subject line that makes your stance on the issue clear.

Headings are single words, short phrases, or complete sentences that indicate the topic in a document section. Headings must be *parallel*—that is, they must use the same grammatical structure—and must cover all the information until the next heading.

The most useful headings are **informative** or **talking heads**, which sum up the content of the section.

Weak:	*Problem:*
	Cause 1
	Cause 2
	Cause 3
Better:	*Communication Problems Between Air Traffic Controllers and Pilots:*
	Selective Listening
	Indirect Conversational Style
	Limitations of Short-Term Memory

Exercises

Write a good subject line for each of the following situations:

1. I'm your new boss
2. I wanted those annual enrolment forms back from you last week
3. Blood donor clinic
4. Not that it will really affect you, but starting next week there will be an opportunity for non-hourly workers (you're hourly) to also get overtime compensation for extra hours worked.
5. We're going to raise your insurance rates

Make the following statements into effective headings using parallel form:

6. Making the Most of Undergraduate Years; Making the Most of Graduate School; Now What?

7. Research; Logistics: What's in It for Us?
8. Pros of Investing in Short-Term Mutual Funds; Cons of Investing in Short-Term Mutual Funds; The Market
9. Clemente Research Group's Five-Year Goals; What We Want to Accomplish in Ten Years; Our Fifteen-Year Goals
10. Overview: Budget; The Problem of Avondale Expanding into Europe

Check your answers to the odd-numbered exercises in the Polishing Your Prose Answer Key.

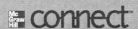

MODULE 18

Writing Formal Reports

Learning Objectives

After reading and applying the information in Module 18, you'll be able to demonstrate

Knowledge of

LO1 The parts of a formal report

LO2 The importance of summaries

LO3 Report formats and style choices

Skills to

LO4 Create a formal report

LO5 Begin to write summaries

LO6 Use PAIBOC to analyze and identify audience-appropriate report formats and style

Employability Skills 2000+ Checklist

Module content builds these Conference Board of Canada Employability Skills 2000+

Communicate   **Participate in Projects and Tasks**

Manage Information   **Be Responsible**

Use Numbers   **Learn Continuously**

Think and Solve Problems   **Work with Others**

Employees in government and scientific organizations produce lengthy, formal reports: multiple audiences, greater accountability, and recommendations that may be expensive and lengthy to implement demand extensive supporting information. Formal reports differ from informal letter and memo reports in length, layout, and their additional components.

LO1 What Does a Formal Report Look Like?

Formal reports are lengthy, use formal language, include illustrations, and begin with an Executive Summary.

A full formal report *may* contain the following components:

- Cover
- Letter or Memo of Transmittal
- Title Page
- Table of Contents
- List of Illustrations
- Executive Summary

FIGURE 18.1   **Parts of the Formal Report**

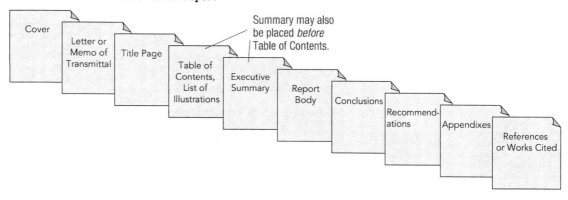

- Report body
  - ✔ Introduction (Purpose and Scope; may also cover Limitations, Assumptions, and Methods.)
  - ✔ Background/History of the Problem (Serves as context for later readers of the report.)
  - ✔ Body (Presents and interprets data in words and visuals. Analyzes the situation or problem, identifies and describes solutions, or evaluates possible solutions. Specific headings depend on the topic of the report.)
- Conclusions (Summarizes main points of the report.)
- Recommendations (Recommends actions to solve the problem. May be combined with Conclusions or may be put before the body rather than at the end.)
- Appendixes (Provides additional material that the careful reader may need: transcripts of interviews, copies of questionnaires, tallies of all the questions, computer printouts, previous reports.)
- References or Works Cited (Lists sources of information used in the report.)

LO4 LO6 How Should I Organize My Time?

Ex.
18.1
18.3–
18.6

Write parts as soon as you can. Spend most of your time on sections that support your recommendations.

Begin by analyzing and identifying your purposes and audiences: PAIBOC analysis will help you decide on the length, structure, organization, content, and language of your report.

FIGURE 18.2   **PAIBOC Questions for Analysis**

P	What are the **purposes** of the report? Are you providing information? Justifying a plan or decision? Providing information and analysis? Rationalizing and recommending change?
	Your purposes come from your organization and your audiences.
A	Who will read/view your report? What are your **audiences'** expectations? What do they already know? What do they need to know? How are they going to use your report?
I	What **information** must the report cover? What is your evidence? What primary research can you use: Observations? Experiments? Experience? Discussions with colleagues, clients or managers, other department personnel? What information will your audience find relevant? What information will convince your audience? Where will you get this information? Will your report include visuals? How can you organize this information for maximum clarity and influence (Module 17)?
B	What reasons or reader **benefits** support your position? What reasons will best appeal to your audience? How do these benefits meet your audience's needs or reinforce your audience's perceptions?
O	What **objections** will occur to your audience as they read your report? What information will your audience perceive as negative? How costly are your recommendations—in time and money? How can you organize the report to overcome audience objections or de-emphasize negative elements (Modules 9 and 17)?
C	What **context** will affect reader response? Consider your relationship to the reader, the reader's values and expectations, the economy, the environment, organizational culture, current morale, social mores, and the time of year.

When you've decided what kind of report you're writing (Modules 16 and 17), break the project into manageable pieces. Use a timeline to plan work on the whole project; start with your report due date, and work backward, establishing specific, realistic dates for each process and product (see Figure 18.3).

LO4 FIGURE 18.3   **Plan Your Report**

May 4	May 12	May 20	May 25	May 27	May 28	May 31	June 4
Report assigned; write working thesis and begin research	Do PAIBOC analysis; draft body	Draft visuals	Have peer read body; start revisions; begin Conclusions and Recommendations	Finish Conclusions, Recommendations, and References	Start Summary	Have peer read Summary, Conclusions, and Recommendations; revise and proof	Report due

To use your time efficiently, think about the parts of the report and jot down draft headings. Mark those that are most important to your reader and to your proof; spend most of your researching and writing time on them. Draft the important sections early so you won't spend all your time on the background or history of the problem. Instead, you'll get to the meat of your report.

How Do I Draft the Report?

Start in the middle: write the body first, then draft the ending sections, then write the beginning parts of the formal report: the summary and the transmittal.

You may want to start by composing the report body, because every other part of the report depends your findings, backed by research. Draft the Conclusions and Recommendations next, because these sections flow naturally out of your research and findings.

As you revise for clarity and conciseness, organize the different report sections to serve your purposes and meet your audience's needs. For example, you might organize the proof in your body section using a comparison/contrast, problem–solution, or elimination of alternatives pattern. However, in your beginning and ending report sections (Transmittal, Summary, Introduction, Conclusions, and Recommendations) you will probably find a chronological development most useful to your purposes and readers (Module 17).

LO1 **LO4** As you read about the content in each section below, you might want to turn to the corresponding pages of the long report in Figure 18.5 to see how each section is organized, and how it relates to the total report.

Report Body

Introduction

The Introduction pulls the reader into the situation, and previews the body; the Introduction contains a statement of purpose and scope, and may include other parameters:

Employability Skills

- **Purpose**: Identify the organizational problem the report addresses, the technical investigations it summarizes, and the rhetorical purposes of the report: to explain, to analyze, to evaluate, to solve, to recommend.
- **Scope**: Identify the topics the report covers. For example, Company TSC is losing money on its line of customized, home-cooked meals. Does the report investigate the quality of the meals? The advertising campaign? The cost of cooking? The market for home-cooked meals? When you define the scope, you *contain* the content of the report: if the report is to examine only advertising, then readers cannot fault the report for not considering other factors.

As policy advisor for the National Round Table on the Environment and the Economy (NRTEE: www.nrtee-trnee.com), Annika Tamlyn researches and writes formal reports that may take up to a year to complete.

- **Limitations**: Limitations usually arise because time or money constraints don't permit full research, and such limitations make the recommendations less valid, or valid only under certain conditions. For example, a campus pizza restaurant considering expanding its menu might not have enough money to take a random sample of students and non-students. Without a random sample, the writer cannot generalize from the sample to the larger population.

  Many feasibility studies and report recommendations remain valid only for a limited time. For example, in a business plan, the business location might be ideal at the time of writing, but economic or demographic changes may cause the location to lose its lustre. Or a store may want to investigate the kinds of clothing that will appeal to university students. The recommendations will remain in force only for a short time: a year from now, styles and tastes may change.

- **Assumptions**: Assumptions are statements whose truth you assume and that you use to support your conclusions and recommendations. If they are wrong, the conclusion will be wrong, too. For example, recommendations about what cars appeal to drivers aged 18 to 34 would be based on assumptions about the economy and gas prices. In a major recession, people wouldn't buy new cars. When gas prices radically rise or fall, young adults want different kinds of cars.

- **Methods**: Here writers describe how they found the report data: what they observed, whom they chose to survey and interview, and how, when, and where respondents were interviewed. Omit methods if your report is based solely on library and online research. Instead, simply cite your sources in the text and document them in the References or Works Cited section. See Module 15 on how to cite and document sources.

Background or History

Although the current audience for the report probably knows the situation, reports are filed and then consulted years later. These later audiences will probably not know the background, although it may be crucial for understanding the options possible.

In some cases, the history section might cover many years. For example, a report recommending that a Quebec consortium purchase an Ontario-based newspaper will probably provide the history of the newspaper's ownership, readership, and any editorial changes. In other cases, the background or history is much briefer, covering just the immediate situation.

Findings

The Findings section of the report provides the proof of your position. Here you present the facts, gathered through primary and secondary research (Modules 14 and 15), to demonstrate that your conclusions are accurate and your recommendations inevitable.

Spend most of your time composing, rewriting, and revising this section. Pay particular attention to the organization: you want to frame the situation and your solutions to influence your readers to your point of view. Through your PAIBOC analysis, you identify reader benefits and objections. Use this information to structure your argument: emphasize benefits through placement of text and headings (Module 17); de-emphasize negatives by offering alternatives (Module 12). Use *talking heads*—headings that describe what is coming next in the text to preview the subsequent content for the reader and contribute to clarity and understanding.

In the sample report (Figure 18.5), the writer's purpose is to provide information to the publisher of GreenZine about what articles her readers will find interesting.

The Report Ending

Conclusions and Recommendations

All communication is an act of creation: after all, when we make meaning, we create order out of chaos. Reports, too, can be creative. However, unlike fiction writing, your report should not contain any surprises for your intended audiences.

Because formal reports are so lengthy, they use a great deal of *repetition for reinforcement.* The ending sections do not introduce any new information; your conclusions and recommendations concisely and clearly summarize information covered in the body.

The Conclusions section sums up the key ideas proven by the facts in the body of the report. Note that you may present your conclusions in paragraphs or single sentences, depending on how full an explanation you have offered in the body, and on your reader's expectations. Use "should" throughout ("Ardene should hire one more full-time staff for the holiday season") because the writer and reader share the assumption that the points have been proven.

The Recommendations section identifies action items that will solve or partially solve the problem. Again, you have already explained these actions in the body, where your skill in finding, organizing, and presenting the relevant facts lead the reader to the inevitability of your recommendations.

Be sure to number the recommendations to make them easy to discuss. If your readers might find your recommendations expensive, difficult, or controversial, give a brief rationale paragraph after each recommendation. If your recommendations are easy for the audience to accept, simply list them without comments or reasons.

Depending on audience expectations, some recommendations use the imperative verb tense. "Do this."

1. *Choose* Positions for Co-op Students
2. *Set* Salaries
3. *Choose* Supervisors and Mentors
4. *Publicize* the Program
5. *Recruit* Students

Formal reports contain a great deal of repetition because of their length and because repeated information increases readability and retention. Therefore, your recommendations also go in the Summary, and if possible, in the Title and the Transmittal.

Appendixes and References or Works Cited

Place supplemental information, including visuals, questionnaires, scientific and survey data, historical documents, and even glossaries in appendixes at the end of the report, before your bibliography. When deciding if you need an appendix, follow the norms of your discourse community: if your readers expect plenty of supporting documentation, provide it.

If you are undecided about where to place such documentation, assess its value to the reader and to your proof. If the data are necessary to prove your point of view, place them in the body. If the information provides useful background to your argument, place it in an appendix. If the information is superfluous to your argument, omit it.

Your report's credibility and your own reputation depend on your careful documentation of sources and resources (Module 15). Again, follow the norms of your discourse community when deciding whether to use endnotes or in-text citations, and APA or MLA formats for your bibliography.

The Report Beginning

Title Page

The title page of a report contains four items: the title of the report, for whom the report is prepared, by whom it is prepared, and the release date. The title of the report should be as informative as possible:

Poor title: New Office Site

Better title: Why St. John's Newfoundland is the Best Site for the New Info.com Office

In many cases, the title states the recommendation in the report: "Improving Productivity at Cambridge International: Updating Communications Policies." However, omit the recommendations in the title when

- The reader will find the recommendations hard to accept
- The recommendations in the title would make the title too long
- The report is not supposed to offer recommendations

If the title does not contain the recommendation, it usually indicates the problem that the report solves: "Best-Practices Analysis, City of Montreal: The Communications Audit."

Letter or Memo of Transmittal

The Transmittal has several purposes: to send the report, to orient the reader to the report, and to influence the reader favourably toward the report and the writer. Use a *memo of transmittal* if you are a regular employee of the organization for which you prepare the report; use a *letter of transmittal* if you are not.

Organize the transmittal in this way:

1. State the report's purpose as well as when and by whom the report was authorized.
2. Summarize your conclusions and recommendations.
3. Indicate minor problems you encountered in your investigation and show how you overcame them.
4. Thank people who helped you.
5. Point out additional research required (if any).
6. Thank the reader for the opportunity to do the work and offer to answer questions. Even if you did not enjoy writing the report, readers expect some positive acknowledgment about the experience. An example of a transmittal memo is included in the long report, Figure 18.5.

Table of Contents

In the Contents, list the headings exactly as they appear in the body of the report. If the report is shorter than 25 pages, list all the headings. In a very long report, list the two or three highest levels of headings. Include your List of Illustrations in your Table of Contents.

List of Illustrations

Report visuals comprise both tables and figures. **Tables** are words or numbers arranged in rows and columns. **Figures** are everything else: bar graphs, pie graphs, maps, drawings, photographs, computer printouts, and so forth (Module 19). Number tables and figures independently, so you may have both a "Table 1" and a "Figure 1." In a report with maps and graphs but no other visuals, the visuals are sometimes called "Map 1" and "Graph 1." Whatever you call the illustrations, list them in the order in which they appear in the report; give the name of each visual as well as its number. See Module 19 for information about how to design and label visuals.

LO2 LO5 Executive Summary

The Executive Summary provides a précis (Module 15) of the whole report. For many readers, the Summary is the most important part of the report; here audiences find immediate answers to their questions.[1]

Although the Summary goes first, you create it last, because to write the Summary, you must know the report's methods, findings, and recommendations. Write and revise the Summary last, as a stand-alone document.

1. In the first paragraph, identify the report's recommendations or main point (purpose). State the situation briefly.
2. In the Summary body, identify the major supporting points for your argument. Include all the information decision makers will need.
3. Briefly describe your research methods.
4. If your report ends with conclusions, provide the conclusions section in the Summary.
5. If your report includes recommendations, provide the recommendations in the Summary.

FIGURE 18.4   **Excerpt from an Executive Summary**

Recommendations are up front in first paragraph of Summary.

To market life insurance to mid-40s urban professionals, Great North Insurance should advertise in upscale publications and use direct mail.

Network TV and radio are not cost-efficient for reaching this market. This group makes up a small percentage of the prime-time network TV audience and a minority of most radio station listeners. They tend to discard newspapers and general-interest magazines quickly, but many of them keep upscale periodicals for months. Magazines with high percentages of readers in this group include *Architectural Digest*, *Bon Appétit*, *Canadian Home*, *Canadian Gardening*, *Golf Digest*, and *Smithsonian*. Most urban professionals in their mid-40s already shop by mail and respond positively to well-conceived and well-executed direct-mail appeals.

Conclusions include focus of the report and findings.

How Should I Submit the Report?

Follow instructions carefully. If you don't know, ask.

Pay attention to the receiver's instructions whenever you send any documents. If you don't, your material may not be read. Many organizations, for example, accept only job applications and resumés sent electronically. Government RFPs define not only the format, content, and organization of vendors' responses, but also the method, date, and cut-off time of submission. The RFP might specify that the vendors' pricing description must be submitted in a separate envelope from that containing the work proposal. Proposals that do not conform to the submission specifications, like those submitted after the designated deadline, are not accepted.

Your organizational culture may have very clearly defined specifications about how to send reports to internal and external audiences. If you don't know the expectations of your discourse community, ask a colleague or your supervisor.

Language FOCUS

RFP means **request for proposal**. Many organizations will ask for proposals from companies to complete necessary work, such as the construction or repair of city roads.

FIGURE 18.5   **Formal Report**

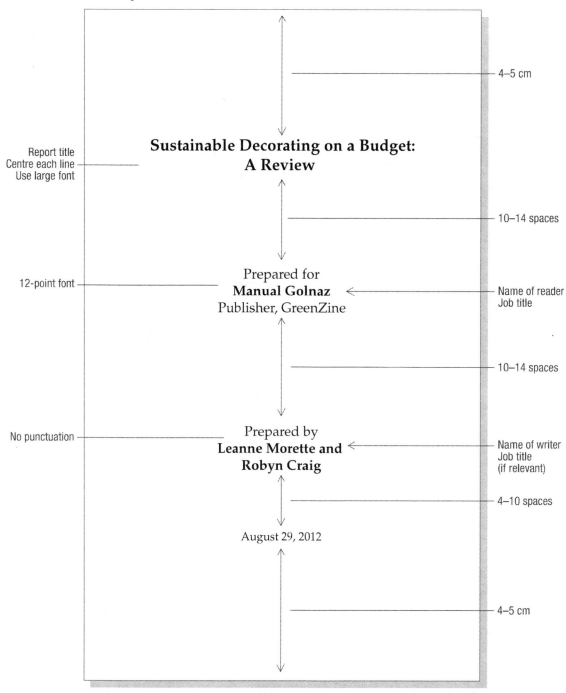

4–5 cm

Report title
Centre each line
Use large font

**Sustainable Decorating on a Budget:
A Review**

10–14 spaces

12-point font

Prepared for
Manual Golnaz
Publisher, GreenZine

Name of reader
Job title

10–14 spaces

No punctuation

Prepared by
**Leanne Morette and
Robyn Craig**

Name of writer
Job title
(if relevant)

4–10 spaces

August 29, 2012

4–5 cm

FIGURE 18.5   **Formal Report (continued)**

Date: August 29, 2012
To: Manual Golnaz
From: Leanne Morette and Robyn Craig
Subject: Sustainable Decorating on a Budget: A Review

Thank you for the opportunity to report on sustainable decorating on a budget. The purpose of this report is to identify eco-decorating trends in the design and renovation industries, suggest resources that allow people to decorate sustainably on a budget, and provide your magazine with ideas for future articles on the topic of sustainable living.

People have become more environmentally conscious and are searching for eco-responsible ways to renovate and decorate. Experts in design and environmental conservation agree that a few simple steps can lead to a more environmentally friendly and sustainable life:

1. Buy recycled and eco-friendly products
2. Shop second-hand whenever possible
3. Use as many energy-efficient products as possible in the home to reduce overall consumption

Through researching and writing this report, we learned that homeowners can make decorating decisions that save money and contribute to sustainability. We also learned that the architecture and design industries are leaders in promoting sustainable living choices, and creating environmentally sound and aesthetically pleasing products.

The information in our report came from our own experiences, from online sources, and from interviews with designer Harvaad Olsen, and Derek Mletzko, Manager, Marketing & Communications, Habitat for Humanity. Their insights were especially helpful.

Please let us know your comments and questions, and thank you again.

FIGURE 18.5 **Formal Report (continued)**

Writer chooses to position Executive Summary before Table of Contents

Executive Summary of whole report includes purpose, focus and findings, and recommendations. All information in Executive Summary comes from the report.

Executive Summary

This report:
1. Describes sustainable living and its benefits
2. Reviews experts' tips on renovating and decorating the home as a "green" space
3. Suggests available resources for someone living within a budget to create a more sustainable home

The report discusses:
- Benefits of sustainable living and sustainable products on the environment
- Quality and price efficiency of recycled goods
- Choices available through second-hand shops and organizations

Findings

Experts agree that reducing our overall consumption will help mitigate environmental damage. Moreover, the contributions of design and renovation experts to increasing consumer awareness—and access to a surfeit of consumer goods—has begun to make it financially as well as ethically attractive to go green in our homes.

Recommendations

For the future, GreenZine should focus on articles that provide readers with specific articles on:
1. How to make informed choices about eco-friendly products and services
2. Where to find—online or at "bricks and mortar" stores—budget-conscious products and services for home and office
3. How to decorate in economically and aesthetically pleasing ways

Information in this report is based on our own experiences, online sources, and interviews with Harvaad Olsen, designer, and Derek Mletzko, Manager, Marketing & Communications, Habitat for Humanity.

iii

FIGURE 18.5   **Formal Report (continued)**

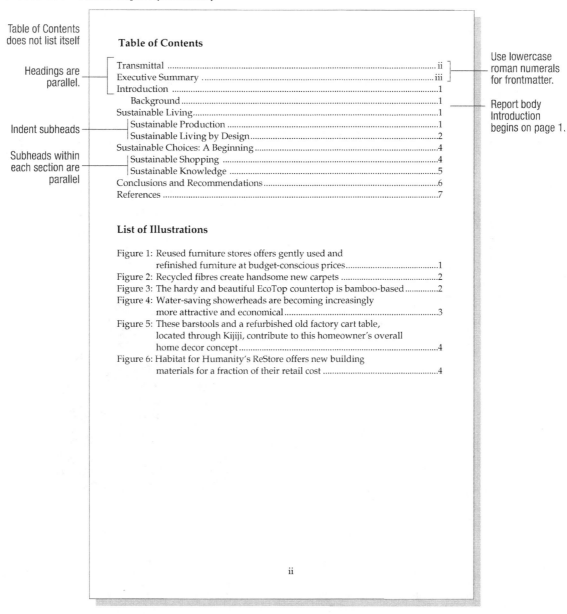

Table of Contents does not list itself

Headings are parallel.

Indent subheads

Subheads within each section are parallel

Use lowercase roman numerals for frontmatter.

Report body Introduction begins on page 1.

Table of Contents

List of Illustrations

ii

FIGURE 18.5   **Formal Report (continued)**

Introduction

Intro paragraph summarizes all the content in this section.

This report explores the practices and benefits of sustainable living—"going green"—and the possibilities of renovating and decorating on a budget. The purpose of this report is to identify eco-decorating trends in the design and renovation industries, suggest resources that allow people to decorate sustainable on a budget, and provide your magazine with ideas for future articles on the topic of sustainable living.

The report describes sustainable living and provides resources for choosing to renovate and decorate in a sustainable way. The report considers the benefits of sustainable living, describes trends in the manufacture of recycled goods and materials, offers tips from designers and renovators for going green, and provides specific resources—both new and used—that consumers can use to renovate and decorate in an environmentally responsible and aesthetically pleasing way.

Background

To reverse the damage done to our environment, and in response to increasingly precarious global economic realities, people are making a conscious effort to live in an environmentally conscious way: to "go green" in their everyday lives. In its sustainable living resource guide, the Middletown Thrall Library defined going green as "pursuing knowledge and practices that can lead to more environmentally friendly and ecologically responsible decisions and life styles, which can help protect the environment and sustain its natural resources for current and future generations" (2010). Happily, the act of going green can also be cost effective, making sustainable renovating and decorating affordable even for those on a budget. This report provides information on sustainable renovating and decorating on a budget, and suggests resources to do so.

Sustainable Living

Talking head

Document sources

Sustainability is at the core of an environmentally conscious lifestyle. Post-consumer waste is the largest contributor to environmental degradation—worse than most post-industrial waste (Tilford, 2000). Therefore, any product that minimizes post-consumer waste by recycling or repurposing, especially while incorporating great design elements, is both an excellent sustainable choice and a sensible budgetary one. People who buy products made from rapidly renewable resources, durable products that will not need replacing, and reused products are helping to protect the environment and sustain our natural resources for current and future generations (Middletown Thrall Library, 2010).

Figure 1: Reused furniture stores offer gently used and refinished furniture at budget-conscious prices

Source: Supertrooper/Dreamstime.com

Sustainable Production

Not only individuals are embracing sustainable living choices; the engineering, manufacturing, architecture, and design industries are leading the way in educating consumers about making responsible and stylish interior design choices, and in creating ecologically responsible products (Harvaad Olsen, personal communication, January 2, 2012). As an example, *Interiors & Sources* magazine and the American Society of Interior Decorators (ASID) have introduced an annual awards program, the Bloom Awards, to honour companies that produce products that reflect both aesthetics and environmental responsibility (*Interiors & Sources*, 2009).

APA uses in-text citations for personal communications. These are not listed in the References.

Report introduction begins on page 1

1

FIGURE 18.5   **Formal Report (continued)**

The Bloom Awards reviews entries in the categories of furniture, flooring, lighting, textiles, and innovative products that, for consideration, must meet specific criteria: "environmental innovation, aesthetics, promotion of sustainability, and recycling and waste management within the manufacturing process and at the end of the products' life-cycle, to name a few" (*Interiors & Sources*, 2009). A recent Bloom Awards winner is "Refresh Fiber," by Universal Fibers; the "Refresh Fiber" is a carpet recycled from carpet fibres, "a breakthrough in recycling nylon 6-6 fibers, a method that was previously impossible and can prevent thousands of yards of carpet from being dumped into landfills" (*Interiors & Sources*, 2009).

Figure 2: Recycled fibres create handsome new carpets.

Source: Universal Fibers

Yet another Bloom Award winner is Klip Biotechnologies for its "EcoTop" countertop that focuses on sustainability by using materials such as bamboo (a tall grass that grows quickly and in abundance) and recycled paper fibres. EcoTop can last for decades and can be used as bio-fuel at the end of its life cycle, unlike many other countertops on the market. Most countertops must be disposed of in a landfill at the end of their life cycle. They can't be recycled because of the chemicals involved in the manufacturing process and cost, on average, $35/sq. foot (Klip Biotechnologies, 2009).

Figure 3: The hardy and beautiful EcoTop counter-top is bamboo based.

Source: www.KlipTech.com

These Bloom Award winners are just two examples of products designed to promote sustainable living in the home at a manage-able cost.

Sustainable Living by Design

Topic sentences begin each paragraph.

With today's attention on sustainable living, designers and renovators now focus on creating green spaces. These designers and renovation experts provide tips on creating healthy and sustainable environments by 1) adopting a few simple changes in personal habits and 2) choosing eco-friendly products and appliances for our homes.

Television host, author, and columnist Sara Snow shares her tips for green living in the article *Going Green with Sara Snow:*

> [Buy] eco-friendly materials like organic cotton for sheets and towels, and bamboo for flooring and countertops, [choose] second hand furniture (which saves the environment and your money), [hang] your clothes to dry (inside or outside), and [cut] down home energy usage by fitting your home with energy-efficient light bulbs. (Berggoetz, 2009, p. 3)

HGTV designer Linda Woodrum, on HGTV's website (2011), also offers similar suggestions for sustainable in-home materials. Woodrum suggests using sustainable woods such as bamboo or eucalyptus for floors and cabinets, shopping for recycled hardware like cupboard handles at flea markets, using natural stone for countertops, using carpet made of natural fibres like organic cotton and wool or recycled materials, and using Energy-Star rated appliances (Woodrum, 2011). Woodrum specifically suggests replacing shower heads and faucets with water-saving attachments, switching to a low-flow toilet, and investing in an energy efficient water heater, such as a instant tankless hot water heater, which heats water when needed rather than constantly heating a tank of water and thus wasting electricity (Woodrum, 2011).

Figure 4: Water-saving showerheads are becoming increasingly more attractive and economical.

Source: David Buffington/ Getty Images

2

FIGURE 18.5   **Formal Report (continued)**

Sustainable Choices: A Beginning

Obviously, newer, eco-friendly products can dramatically decrease the impact that we all person-ally make daily on the environment. In many cases, however, cutting back our consumption is a first and very important step in adopting a sustainable lifestyle. Josh Dorfman, host of The Sundance Channel's *The Lazy Environmentalist*, affirms that "whether people realize it or not, cutting back has made them accidental environmentalists." Dorfman goes on to identify the prime motivator in people's decision to embrace sustainability: "saving money is more important to most people than going green" (Judkis, 2010). Increasingly, therefore, designers, builders, renovators, and manufacturers must source and choose sustainable materials and methods that do not cost the conservationist consumer more, while emphasizing the global benefits of these choices: diverting waste from landfills, preserving our natural resources, and reducing the damage already done to our planet.

(margin note: Start major headings on a new page for emphasis)

Sustainable Shopping

Shopping for second-hand renovating and decorating materials and furnishings is a first, economi-cal step in choosing an environmentally responsible lifestyle. To find second-hand or gently used products, consumers can venture to flea markets, rummage sales, garage sales, thrift stores such as The Salvation Army, Goodwill, or Value Village, or a Habitat for Humanity ReStore location. Consumers can also source decor finds through Craigslist or Kijiji.

(margin note: Create sub-headings to increase readability when introducing more specific information)

Figure 5: These barstools and a refurbished old factory cart table, located through Kijiji, contribute to this homeowner's overall home decor concept.

Source: Robyn Craig

Habitat for Humanity's ReStore is one of the best options for a one-stop shop to meet renovators' green and budget decorating needs. Consumers not only save money and the environment by shopping at the ReStore; a large portion of the money consumers spend there goes towards funding for Habitat for Humanity projects in local communities (Habitat for Humanity, 2011).

Commonly found items available at the ReStore include sinks, windows, doors, paint, hardware, lumber, tools, lighting fixtures, and appliances, all at a fraction of their original cost. Much of what is sold is new, gently used, or retail customer returns that would otherwise end up in a landfill (Habitat for Humanity, 2011). In fact, in 2010 alone "ReStore locations across Canada kept 20,000 tonnes of materials out of landfills through taking donations from the public and re-selling them at ReStore locations" (Habitat for Humanity, 2011).

Figure 6: Habitat for Humanity's ReStore offers new building materials for a fraction of their retail cost

Source: Habitat for Humanity

3

FIGURE 18.5   **Formal Report (continued)**

Longer quotations are introduced with colons

Furthermore, Habitat for Humanity uses its ReStores to model sustainable building as well as waste management processes:

> [A] lot of our product is new end-of-line that comes directly from retailers. While encouraging many customers to visit our stores, this is also a green practice, as retailers would often otherwise dispose of this product in a landfill.
>
> Many of our homes are also built to recognized green building standards (making the green impact exponential!). In 2012, we expect 90% of our homes to be constructed to recognized green building standards, and for 75% of these to be certified. (Derek Mletzko, Manager, Marketing & Communications, Habitat for Humanity Canada, personal communication, August 24, 2012)

Longer quotations are indented.

Clearly the environmental and community benefits—and the choices and potential savings—of shopping for used and recycled goods from stores such as the Habitat for Humanity's ReStore make a strong case for choosing sustainable decorating.

Sustainable Knowledge

Consumers need to be aware, however, that some used building materials and appliances may not be the best environmental choice, although they may be budget friendly. Used older appliances are not energy efficient. Repurposed furniture may also contain lead paint or other health hazards. Eco-decorators need to be knowledgeable buyers, according to renovation expert and sustainable building advocate Mike Holmes:

Subheadings within each section are parallel.

> You need to be aware of the real differences between surplus new, used, and antique before you start shopping…[I]f you are buying an antique, you definitely won't have windows or doors with high thermal value. That's probably not a sensible idea, given the ever-climbing cost of energy….An old window might be framed in wood that's rotten. And older glass is typically single-glazed and much less energy-efficient than newer designs. So I'd use an antique window as an interior accent, or in non-heated space like a shed or porch. (Holmes, 2008)

Holmes goes on to suggest that a *knowledgeable*, budget-conscious eco-shopper can make informed sustainable choices: "A better idea, if you are looking to save on windows, would be to search the re-use centre for surplus new models that still might be perfect for your renovation needs" (Holmes, 2008).

4

Conclusions and Recommendations

Faced with harsh environmental and economic realities, people are becoming more eco-conscious in their lifestyle, renovating, and decorating choices. Experts in environmental conservation, renovation, and design all agree on a few simple key steps to begin to adopt an inexpensive approach to living a sustainable life:

Use bullets for readability

- Buy recycled and eco-friendly products
- Shop second-hand, whenever possible
- Fit homes with as many energy efficient products as possible

This reduction in overall consumption will help reverse the human-generated damage to our planet. Design and renovation experts have helped to increase consumer awareness. This awareness, combined with access to a surfeit of consumer goods, has begun to make it financially as well as ethically attractive to go green in our homes.

It is the recommendation of this report that, to ensure topicality and relevance, GreenZine should focus on articles that provide readers with specific articles on:

1. How to make informed choices about eco-friendly products and services
2. Where to find—online or at bricks-and-mortar stores—budget-conscious products and services for home and office
3. How to decorate in economically and ascetically pleasing ways

5

FIGURE 18.5 **Formal Report (continued)**

References

Berggoetz, B. (2009). Going green with Sara Snow. *Saturday Evening Post, 281*(2), pp. 56–59. Retrieved from http://search.ebscohost.com/login.aspx?direct=true&db=a9h&AN=36611455&site=ehost-live&scope=site

Habitat for Humanity (2011). *ReStore building supplies*, Habitat for Humanity Canada. Retrieved October 11, 2011, from www.habitat.ca/en/community/restores

Holmes, M. (2008, October 3). How green is your reno? *Globe and Mail*, G10.

Holmes, M. (2011, March 15). Using salvaged materials makes sense. *Globe and Mail*. Retrieved from http://m.theglobeandmail.com/life/home-and-garden/renovations/renovations-green/using-salvaged-materials-makes-sense/article44274/?service=mobile

Interiors & Sources (2009). The bloom awards. 16(4), pp. 71–76. Retrieved from Full Text HTMLWilson-Link HTML: http://vnweb.hwwilsonweb.com/hww/jumpstart.jhtml?recid=0bc05f7a67b1790e841a46ab33283c14bde461c4288200bdc7035f2d296f36c69eb183133fcd2904&fmt=H

Judkis, M. (2010). 10 ways to save by going green. *U.S. News & World Report, 147*(3), pp. 34–35. Retrieved from http://search.ebscohost.com/login.aspx?direct=true&db=a9h&AN=48174339&site=ehost-live&scope=site

Klip Biotechnologies. (2009). *Interiors & Sources* (2009), 16(2), p. 37. Retrieved from Full Text HTML-WilsonLink HTML: http://vnweb.hwwilsonweb.com/hww/jumpstart.jhtml?recid=0bc05f7a67b1790e841a46ab33283c14bde461c4288200bdaaf1e06837196cfd227652fe9410fe37&fmt=H

McAllister, C., & Ryan, J. (2011). It's worth a walk around the block. *yourhome.ca*, Retrieved August 12, 2012, from www.yourhome.ca/homes/article/1080803

Middletown Thrall Library (2010). *Going green: Sustainable living resource guide.* (2010), Retrieved October 16, 2011, from www.thrall.org/special/goinggreen.html

Tilford, D. (2000). Sustainable consumption: Why consumption matters. *Sierra Club*, www.sierraclub.org/sustainable_consumption/tilford.asp

Woodrum, L. (2011). Green decorating basics from Linda Woodrum. HGTV. Retrieved October 11, 2011, from www.hgtv.com/green-home/green-decorating-basics-from-linda-woodrum/index.html

6

EXPANDING A CRITICAL SKILL

L03 Choosing a Long Report Format and Style

Many types of long reports exist in the workplace. Their formats and styles vary according to purpose, audience expectations, organization, and context.

Corporate annual reports are typically printed on glossy stock, filled with colour photos, charts, and graphs, and focused on information, like financial statistics, that is important to investors. These reports may have dozens of pages and be bound like a magazine or paperback book. Other organizations choose to use fewer colours and pages, and inexpensive binding. Still other organizations put their reports online only, saving money and paper.

Reports on scientific and engineering projects, like soil contamination remediation, highway repair efforts, or technology research and development, are frequently text-heavy, including jargon, but relatively light on visuals, which may be only the most technical of diagrams. They may have hundreds of pages and be bound in three-ring binders. A government report on the bereavement industry or tax law revisions might also be dense with text. Plain covers and paper stock closer to copy bond are typical.

Text in reports may be arranged in single or multiple columns, and feature a "drop cap"—an enlarged letter at the beginning of an opening paragraph—and "pull quotes"—portions of the body text repeated and set apart graphically from the rest. Online reports routinely include hypertext links to other documents.

Long reports are written formally. They

- Use the third person (*employees, waste management services, the retail sales team, finance graduates*).

- Are impersonal: long reports avoid *I* and *you* because the data are more important than the writer; the facts are supposedly objective; in a document to multiple, even global audiences, it is not clear who "you" is.
- Avoid contractions: use *they will* instead of *they'll*; *it is* instead of *it's*.

Use your resources to decide on the appropriate format and style:

- Start with PAIBOC analysis.
- Review organizational models. Many organizations have a databank of reports and generic report templates. Writers customize these for their purposes and audiences.
- Many organizations publish reports online, and some public and post-secondary libraries keep copies of government and annual reports. Use your research techniques to find these.
- Look at the report templates online: Microsoft Office Online provides a variety of templates; BDC offers templates and user guides to help writers prepare a business plan (www.bdc.ca/en/business_tools/business_plan/default.htm).
- Consult texts on writing reports, experts in your organization, or professional writers and graphic designers.
- Test your drafts with colleagues, and where possible, with audiences similar to ones that will read your report.

The more specialized the report, the more likely experienced employees will write it. However, many organizations expect novice writers to participate. Use this opportunity to begin to learn a valuable transferable skill.

MODULE SUMMARY

- Long formal reports might include a Transmittal, Executive Summary, Table of Contents with List of Illustrations, the body of the report itself, and Conclusions and Recommendations.

- Writing a long report takes time and organization:
  ○ Create a timeline for parts of the report.
  ○ Write the report in sections, starting with the body, where you present facts that prove your position.
  ○ Jot down potential headings, both for the whole report, and for the sections in the body (The Problem, The Results, The Solution, The Benefits).
  ○ When you revise the report, reshape the headings into talking heads to preview the subsequent content for the reader and contribute to clarity and understanding.
  ○ As you research and analyze your information, prepare a bibliography of your sources. Use APA or MLA documentation according to the standards of your discourse community (Module 15).

- All reports should include an overview, to preview the report's contents for the reader. In a formal report, this overview is called a **Summary** or **Executive Summary**. The Summary
  ○ Sums up the whole report and includes conclusions and recommendations
  ○ Goes first, on a separate page
  ○ Is about one-tenth the length of the whole report

- **Introduction**: statement of Purpose and Scope. The **Purpose** statement includes the situation the report addresses, the investigations it summarizes, and the rhetorical purposes (to explain, to describe, to recommend). The **Scope** statement identifies the topics the report covers. The Introduction may also include the following:

- **Limitations**: factors or problems that limit the scope of the report or the validity of the recommendations

- **Assumptions**: statements whose truth you assume, and that you use to prove your ideas

- **Methods**: explanations of how you gathered your data

- **Background** or **History**: this section is information for audiences who may need to read the report years later.

- **Conclusions**: a summary of the main ideas you make in the report body. All reports offer Conclusions.

- **Recommendations**: action items that would solve, or partially solve, the problem.

- Add additional appendixes, responses to questionnaires, figures and tables, and background information only if they are useful to the reader.

- Your choice of report format, style, and method of submission are as important as your content. Pay attention to the rules and norms of your discourse community. If you are unsure, ask someone who knows.

ASSIGNMENTS FOR MODULE 18

Questions for Critical Thinking

18.1 How do you decide on the length and formality of a report?

18.2 How do you decide how much background information to provide in a report?

18.3 How much evidence do you need to provide for each recommendation you make?

Exercises and Problems

As your instructor directs

Submit the following documents for Problems 18.4 through 18.8:

a. The approved proposal
b. Two copies of the report, including
  - Cover
  - Letter or Memo of Transmittal

- Title Page
- Table of Contents
- List of Illustrations
- Executive Summary
- Body (Introduction, all information). Your instructor may specify a minimum length, a minimum number or kind of sources, and a minimum number of visuals.

- Conclusions and Recommendations
- Appendixes, if useful or relevant
- References or Works Cited
c. Your notes and rough drafts

18.4 Writing a Feasibility Study

Write an individual or group report evaluating the feasibility of a plan or idea. Explain your criteria clearly, evaluate each alternative, and recommend the best course of action. Possible topics include the following:

1. What is the feasibility of your business idea? Write a business plan evaluating the opportunity for the start-up of an entrepreneurial business.
2. What is the feasibility of the electric car for common use in your province?
3. What is the feasibility of high-speed commuter trains in your province? If such trains already exist, what is the feasibility of increasing their use, so that they become the primary mode of transportation throughout your province?
4. What is the feasibility of starting a blog for students in your program or for employees in your organization?
5. What is the feasibility of starting a mentorship affiliation in your organization, or in your college/university program? What businesses or non-profits might you affiliate with? What benefits would the mentors enjoy?
6. With your instructor's permission, choose your own topic.

18.5 Writing a Research Report

Write an individual or group library research report. Possible topics include the value of Wikipedia, social networking, your province's healthcare policies, your city's strategies for providing homeless shelters, Canadian copyright or defamation legislation related to Internet material, your province's small business support resources, or your province's welfare strategies. Or, with your professor's permission, choose your own topic.

Start the project by finding the most current information available online and in print.

18.6 Writing a Recommendation Report

Write an individual or group recommendation report. Possible topics are the following:

1. *Recommending courses*: What skills are in demand in your community? What courses at what levels should the local college or university offer? What accreditation courses should graduates in your programs pursue to increase their marketability and salaries?

2. *Improving sales and profits*: Recommend ways a small business in your community can increase sales and profits. Focus on one or more of the following: the products or services it offers, its advertising, its decor, its location, its accounting methods, its cash management, or anything else that may be keeping the company from achieving its potential. Address your report to the owner of the business.
3. *Increasing student involvement*: How might an organization on campus persuade more of the students who are eligible to join or to become active in its programs? Do students know that it exists? Is it offering programs that interest students? Is it retaining current members? What changes should the organization make? Address your report to the officers of the organization.
4. *Evaluating a potential employer*: What training is available to new employees? How soon is the average entry-level person promoted? How much travel and weekend work are expected? Is there a "busy season," or is the workload consistent year-round? What fringe benefits are offered? What is the corporate culture? Is the climate open, friendly, and encouraging? Non-discriminatory? How economically strong is the company? How is it affected by current economic, demographic, and political trends?

Address your report to your college or university placement office; recommend whether the placement office should encourage students to work at this company.

Or, with your professor's permission, choose your own topic. Start the project by finding the most current information available online and in print.

18.7 Writing Up a Survey

Survey two groups of people on a topic that interests you. (For help in creating your survey, go to http://ezinearticles.com/?20-Top-Tips-To-Writing-Effective-Surveys&id=2622.) Possible groups are men and women, people in business and in English programs, younger and older students, students and non-students. Non-random samples are acceptable.

As your instructor directs

a. Survey 40 to 50 people.
b. Team up with your classmates. Survey 50 to 80 people if your group has two members, 75 to 120 people if it has three members, 100 to 150 people if it has four members, and 125 to 200 people if it has five members.
c. Keep a journal during your group meetings and submit it to your instructor.
d. Write a memo to your instructor. (See Module 21, Working and Writing in Teams.)

As you conduct your survey, make careful notes about what you do so that you can use this information when you write your report. If you work with a group, record who does what. Use a memo format. Your subject line should be clear. Omit unnecessary words such as "Survey of." Your first paragraph serves as an introduction, but it needs no heading. The rest of the body of your memo might be divided into four sections with the following headings: Purpose, Procedure, Results, and Discussion. Alternatively, make your survey report more interesting by using talking headings.

In your first paragraph, briefly summarize (not necessarily in this order) who conducted the experiment or survey, when it was conducted, where it was conducted, who the subjects were, what your purpose was, and what you found out.

In your **Purpose** section, explain why you conducted the survey. What were you trying to learn? Why did this subject seem interesting or important? In your **Procedure** section, describe in detail exactly what you did. In your **Results** section, first indicate whether or not your results supported your hypothesis. Use both visuals and words to explain what your numbers show. (See Module 19 on how to design visuals.) Process your raw data in a way that will be useful to your reader. In your **Discussion** section, evaluate your survey and discuss the implications of your results. Consider these questions:

1. Do you think a scientifically valid survey would have produced the same results? Why or why not?
2. Were there any sources of bias either in the way the questions were phrased or in the way the subjects were chosen? If you were running the survey again, what changes would you make to eliminate or reduce these sources of bias?

3. Do you think your subjects answered honestly and completely? What factors may have intruded? Is the fact that you did or didn't know them, or that they were or weren't of the same gender, relevant?
4. What causes the phenomenon your results reveal? If several causes together account for the phenomenon, or if it is impossible to be sure of the cause, admit this. Identify possible causes and assess the likelihood of each.
5. What action should the reader take?

The discussion section gives you the opportunity to analyze the significance of your survey. Its insight and originality lift the otherwise well-written memo from merely satisfactory to the ranks of the above average and the excellent.

18.8 Writing Summaries

Go to www.transcanada.com/keystone.html to view the TransCanada Corporation's overview of the Keystone Pipeline Project. Read any of the following sections: *Keystone Pipeline Project, Energy Security, Pipeline Safety, Environmental Responsibility,* or *Landowner Relations.* Create a one-paragraph Executive Summary for the section you chose.

As your instructor directs

1. Form a team with two other students who chose the same section to create their Summary.
2. Read and discuss your versions of the Executive Summary.
3. Together, rewrite and revise to create your team's version of the Executive Summary.
4. Hand in for grading.

POLISHING YOUR PROSE

Improving Paragraphs

Good paragraphs demonstrate unity, detail, and variety. The following paragraph from a sales letter illustrates these three qualities:

> The best reason to consider a Schroen Heat Pump is its low cost. Schroen Heat Pumps cost 25 percent less than the cheapest competitor's. Moreover, unlike the competition, the Schroen Heat Pump will pay for itself in less than a year in energy savings. That's just 12 months. All this value comes with a 10-year unlimited warranty—if anything goes wrong, we'll repair or replace the pump at no cost to you. That means no expensive repair bills and no dollars out of your pocket.

A paragraph is **unified** when all its sentences focus on a single central idea. As long as a paragraph is about just one idea, a topic sentence expressing that idea is not required. However, using a topic sentence makes it easier for the reader to skim the document. (Essays use a *thesis statement* for the central idea of the entire document.) Sentences throughout the paragraph should support the topic sentence, or offer relevant examples.

Transitions connect ideas from one point to another. Common transitions are *and, also, first, second, third, in addition, likewise, similarly, for example (e.g.), for instance, indeed, to illustrate, namely, specifically, in contrast,* and *on the other hand.*

Detail makes your points clearer and more vivid. Good details express clearly and completely what you mean. Use concrete words, especially strong nouns, verbs, adjectives, and adverbs that paint a picture in the reader's mind and say what you mean. Avoid unnecessary repetition.

Variety is expressed first in sentence length and patterns and second in the number of sentences in each paragraph. Most sentences in business writing should be 14 to 20 words, but an occasional longer or very short sentence gives punch to your writing.

The basic pattern for sentences is subject+verb+object (SVO): *Our building supervisor sent the forms.* Vary the SVO pattern by changing the order, using transitions and clauses, and combining sentences.

Also, vary paragraph length. First and last paragraphs can be quite short. Body paragraphs will be longer. Whenever a paragraph runs eight typed lines or more, think about dividing it into two paragraphs.

Exercises

Rewrite the following paragraphs to improve unity, detail, and variety.

1. I used to work for McCandless Realty as a receptionist. My many experiences in the accounting field make me an ideal candidate for a position as senior administrative assistant with Graham, Chang, and Associates. I answered phones at McCandless. I typed there. I worked at Dufresne Plastics as a secretary. At McCandless, I also handled payroll. There are a lot of reasons why I liked Dufresne. These included the opportunity for training in data entry and Microsoft Word. I learned to type 70 wpm with no mistakes.

2. Mr. Walter Pruitt visited our business communication class yesterday. He spoke about the importance of co-op placements. Mr. Pruitt works for Global Energy. Global Energy provides network and service management to companies around the world. Mr. Pruitt, who works for Global Energy, told us he got his first job because of a co-op. A co-op is an opportunity for students to work with a company for a period of time to get business experience. Mr. Pruitt went to university and worked at a co-op placement for Global Energy. At first, Global Energy only wanted him to work for 10 weeks. Mr. Pruitt did such a good job, they kept him on another 10 weeks and another. Mr. Pruitt was offered a job by Global Energy when he graduated.

Check your answers to the odd-numbered exercises in the Polishing Your Prose Answer Key.

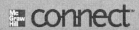

MODULE
19

Using Visuals

Learning Objectives

After reading and applying the information in Module 19, you'll be able to demonstrate

Knowledge of

LO1 How visuals create stories

LO2 How to choose appropriate visuals

Skills to

LO3 Choose visuals to tell a story

LO4 Match the visual to your story

LO5 Choose ethical visuals

LO6 Use visuals in your documents and presentations

Employability Skills 2000+ Checklist

Module content builds these Conference Board of Canada Employability Skills 2000+

Communicate   **Think & Solve Problems**

Manage Information   **Participate in Projects & Tasks**

Pictures tell stories: charts and graphs make numbers meaningful; mall maps tell us where we are; your graduation photos document a rite of passage. Using visuals and text together "as tools to increase understanding" can "get our message across with great efficiency."[1]

LO1 LO3   Why Use Visuals?

Appropriate, attractive visuals create immediate stories: they are faster and easier to understand and remember.

Visuals condense and clarify data; visuals are a reader-friendly way to communicate your points.

Formal visuals are divided into tables and figures. **Tables** are numbers or words arranged in rows and columns; **figures** are everything else. In a document, formal visuals have both numbers and titles: Figure 1, The Falling Cost of Computer Memory, 2004–2012. In an oral presentation, the title is usually used without the number: The Falling Cost of Computer Memory, 2004–2012. The title puts the story in context, indicating what your audience should look for in the visual, and why it is important. Informal or spot visuals are inserted directly into the text; they do not have numbers or titles.

In your rough draft, use visuals

- *To see that ideas are presented completely.* A table, for example, can show you whether you've included all the items in a comparison.
- *To find relationships.* For example, charting sales on a map may show that the sales representatives who made their quotas all have territories on the west coast or in the Atlantic provinces. Is the product one that appeals to coastal lifestyles? Is advertising reaching the coasts but not the prairie provinces, Ontario, or Quebec? Even if you don't use the visual in your final document, creating the map may lead you to questions you wouldn't otherwise ask.

In the final presentation or document, use visuals

- *To make points vivid.* Readers skim memos and reports; a visual catches the eye. The brain processes visuals immediately. Understanding words—written or oral—takes more time.
- *To emphasize material* that might be skipped if it were buried in a paragraph.
- *To present material more compactly and with less repetition* than words alone can.

The number and type of visuals you need depend on your purposes, your information, and the audience. You'll use more visuals when you want to show relationships, to persuade when the information is complex or contains extensive numerical data, and when the audience values visuals.

Your visual is only as good as the underlying data. Check to be sure that your data come from a reliable source (Module 14).

FIGURE 19.1   **PAIBOC Questions for Analysis**

P	What are your **purposes** in communicating with visuals? Why are you using illustrations? Your purposes come from you, your organization, and the information you intend to convey.
A	Who is your **audience**? Who will read your message? What do they need to know? How will they use your visuals? Will they use them to follow instructions? to understand directions? to assemble something? to understand how a machine, a department or a process works? to see the future if they act a certain way now? What graphics/illustrations would most appeal to your audience? Why? What visuals would maximize your audience's understanding? Why?
I	What **information** must your visual include? What visual will cause your readers to think or do as you want them to? What images could tell your story dramatically and immediately? What numerical or quantitative data are you representing? What visuals would best convey that information?
B	What reasons or reader **benefits** support your position? What visuals would emphasize those benefits?
O	What audience **objections** do you anticipate? How can you use visuals to de-emphasize or overcome audience objections?
C	What **context** will affect reader response? Consider your relationship to your readers, organizational culture, the economy, recent organizational developments, current morale, and the time of year. When choosing your illustrations, consider also your audience demographic, cultural values, and norms.

What Are Stories, and How Do I Find Them?

A story interprets something that is happening or will happen. Look for relationships, patterns, and changes.

Stories are made up of symbols—words, images, colours, and icons—that enable us to create and translate meaning. The garbage-can icon by the words "Recycle Bin" translates the computer's binary code into a story about what happens when we hit Delete. An organization's brand tells the story of its purposes and values.

Every visual should tell a story that is meaningful to your audience. Use the title of the visual to give your story context and emphasis.

Not a story:	Asian Exports, 2007–2012
Possible stories:	China and India Rule Export Trade
	Chinese Garlic Exports Flood Canadian Market

Stories that tell us what we already know are rarely interesting. Instead, good stories do at least one of several things:

- Support a hunch you have
- Surprise or challenge so-called common knowledge
- Show trends or changes you didn't know existed
- Have commercial, cultural, or social significance
- Provide information needed for action
- Have personal relevance to you and the audience

You can find stories in three ways:

1. *Focus on a topic* (starting salaries, alternative music choices, Twitter demographics).
2. *Simplify the data* on that topic and convert the numbers to simple, easy-to-understand units.

3. *Look for relationships and changes.* For example, compare two or more groups: Do men and women have the same attitudes? Look for changes over time. Look for items that can be seen as part of the same group; for example, to find stories about Internet ads, you might group ads in the same product category—ads for cars, for food, for beverages.

When you think you have a story, test it against all the data to be sure it's accurate.

Some stories are simple straight lines: "Workweek Comparison," as illustrated in Figure 19.2. But other stories are more complex, with exceptions or outlying cases. Such stories will need more vivid illustration to do them justice. And sometimes the best story arises from the juxta-position of two or more stories. In Figure 19.3, for example, the bar graphs compare Canadians' feelings about the influence of social networking sites on their reputations with the attitudes of teachers. Whatever the story, your audience should be able to see what the visual says:

> Does the chart support the title, and does the title reinforce the chart? So if I say in my title "sales have increased significantly," I want to see a trend moving up at a sharp angle. If not, if the trend parallels the baseline, it's an instant clue that the chart needs more thinking.[2]

Checkpoint

The Six Components of Every Visual

1. A title that tells the story that the visual shows
2. A clear indication of what the data are
3. Clearly labelled units
4. Labels or legends identifying axes, colours, symbols, and so forth
5. The source of the data, if you created the visual from data someone else gathered and compiled
6. The source of the visual, if you reproduce a visual that someone else created

FIGURE 19.2   **EU Countries' Workweek Comparison** ◀——— Title tells the story

Average usual hours worked, full-time workers, April to June 2011, selected European countries ◀——— Clear description of data

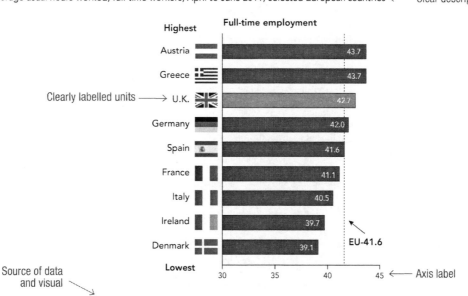

Source: Labour Force Survey — Office for National Statistics, Eurostat. © European Union, 1995-2012.

FIGURE 19.3   **Bar Graphs Tell a Story**

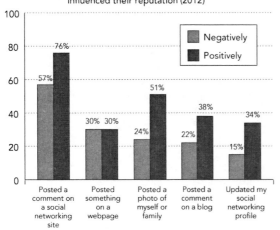

Online activities Canadians feel negatively/positively influenced their reputation (2012)

Source: Microsoft
Graph by: gdsourcing.com

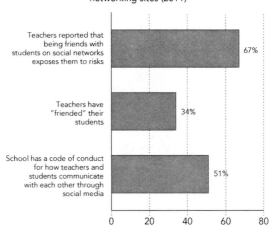

Canadian teachers and social networking sites (2011)

Source: Symantec
Graph by: gdsourcing.com

For optimum audience impact, use the "tell, show, tell" rule:

- first, *tell* your readers or listeners what they are about to see
- next, *show* your audience what you promised to show them
- finally, *tell* them the significance of the visual

And, of course, the visual must depict exactly what you said it would.

Almost every data set allows you to tell several stories. Choose the story you want to tell based on your PAIBOC analysis.

Ex. 19.1– 19.6

LO2 LO4 # Does It Matter What Kind of Visual I Use?

Yes! The visual must match the kind of story.

Visuals are not interchangeable. Use visuals that best present the data.

Whenever possible, create your own, original visuals. Use software to make charts, graphs, tables, and figures; use a digital camera to capture stories.

- Use **maps**, **diagrams**, and **graphics** to convey complex information (see Figure 19.3).
- Use **images** and **artwork** to reinforce themes (see Figure 19.4).
- Use **tables** when the reader needs to be able to identify exact values (see Figure 19.5a).
- Use a chart or graph when you want the reader to focus on relationships.[3]
  - To compare a part to the whole, use a **pie graph** (see Figure 19.5b).
  - To compare one item to another item, or items over time, use a bar graph or a line graph (see Figures 19.5c and 19.5d).

Language FOCUS

The word **data** is the plural form of the Latin word datum, which is related to the verb "to give."

FIGURE 19.4   **Visual Imagery That Tells the Story of Data Management**

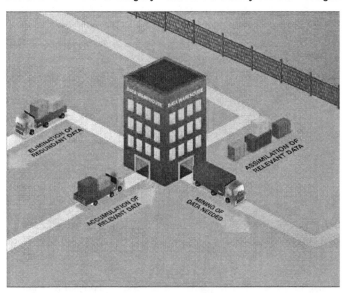

FIGURE 19.5   **Choose the Visual to Fit the Story**

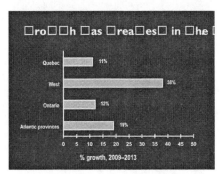

Canadian sales reach $44.5 million.			
	Millions of Dollars		
	2010	2011	2012
British Columbia	10.2	10.8	11.3
Ontario and Quebec	7.6	8.5	10.4
Prairie provinces	8.3	6.8	9.3
Atlantic provinces	11.3	12.1	13.5
Total	37.4	38.2	44.5

a. Tables show exact values.

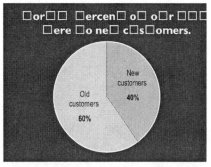

b. Pie graphs compare a component to the whole.

c. Bar graphs compare items or show distribution or correlation.

d. Line charts compare items over time or show distribution or correlation.

Tables

Use tables only when you want the audience to focus on specific numbers.

- Round off to simplify the data (e.g., 35 percent rather than 35.27 percent; 34 000 rather than 33 942). Provide column and row totals or averages when they're relevant.
- Put the items you want readers to compare in columns rather than in rows to facilitate mental subtraction and division.
- When you have many rows, screen alternate entries or double-space after every five entries to help readers line up items accurately.

Pie Graphs

Graphs convey less specific information but are always more memorable.

Pie graphs force the audience to measure area. Research shows that people can judge position or length (which a bar graph uses) much more accurately than they can judge area. The data in any pie graph can be put in a bar graph.[4] Therefore, *use a pie graph only when you are comparing one segment* to the whole. When you are comparing one segment to another, use a bar graph, a line graph, or a map—even though the data may be expressed in percentages.

- Start at 12 o'clock with the largest percentage or the percentage you want to focus on. Go clockwise to each smaller percentage or to each percentage in some other logical order.
- Make the graph chart a perfect circle. Perspective circles distort the data.
- Limit the number of segments to five or seven. If your data have more divisions, combine the smallest or the least important into a single "miscellaneous" or "other" category.
- Label the segments outside the circle. Internal labels are hard to read.

Bar Graphs

Bar graphs are easy to interpret, because they ask people to compare distance along a common scale, which most people judge accurately. Bar graphs are useful in a variety of situations: to compare one item to another, to compare items over time, and to show correlations.

FIGURE 19.6   **A Grouped Bar Graph Allows You to Compare Several Items over Time**

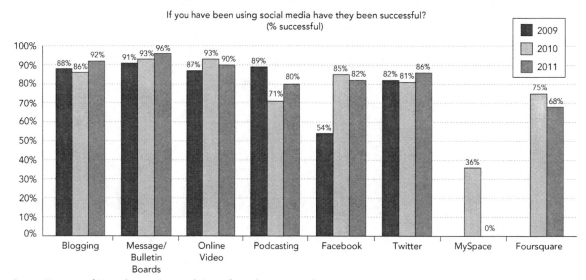

Source: University of Massachusetts, Dartmouth Centre for Marketing Research.

Use horizontal bars when your labels are long; when the labels are short, either horizontal or vertical bars will work.

- Order the bars in a logical or chronological order.
- Put the bars close enough together to make comparisons easy.
- Label both horizontal and vertical axes.
- Put all labels inside the bars or outside them. When some labels are inside and some are outside, the labels carry the visual weight of longer bars, distorting the data.
- Make all the bars the same width.
- Use different colours for different bars only when their meanings are different: estimates as opposed to known numbers, negative as opposed to positive numbers.
- Avoid using perspective. Perspective makes the values harder to read and can make comparison difficult.

Several varieties of bar graphs exist:

- **Grouped bar graphs** allow you to compare several aspects of each item or several items over time.
- **Segmented, subdivided, or stacked bars** sum the components of an item. It's hard to identify the values in specific segments; grouped bar charts are almost always easier to use.
- **Deviation bar graphs** identify positive and negative values, or winners and losers.
- **Paired bar graphs** show the correlation between two items.
- **Histograms** or **pictographs** use images to create the bars.

Line Graphs

Line graphs are also easy to interpret. Use line graphs to compare items over time, to show frequency or distribution, and to show correlations.

- Label both horizontal and vertical axes.
- When time is a variable, put it on the horizontal axis.
- Avoid using more than three different lines on one graph. Even three lines may be too many if they cross each other.
- Avoid using perspective. Perspective makes the values harder to read and can make comparison difficult.

Checkpoint

Tables are numbers or words arranged in rows and columns; **figures** are everything else. In a document, formal visuals have both numbers ("Figure 1") and titles. In an oral presentation, the title is usually used without the number.

What Design Conventions Should I Follow?

Ex. 19.4 19.5

Tell your story effectively and ethically. Provide the context. Cite your sources.

Tell Your Story Effectively

Plan your visuals to achieve your purposes, and meet audience needs (Modules 5 and 17). The best visuals

- Use clear, simple, and relevant images
- Use metaphors and pictures that make connections and patterns obvious
- Put people in the picture: show people working well in teams, using the new software, driving further and cleaner in the hybrid
- Blend seamlessly and are balanced with the text[5]

Provide the Context

Every visual should

1. Give a title that tells the story the visual shows
2. Clearly indicate the data
3. Clearly label units
4. Provide labels or legends identifying axes, colours, symbols, and so forth
5. Give the source of the data, if you create the visual from data someone else gathered and compiled
6. Give the source of the visual, if you reproduce a visual that someone else created

Cite Your Sources   Like all intellectual property, visuals are protected by copyright. Whenever you use secondary sources, you must credit the author. Information on how to cite images correctly is available online, in style guide sites, and on your local and university and college library sites (Modules 14 and15).

Can I Use Colour and Clip Art?

Use colour and clip art carefully.

Colour makes visuals more dramatic, but creates at least two problems. First, readers try to interpret colour, an interpretation that may not be appropriate. Second, meanings assigned to colours differ depending on the audience's culture and profession.

Connotations for colour vary from culture to culture and within cultures (Module 3). Blue suggests masculinity in North America, criminality in France, strength or fertility in Egypt, and villainy in Japan. Red is sometimes used to suggest danger or stop in North American culture; it means go in China and is associated with festivities. Yellow suggests caution or cowardice in North America, prosperity in Egypt, grace in Japan, and femininity in many parts of the world.[6]

Corporate, national, or professional associations may override these general cultural associations. Some people associate blue with IBM or Hewlett-Packard and red with Coca-Cola, communism, or Japan. People in specific professions learn other meanings for colours. Blue suggests *reliability* to financial managers, *water* or coldness to engineers, and *death* to healthcare professionals. Red means *losing money* to financial managers, *danger* to engineers, but *healthy* to healthcare professionals. Green usually means *safe* to engineers, but infected to healthcare professionals.[7]

These various associations suggest that colour is safest with a homogenous audience that you know well. In an increasingly multicultural workforce, colour may send signals you do not intend.

When you do use colour in visuals, experts suggest the following guidelines:[8]

- Use no more than five colours when colours have meanings.
- Use glossy paper to make colours more vivid.
- Be aware that colours always look brighter on a computer screen than on paper, because the screen sends out light.

In any visual, use as little shading and as few lines as are necessary for clarity. Don't clutter up the visual with extra marks. When you design black-and-white graphs, use shades of grey rather than stripes, wavy lines, and checks to indicate different segments or items. Test print to ensure your chosen shades of grey make your story obvious to the reader.

Clip Art

In memos and reports, resist the temptation to make your visual "artistic" by turning it into a picture or adding clip art. A small drawing of a car in the corner of a line graph showing the number of kilometres driven might be acceptable in an oral presentation or a newsletter, but is out of place in a written report. Indeed, because of its blandness and ubiquity, clip art can diminish and trivialize content.

Statistician and visual design expert Edward Tufte uses the term **chartjunk** for visual details—"the encoded legends, the meaningless color[,] the logo-type branding"—that at best are irrelevant to

EXPANDING A CRITICAL SKILL

Integrating Visuals into Your Text

To keep your reader in your story, tell, show, tell: refer to every visual in your text.

> ING Direct Canada ranks first in mid-size retail banks for customer satisfaction, as Figure 1, below, indicates.

FIGURE 1   ING Direct Canada Customer Satisfaction Standing

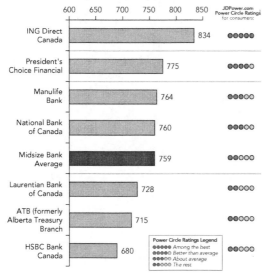

J.D. Power and Associates
2012 Canadian Retail Banking Customer Satisfaction Study^{SM}

Customer Satisfaction Index Ranking
Midsize Bank Segment
(Based on a 1,000-point scale)

Note: Altema Bank is included in the study but not ranked due to small sample size.

Charts and graphs extracted from this press release must be accompanied by a statement identifying J.D. Power and Associates as the publisher and the J.D. Power and Associates 2012 Canadian Retail Banking Customer Satisfaction Study^{SM} as the source. Rankings are based on numerical scores, and not necessarily on statistical significance. JDPower.com Power Circle Ratings^{TM} are derived from consumer ratings in J.D. Power studies. For more information on Power Circle Ratings, visit jdpower.com/faqs. No advertising or other promotional use can be made of the information in this release or J.D. Power and Associates survey results without the express prior written consent of J.D. Power and Associates.

Source: J.D. Power and Associates 2012 Canadian Retail Banking Customer Satisfaction Study^{SM}

Normally give the table or figure number in the text but not the title. Put the visual as soon after your reference as space and page design permit. If the visual must go on another page, tell the reader where to find it:

> As Figure 3 shows (p. 10)…
> (See Table 2 on page 3.)

Summarize the main point of a visual before you present the visual itself. Then when readers get to it, they'll see it as confirmation of your point.

Weak: Listed below are the results.

Better: As Figure 4 shows, sales doubled in the last decade.

How much discussion a visual needs depends on the audience, the complexity of the visual, and the importance of the point it makes. If the material is new to the audience, you'll need a fuller explanation than if similar material is presented to this audience every week or month. Help the reader find key data points in complex visuals. If the point is important, discuss its implications in some detail.

In contrast, one sentence about a visual may be enough when

- the audience is already familiar with the topic and data
- the visual is simple and well designed
- the information in the visual is a minor part of your proof

When you discuss visuals, spell out numbers that fall at the beginning of a sentence. If spelling out the number or year is cumbersome, revise the sentence so that it does not begin with a number.

Correct: Forty-five percent of the cost goes to pay wages and salaries.

Correct: The year 2011 marked the EU economic crisis.

the visual, and at worst mislead the reader.[9] Turning a line graph into a highway to show kilometres driven makes it more difficult to read: it's hard to separate the data line from lines that are merely decorative. Similarly, MS Office charts can create distortion—especially the 3D options for pie charts and the shadowing options for bar charts.

If you use clip art, do so ethically: make it relevant to your content, be sensitive to your audience's pluralistic interpretations, and be sure that the images of people show a good mix of both sexes, various races and ages, and various physical conditions (Module 3).

L05 What Else Do I Need to Check For?

Be sure that the visual is accurate and ethical.

Always double-check your visuals to be sure that the information is accurate. Be aware, however, that many visuals have accurate labels but misleading visual shapes. Visuals communicate quickly; audiences remember the shape, not the labels. If the reader has to study the labels to get the right picture, the visual is unethical even if the labels are accurate.

People manipulate images for a variety of reasons, some artistic, many commercial. Only the informed person qualifies for citizenship in the global marketplace. Be prepared to question the validity of all data; your personal and professional well-being depend on these critical thinking skills.

Even simple bar and line graphs may be misleading if part of the **scale** is missing, or **truncated**. Truncated graphs are most acceptable when the audience knows the basic data set well. For example, graphs of the stock market almost never start at zero; they are routinely truncated. This omission is acceptable for audiences who follow the market closely.

Data can also be distorted when the context is omitted. For example, a drop may be part of a regular cycle, a correction after an atypical increase, or a permanent drop to a new, lower plateau.

You can do several things to make your visuals more accurate:

- Differentiate between actual and estimated or projected values.
- When you must truncate a scale, do so clearly with a break in the bars or in the background.
- Avoid perspective and three-dimensional graphs.
- Avoid combining graphs with different scales.
- Use images of people carefully in histograms to avoid sexist, racist, or other exclusionary visual statements.

L06 Can I Use the Same Visual in My Document and in My Presentation?

Use it in both only if the table or graph is simple.

For presentations, simplify paper visuals. To simplify a complex table, cut some information, round off the data even more, or present the material in a chart rather than in a table.

Visuals for presentations should have titles but don't need figure numbers. Know where each visual is so that you can return to one if someone asks about it during the question period. Use clip art only if it's relevant, and does not obscure the story you're telling with the visual.

MODULE SUMMARY

- Appropriate, attractive visuals tell stories concisely and immediately: visuals are faster and easier to understand, and more memorable.

- In your rough draft, use visuals to see that ideas are presented completely, and to identify patterns and relationships. In your reports and presentations, use visuals to make points vivid, to emphasize material the audience might overlook, and to present material more efficiently and more compactly than words alone can do.

- Use more visuals when you want to show relationships, when the information is complex, or contains extensive numerical data, and when the audience values visuals.

- Pick data to tell a story, to make your point. To find stories, look for relationships and changes. Writers and illustrators create worthy stories through research: they
  - ○ Follow up on hunches
  - ○ Find data that challenge accepted wisdom, have commercial, cultural or social significance, or indicate new trends
  - ○ Identify information that requires immediate action, or has personal relevance for them and their audiences

- When you think you have a story, test it against all the data to be sure it's accurate.

- Formal visuals are divided into tables and figures. Tables are numbers or words arranged in rows and columns; figures are everything else, including clip art and photographs.

- Choosing the best visual depends on the kind of data and the point you want to make with the data.

- Visuals represent a point of view; they are never neutral. You are legally and ethically responsible for creating and using visuals that
  - ○ Represent data accurately, both literally and by implication
  - ○ Avoid chartjunk: decorations and details that are irrelevant or misleading
  - ○ Give the source of the data

- Appropriate visuals are both accurate and ethical. They
  - ○ Give a title that tells the story the visual shows
  - ○ Clearly indicate the data
  - ○ Clearly label units
  - ○ Provide labels or legends identifying axes, colours, symbols, and so forth
  - ○ Give the source of the data, if you created the visual from data someone else gathered and compiled
  - ○ Give the source of the visual, if you reproduce a visual someone else created

ASSIGNMENTS FOR MODULE 19

Questions for Critical Thinking

19.1 Identify three specific types of reports that rely heavily on visuals.

19.2 How do MS chart styles create distortion? Find an example of a ready-made chart that distorts the data.

19.3 How could you take a photograph to tell a story?

19.4 Is it ethical to use dramatic pictures and visual metaphors to motivate people to give to charity? Why or why not?

Exercises and Problems

19.5 Reviewing Expert Advice on Creating Visuals

Review Tufte's Rules—Professor Tuft's compendium for creating the best visuals—at www.sealthreinhold.com/class_sites/tuftes_rules/rule_one.php.

On the basis of your review, create a summary of the rules.

Apply your summary to Exercises 19.6 through 19.9.

19.6 Evaluating Text and Images

Evaluate the following student report excerpt using these criteria:

1. The visuals tell a story.
2. The writer has used the best visuals to convey the story.
3. The visuals use clear, simple, and relevant images.
4. The writer balances visuals and text.
5. The writer integrates visuals and text.
6. The visuals and text together communicate the message compactly.

The Career Centre's brochures and information sheets are helpful for students.						
	Total		Male		Female	
	Number	Percentage	Number	Percentage	Number	Percentage
Agree strongly	25	25%	14	28%	11	22%
Agree somewhat	56	56%	27	54%	29	58%
Disagree somewhat	11	11%	5	10%	6	12%
Disagree strongly	8	8%	4	8%	4	8%
Total	**100**	**100%**	**50**	**100%**	**50**	**100%**

Source: Reprinted by permission of Lindsay Hopton-Piché, Sheridan Graduate and Silver Medallist, Business Administration Finance.

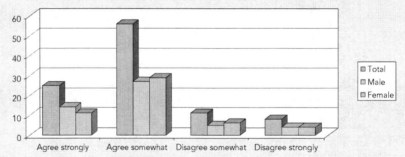

Source: Reprinted by permission of Lindsay Hopton-Piché, Sheridan Graduate and Silver Medallist, Business Administration Finance.

When asked to indicate if they felt that the Career Centre's brochures and information sheets are helpful for students, 56 percent of respondents agreed somewhat with this statement; of these respondents, 27 were male and 29 female. Twenty-five percent of respondents agreed strongly that the Career Centre's brochures and information sheets are helpful for students; of these respondents, 14 were male and 11 female. Eleven percent of respondents somewhat disagreed that the Career Centre's brochures and information sheets are helpful for students; of these respondents, 5 were male and 6 female. Eight percent of respondents strongly disagreed that the Career Centre's brochures and information sheets are helpful for students; of these respondents, 4 were male and 4 female. This data suggests that the large majority of respondents believe that the Career Centre's brochures and information sheets are helpful for students, and that the same number of males and of females feel this way.

How likely are you to use the Career Centre in the future?						
	Total		Male		Female	
	Number	Percentage	Number	Percentage	Number	Percentage
Very likely	37	37%	18	36%	19	38%
Somewhat likely	55	55%	29	58%	26	52%
Not likely	8	8%	3	6%	5	10%
Total	**100**	**100%**	**50**	**100%**	**50**	**100%**

Source: Reprinted by permission of Lindsay Hopton-Piché, Sheridan Graduate and Silver Medallist, Business Administration Finance.

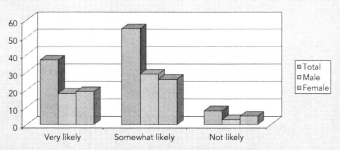

Source: Reprinted by permission of Lindsay Hopton-Piché, Sheridan Graduate and Silver Medallist, Business Administration Finance.

When asked to indicate how likely they are to use the Career Centre in the future, 55 percent of respondents indicated that they are somewhat likely to use the Career Centre in the future; of these respondents, 29 were male and 26 female. Thirty-seven percent of respondents indicated that they will be very likely to use the Career Centre in the future; of these respondents, 18 were male and 19 female. Eight percent of respondents indicated that they will not likely use the Career Centre in the future; of these respondents, 3 were male and 5 female. These data suggest that most students are likely to use the Career Centre in the future, and that males and females are almost equally likely to use the Career Centre in the future.

19.7 Matching Visuals with Stories

What visual(s) would make it easiest to see each of the following stories?

1. In Canada, the gap between rich and poor is widening.
2. An increasing number of young adults (ages 7 to 24) are politically active.

3. The Facebook Nation: Canadians are the largest population on Facebook.
4. Vegetarianism is becoming a lifestyle choice among young adults.
5. Canada's population is aging.
6. Number of years of postsecondary education correspond to employment success.

19.8 Evaluating Visuals

Evaluate each of the following visuals using Tufte's rules and these questions:

- Is the visual's message clear?
- Is it the right visual for the story?
- Is the visual designed appropriately? Is colour, if any, used appropriately?
- Is the visual free from chartjunk?
- Does the visual distort data or mislead the reader in any way?

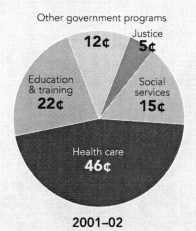

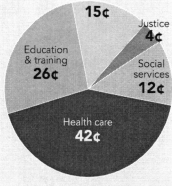

Source: Reprinted with permission. Torstar Syndication Services.

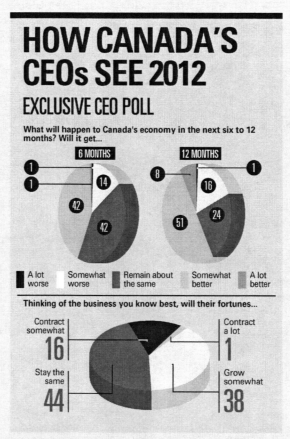

HOW CANADA'S CEOs SEE 2012

EXCLUSIVE CEO POLL

What will happen to Canada's economy in the next six to 12 months? Will it get...

6 MONTHS

1
1
14
42
42

12 MONTHS

8
1
16
51
24

| A lot worse | Somewhat worse | Remain about the same | Somewhat better | A lot better |

Thinking of the business you know best, will their fortunes...

Contract somewhat
16

Contract a lot
1

Stay the same
44

Grow somewhat
38

Source: COMPAS Research www.compas.ca. *Canadian Business,* February 20, 2012 p. 13.

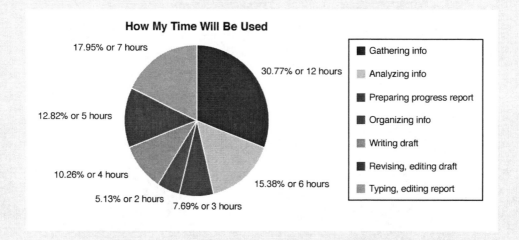

How My Time Will Be Used

17.95% or 7 hours

30.77% or 12 hours

12.82% or 5 hours

15.38% or 6 hours

10.26% or 4 hours

5.13% or 2 hours

7.69% or 3 hours

- Gathering info
- Analyzing info
- Preparing progress report
- Organizing info
- Writing draft
- Revising, editing draft
- Typing, editing report

A Year of Soda: 44.7 Gallons

Here's what carbonated soft drink consumption — sugared and diet sodas — looked like in 2010. The average American chugged the equivalent of 48 two-liter bottles and 206 12-ounce cans of soft drinks (one of many possible container combinations that add up to about 44.7 gallons):

Soda Is Cheap, and Staying Cheap

THE PRICE of carbonated drinks in the U.S. has crept up, but more slowly than overall prices — in effect, making them ever cheaper relative to other goods. Fruits and vegetables have become more expensive at a much faster rate.

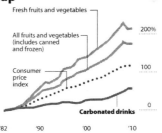

Fresh fruits and vegetables

All fruits and vegetables (includes canned and frozen)

Consumer price index

200%

100

0

Carbonated drinks

'82   '90   '00   '10

What a Small Federal Tax Could Do

Her is the revenue from a levy on sugar-sweetened beverages, in effect next year, according to Yale University's Rudd Center for Food Policy and Obesity.

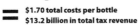 If a 20-ounce bottle of soda costs $1.50 **+** it carries a one-cent tax per ounce

$1.70 total costs per bottle
$13.2 billion in total tax revenue
from this and other sugar-sweetened beverages in 2012

Sources: Beverage Marketing Corporation, Advertising Age (consumption); U.S. Dept. of Agriculture (food inflation); Rudd Center for Food Policy and Obesity, Yale University (federal tax)

The iPhone: Designed in the U.S. ...	...Made Overseas...			...Assembled in China
		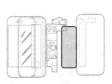		
	DISPLAYS	**SEMICONDUCTOR (CHIPS)**	**BATTERIES**	**ASSEMBLY**
27,300	**5,000 – 10,000**	**7,000 – 20,000**	**300 – 1,000**	**200,000**
non retail jobs in the U.S.	jobs in South Korea and other Asian countries	jobs in Taiwan, Singapore, Malaysia, Japan, Europe and elsewhere	jobs in China	jobs in China

Dreamed up in California	**An Industry lost**	**An industry outsourced**	**No catching up**	**It's not just cheap labor**
Apple once boasted that its products were manufactured in the United States. No longer. Specifics differ between versions, but an estimated 90 percent of iPhone components are manufactured overseas, by workers in Germany, Singapore, Korea, Taiwan China and elsewhere.	America was once a leader in television and other display manufacturing. Today, virtually no displays are made in the United States. They mostly come from Asia, especially South Korea and Japan, where wages are not much cheaper but technical manufacturing has outpaced American capabilities.	The semiconductor was essentially invent in the United States. Then foreign nations discovered that semiconductor manufacturing could jump-start technology industries. In the 1960s, assembly was outsourced to Asia. higher-skilled jobs soon followed. Although the latest iPhone processor is made in Texas, most of its other chips are made abroad.	Sony helped develop the lithium-ion battery in the early 1980s for use in its consumer electronics devices, including the Walkman. Japan came to dominate the manufacturing of these batteries. Energizer tried to open a battery factory in Florida in the 1990s, but raw material costs and labor rates made it unable to compete with Japan and other Asian countries.	The iPhone is assembled in China by Foxconn, the largest electronics assembler in the world. U.S. executives say they cannot function without companies like Foxconn. The Taiwanese company has a million workers, many willing to live in company dorms, work midnight shifts and spend 12 hours in a factory, six days a week. Chinese workers are cheaper they their American Counterparts — but just as important, they are more flexible and plentiful, and thousands can be hired overnight.

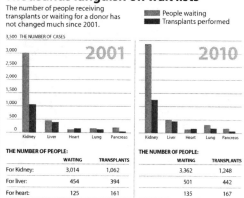

Thousands languish on wait lists

The number of people receiving transplants or waiting for a donor has not changed much since 2001.

■ People waiting
■ Transplants performed

3,500 THE NUMBER OF CASES

2001

2010

Kidney Liver Heart Lung Pancreas

THE NUMBER OF PEOPLE:

	WAITING	TRANSPLANTS
For Kidney:	3,014	1,062
For liver:	454	394
For heart:	125	161
For lung:	163	126
For pancreas:	204	47

THE NUMBER OF PEOPLE:

	WAITING	TRANSPLANTS
	3,362	1,248
	501	442
	135	167
	310	179
	175	74

Source: Reprinted with permission. Torstar Syndication Services.

CMA gains/losses

Biggest and smallest percentage population changes among Canada's 33 census metropolitan areas:

Rank	Metropolitan area	Population	% change since previous census
1.	Calgary	1,214,839	+12.6%
2.	Edmonton	1,159,869	+12.1%
3.	Saskatoon	260,600	+11.4%
4.	Kelowna, B.C.	179,839	+10.8%
5.	Moncton, N.B.	138,644	+9.7%
6.	Vancouver	2,313,328	+9.3%
7.	Toronto	5,583,064	+9.2%
29.	Sudbury	160,770	+1.6%
30.	Saguenay, Que.	157,790	+1.0%
31.	St. Catharines, Ont.	392,184	+0.5%
32.	Thunder Bay	121,596	−1.1%
33.	Windsor	319,246	−1.3%

Canadian communities

Canadian communities with highest and lowest percentage growth rates, 2006–2011:

GAINERS	Population	% change since previous census
Milton, Ont.	84,362	+56.5%
Martensville, Sask.	7,716	+55%
Whitchurch-Stouffville	37,628	+54.3%
Sainte-Brigitte-de-Laval	5,696	+50.35
Chestermere, Alta	14,824	+49.4%

LOSERS		
Thunder Bay, Ont.	5,909	−10.3%
Inverness, N.S.	5,280	−9.9%
Hearst, Ont.	5,090	−9.4%
Lac la Biche, Alta.	8,402	−7.9%
Kitmat, B.C.	8,335	−7.3%

Canada's population history

35 Population/millions

2011: **33,476,688**

1851 71 91 11 31 51 71 81 91 01 11
      1901

Fastest growing provincial populations

PER CENT CHANGE IN POPULATION BETWEEN 2006/2011 CENSUSES

■ 9% to 12%
■ 6% to 9%
■ 3% to 6%
□ less than 3%

	2001	2006	% increase since 2001	2011	% increase since 2006
Nfld./Labrador	512,930	505,469	−1.5%	514,536	1.8%
P.E.I.	135,294	135,851	0.4	140,204	3.2
Nova Scotia	908,007	913,462	0.6	921,727	0.9
New Brunswick	729,498	729,997	0.1	751,171	2.9
Quebec	7,237,479	7,546,131	4.3	7,903,001	4.7
Ontario	11,410,046	12,160,282	6.6	12,851,821	5.7
Manitoba	1,119,583	1,148,401	2.6	1,208,268	5.2
Saskatchewan	978,933	968,157	−1.1	1,033,381	6.7
Alberta	2,974,807	3,290,350	10.6	3,645,257	10.8
British Columbia	3,907,738	4,113,487	5.3	4,400,057	7.0
Yukon	28,674	30,372	5.9	33,897	11.6
Northwest Territories	37,360	41,464	11	41,462	0.0
Nunavut	26,745	29,474	10.2	31,906	8.3
CANADA	**30,007,094**	**31,612,897**	**5.4**	**33,476,688**	**5.9**

Source: Reprinted with permission. Torstar Syndication Services.

T.O. is the tops

Vibrant labour market and lower bankruptcy rates helped city outscore 25 other major metropolitan areas in economic growth, CIBC says.

■ Toronto
■ Canada

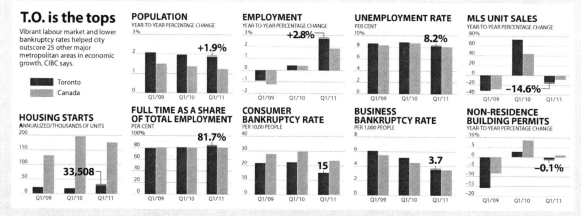

POPULATION
YEAR-TO-YEAR PERCENTAGE CHANGE
3%
+1.9%
Q1/09 Q1/10 Q1/11

EMPLOYMENT
YEAR-TO-YEAR PERCENTAGE CHANGE
3%
+2.8%
Q1/09 Q1/10 Q1/11

UNEMPLOYMENT RATE
PER CENT
10%
8.2%
Q1/09 Q1/10 Q1/11

MLS UNIT SALES
YEAR-TO-YEAR PERCENTAGE CHANGE
80%
−14.6%
Q1/09 Q1/10 Q1/11

HOUSING STARTS
ANNUALIZED/THOUSANDS OF UNITS
200
33,508
Q1/09 Q1/10 Q1/11

FULL TIME AS A SHARE OF TOTAL EMPLOYMENT
PER CENT
100%
81.7%
Q1/09 Q1/10 Q1/11

CONSUMER BANKRUPTCY RATE
PER 10.00 PEOPLE
40
15
Q1/09 Q1/10 Q1/11

BUSINESS BANKRUPTCY RATE
PER 1,000 PEOPLE
8
3.7
Q1/09 Q1/10 Q1/11

NON-RESIDENCE BUILDING PERMITS
YEAR-TO-YEAR PERCENTAGE CHANGE
10%
−0.1%
Q1/09 Q1/10 Q1/11

Source: Reprinted with permission. Torstar Syndication Services.

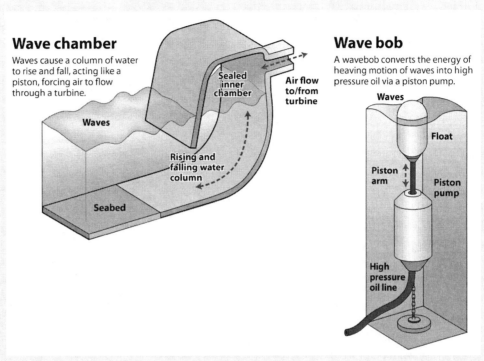

Wave chamber

Waves cause a column of water to rise and fall, acting like a piston, forcing air to flow through a turbine.

Sealed inner chamber

Air flow to/from turbine

Waves

Rising and falling water column

Seabed

Wave bob

A wavebob converts the energy of heaving motion of waves into high pressure oil via a piston pump.

Waves

Float

Piston arm

Piston pump

High pressure oil line

Source: Reprinted with permission. Torstar Syndication Services.

Table 2 **The contribution of background family characteristics**	
	Median number of months between high school graduation and start of first postsecondary education program number
Parents' highest level of educational attainment	
High school or less	14
Some postsecondary	13
Postsecondary graduate	3
Importance to parents that child obtains a postsecondary education	
Not important at all / slightly important	27
Fairly important	15
Very important	3
Frequency with which youth and parent talked about future education and career options	
Never	14
Less than once a year	15
A few times a year	4
A few times a month	3
A few times a week / daily	7

Source: Statistics Canada. Youth in Transition Survey. Cohort B.

Cumulative proportion of high school graduates who started postsecondary education by age 28

Proportion starting PSE by month

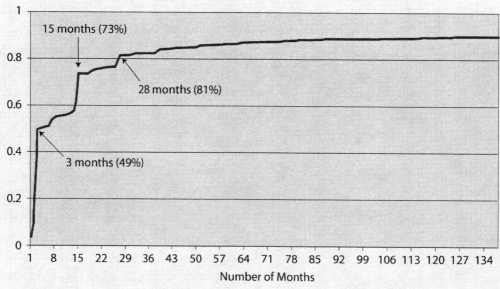

Note: Restricted to youth who graduated high school.
Source: Statistics Canada. Youth in Transition Survey. Cohort B. Cycle 5.

19.9 Graphing Data from the Web

Find data on the Web about a topic that interests you. Sites that provide data include

- www.canoe.ca
- www.statcan.ca
- www.findarticles.com
- Graphic, Visualization, & Usability Center's WWW surveys: www.cc.gatech.edu/gvu/user_surveys/

As your instructor directs,

a. Identify at least seven stories in the data.
b. Create visuals for three of the stories.
c. Write a memo to your instructor explaining why you chose these stories and why you chose these visuals to display them.
d. Write a short report to some group that might be interested in your findings, presenting your visuals as part of the short report.
e. Print out the data and include it with a copy of your memo or report.

POLISHING YOUR PROSE

Being Concise

Being concise in business writing means using only necessary words to make your point, without sacrificing courtesy or clarity. Wordy sentences may confuse or slow readers:

Wordy: All of our employees at Haddenfield and Dunne should make themselves available for a seminar meeting on the 5th of August 2012, at 10 o'clock in the morning. Please make sure you come to the conference room on the 2nd Floor of the Main Complex.

Concise: Please plan to attend a seminar at 10 a.m., August 5, 2012, in the Main Complex 2nd Floor conference room.

Being concise does not mean eliminating necessary information. Sometimes you'll have to write longer sentences to be clear.

Nor does being concise mean using short, choppy sentences.

Choppy: We have a new copier. It is in the supply room. Use it during regular hours. After 5 p.m., it will be shut down.

Concise: A new copier is available in the supply room for use before 5 p.m.

Use concrete words. Instead of vague nouns and verbs with strings of modifiers, use specifics.

Vague: The person who drops off packages talked about the subject of how much to charge.

Concrete: The delivery person discussed fees.

Avoid vague or empty modifiers. Words like *very, some, many, few, much, kind of/sort of,* and so forth, usually can be cut.

Cut redundant words or phrases. Don't say the same thing twice. *Cease and desist, first and foremost, the*

newest and latest, official company policy, 24 storeys tall, said out loud, and *return back* are all redundant.

Avoid unnecessarily complex constructions. Instead of *the bid that won the contract,* use *the winning bid.*

Stick to simple verb tenses. Standard edited English prefers them. Instead of "I *have been attending* Royal Roads University" use "I *attend* Royal Roads University." Instead of "By 2013, I *will have completed my degree*" use "I *will graduate* by 2013."

Exercises

Rewrite the following sentences to make them concise.

1. It would be in your best interest to return the order form to us as quickly as possible.
2. Our official records show that you are a very responsible person.
3. The automobile that is blue belongs to the woman in charge of legal affairs.
4. The mainframe computer is located in our subterranean basement.
5. Call us on the telephone if you want to confirm your order.
6. We faxed a reproduced copy of the application on the fax machine.
7. Enclosed along with the rest of this job application letter is a list of references who can talk about my job qualifications because I used to work for them.
8. I enjoyed the presentation very much.
9. To begin with, let me start by telling you some stories about our guest of honour.
10. The guy that runs our advertising department yelled loudly across the parking lot that a delivery truck had left its two headlights on.

Check your answers to the odd-numbered exercises in the Polishing Your Prose Answer Key.

connect

Practise and learn online with Connect. Connect allows you to practise important skills at your own pace and on your own schedule, with 24/7 online access to an eBook, practise quizzes, interactives, videos, study tools, and additional resources.

Making Oral Presentations

Learning Objectives

After reading and applying the information in Module 23, you'll be able to demonstrate

Knowledge of

LO1 The differences between written and oral messages

LO2 Types of presentations

LO3 The criteria for effective presentations

Skills to

LO4 Reframe written material into an oral presentation

LO5 Plan and deliver oral presentations

LO6 Develop a good speaking voice

LO7 Prepare and deliver group presentations

Employability Skills 2000+ Checklist

Module content builds these Conference Board of Canada Employability Skills 2000+

Communicate

Be Adaptable

Think and Solve Problems

Work with Others

Demonstrate Positive Attitudes and Behaviours

Participate in Projects and Tasks

In every new communication situation, you have fewer than 90 seconds to make that first—and lasting—impression. How are you going to make that a positive one? Effective presenters make that 90 seconds work for them.

Most presentations serve more than one purpose, and every presentation contains an element of persuasion: you must know how to attract and hold your audience's attention if you want to achieve your purposes. The best oral presentations inform and influence people positively.

LO2 What Kinds of Presentations Are There?

Informative presentations inform or teach the audience. For example, health and safety training sessions are primarily informative. Secondary purposes may be to conform to legislation, to meet ISO standards, to persuade employees to follow organizational procedures, and to orient new employees (Module 2).

The goal of most presentations is to get to *yes*.

Persuasive and **sales presentations** motivate the audience to act or to believe. Giving information and evidence persuades through appeals to credibility and reason (Module 10). The speaker must also build goodwill by appearing trustworthy and sensitive to the audience's needs.

In business presentations, speakers want to persuade the audience to buy their product, proposal, or idea. Sometimes the goal is to change attitudes and behaviours, or to reinforce existing attitudes. Thus, a speaker at a workers' compensation and benefits information meeting might stress the importance of following safety procedures; a speaker at a city council meeting might talk about the problem of homelessness in the community to try to build support for homeless shelters.

Goodwill presentations entertain and validate the audience. In an after-dinner speech, the audience wants to be entertained. Presentations at sales meetings may be designed to stroke the audience members' egos and to validate their commitment to organizational goals.

As Thornhill, Ontario, brothers Craig and Marc Kielburger—founders of Me to We and Free the Children—know, all successful presentations are persuasive.

Regardless of the presentation purpose, the best presenters work the three Ps: plan, prepare, and practise:

1. **Plan** a strategy by analyzing the situation (PAIBOC analysis, Figure 23.1)
2. **Prepare** stories and examples relevant to your audience
3. **Practise** until you are completely comfortable with the content

All this preparation increases confidence and reduces the anxiety most speakers feel.

FIGURE 23.1   PAIBOC Questions to Plan Powerful Presentations

P	What is the **purpose** of your presentation? What do you want to happen because of your presentation? What do you want your audience to think, say, or do?
A	Who is your **audience**? What do they already know? What do they need to know? What do they care about? What will motivate them to do as you want? How do members of your audience differ? What cultural/corporate values and norms shape their perceptions? How can you grab your audience's attention positively? What's in it for them?
I	What is your key message? What idea do you want the audience members to take away with them? What do you have to say that is important to them? How can you make the **information** relevant and achieve your purpose(s)? How long is your presentation? What information can you omit?
B	What **benefits** does your message offer the audience? How can you highlight these benefits?
O	What **objections** will your audience have to your message? How will you overcome those objections? What are the negative aspects of your message? How can you de-emphasize, compensate for, or overcome these negatives?
C	What is the **context** of your message? What economic, environmental, professional, and/ or personal realities will affect how your audience perceives your message? What time of day is your presentation? In what kind of room is it? How can you make your presentation interactive, engaging, and stimulating? What technology will you use, and why?

What Decisions Do I Need to Make as I Plan a Presentation?

Choose your main point, the kind of presentation, and ways to involve your audience.

An oral presentation needs to be simpler than a written message to the same audience. Identify the one idea—or critical takeaway—you want the audience to remember. Then phrase your idea so that it offers a specific benefit to the audience.

Weak:	The purpose of my presentation is to discuss saving for retirement.
Better:	The purpose of my presentation is to persuade my audience to put their retirement funds in stocks and bonds, not in money market accounts and GICs.
Or:	The purpose of my presentation is to explain how to calculate how much money someone needs to save in order to maintain a specific lifestyle after retirement.

Note: Your purpose is *not* the introduction of your talk; it is the principle that guides your decisions as you plan your presentation.

Ex.
23.5
23.6
23.9

Always tell your audience what's in it for them.

Now reinforce that idea through clarity, repetition, and emphasis:

- Simplify your supporting detail so it's easy to follow
- Use visuals that can be taken in at a glance
- Choose concrete words and brief sentences that are easy to understand

Analyze your audience for an oral presentation just as you do for a written message. If you'll be speaking to co-workers, talk to them about your topic or proposal to find out what questions or objections they have. For audiences inside the organization, the biggest questions are often practical ones: Will it work? How much will it cost? How long will it take?[1]

And always answer for your audience: What's in it for them?

Before you begin planning your presentation, you need to know *for how long*, *where*, and *when* you will be speaking. Your time and the audience's expectations shape both the content and the kind of presentation you will give. The size and comfort of the room will affect the success of your presentation, as will the time of day.

What size is the room? What equipment will be available? Will the audience be tired at the end of a long day of listening? Sleepy after a big meal? Will the group be large or small? The more you know about your audience and your environment, the better you can shape your presentation for maximum persuasive impact. And that knowledge is power: the more you know, the more in control you will feel.

LO2 Choosing the Kind of Presentation

When you have identified your *purpose*, including the results you want to achieve, analyzed your audience's needs, and considered your time, you can decide on the kind of presentation you will give. Table 23.1 identifies the speaker's role in three kinds of presentations: monologue, guided discussion, and sales.

TABLE 23.1   **Guidelines for Choosing Your Presentation Role**

Chair When You Want To:	Facilitate When You Want To:
Exchange information	Increase participation
Get informal feedback	Deal with group dynamics
Hear members report back	Have members problem solve
Review the current agenda	Have members make decisions
Set the parameters of the discussion	Have members create action plans
Review meeting objectives with members	Shift ownership and commitment levels

Source: Michael Goldman (2001, January/February), To chair or to facilitate, that is the question, *The Training Report*, 13.

A Question of Ethics

Politicians do it. Movie stars do it. Why shouldn't you do it? You can pay to pad your Twitter follower numbers to impress real friends and clients. What ethical considerations might make you hesitate to do so?

[LO5] How Should I Organize a Presentation?

As always, you organize your message based on the results of your PAIBOC analysis. To meet audience needs, you often start with the main point, then use one of five standard organizational patterns.

Most presentations use a direct pattern of organization, even when the goal is to persuade a reluctant audience. Audience members know that you want to persuade them. Be honest about your goals, and prepare your opening to demonstrate that your goal dovetails with the audience's needs. Start with your strongest point, your best reason. If you're making more than one point, put the weakest one in the middle. End on a strong note, and if time permits:

- Give additional reasons
- Anticipate and respond to possible objections

Based on your purpose and audience analysis, use one of five standard patterns of organization:

- **Chronological**: Start with the past, move to the present, and end by looking ahead.
- **Problem/causes/solution**: Explain the symptoms of the problem, identify its causes, and suggest a solution. This pattern works best when the audience will find your solution easy to accept.
- **Exclude alternatives**. Explain the symptoms of the problem. Explain the obvious solutions first and show why they won't solve the problem. End by discussing a solution that will work. This pattern may be necessary when the audience will find the solution hard to accept.
- **Pro/con**: Give all the reasons in favour of something, then those against it. This pattern works well when you want the audience to see the weaknesses in its position.
- **1-2-3**. Discuss three aspects of a topic. This pattern works well to organize short informative briefings. "Today I'll review our sales, production, and profits for the last quarter."

Because people have limited attention spans, the best presentations use **repetition for reinforcement**: tell 'em, tell 'em, and tell 'em again. Early in your talk—perhaps immediately after your opener—provide an agenda or overview of the main points you will make. Include a presentation duration time, and end when you promised you would:

> In the next 20 minutes, I'm going to describe how you can make our city a safer, saner place. First, I'd like to talk about the people who are homeless on Vancouver's East Side. Second, I'll talk about the services the Open Shelter provides. Finally, I'll talk about what you—either individually or as a group—can do to help.

An overview provides a mental peg that hearers can hang each point on. It can also prevent someone missing what you are saying because he or she wonders why you aren't covering a major point that you've saved for later.[2]

Offer a clear signpost or **transition** as you come to each new point. A signpost is an explicit statement of the point you have reached. Choose wording that fits your style. The following statements provide four different ways that a speaker could introduce the last of three points:

> Now we come to the third point: what you can do as a group or as individuals to help homeless people in Vancouver.
>
> So much for what we're doing. Now let's talk about what you can do to help.
>
> You might be wondering, what can I do to help?
>
> As you can see, the shelter is trying to do many things. We could do more with your help.

LO4 LO5 How Do I Adapt My Ideas to the Audience?

Remember that *people can take in only so much information before they shut down!* If you want people to listen, tell them a meaningful story. If your audience is indifferent, skeptical, or hostile, focus on the part of your message the audience will find most interesting and easiest to accept. Here's an example of a story from a speech about world hunger to an audience of college students:

> When was the last time you were hungry? Maybe you remember being hungry while you were on a diet, or maybe you had to work late at a lab and didn't get back to the dorm in time for dinner.

Remember to make your ideas relevant to your audience by

1. Linking what you have to say to the audience's experiences, interests, and needs
2. Showing your audience members that the topic affects them directly
3. Using language the audience knows and understands
4. Relating your purposes to some everyday experience

LO3 LO5 How Can I Create a Strong Opening and Closing?

Use your introduction and your conclusion as points of emphasis.

The beginning and the end of a presentation, like the beginning and end of a written document, are positions of emphasis. Use those key positions to interest the audience and emphasize your main point. You'll sound more natural and more effective if you write out your opening and closing in advance and memorize them. Keep them short: just a sentence or two.

Begin with...

Your introduction is particularly important. To catch and hold audience attention, try these strategies:

- Stand still
- Focus on your audience
- Attract their interest with a **dramatic statement**, **story**, **question**, or **quotation**
- Make the hook or grabber relevant to them

The more you can do to personalize your opener for your audience, the better. Recent events are better than things that happened long ago; local events are better than events at a distance; people they know are better than people who are only names.

Dramatic Statement

> Twelve of our customers have cancelled orders in the past month.

This presentation to a company's executive committee went on to show that the company's distribution system was inadequate and to recommend an additional warehouse located in the Prairies.

Story

A mother was having difficulty getting her son up for school. He pulled the covers over his head.

"I'm not going to school," he said. "I'm not ever going again."

"Are you sick?" his mother asked.

"No," he answered. "I'm sick of school. They hate me. They call me names. They make fun of me. Why should I go?"

"I can give you two good reasons," the mother replied. "The first is that you're 42 years old. And the second is you're the school principal."[3]

This speech given at a seminar for educators went on to discuss "the three knottiest problems in education today." Educators had to face those problems; they couldn't hide under the covers.

Question

Are you going to have enough money to do the things you want to when you retire?

This presentation to a group of potential clients discusses the value of using the services of a professional financial planner to achieve retirement goals.

Quotation

According to Towers Perrin, the profits of Fortune 100 companies would be 25 percent lower—they'd go down $17 billion—if their earnings statements listed the future costs companies are obligated to pay for retirees' health care.

This presentation on options for health care for retired employees urges executives to start now to investigate options to cut the future cost.

Your opener must interest the audience and establish rapport. Some speakers use humour to achieve those goals. However, an inappropriate joke can turn the audience against the speaker. Never use humour directed against the audience. In contrast, speakers who make fun of themselves usually succeed:

It's both a privilege and a pressure to be here.[4]

Humour isn't the only way to put an audience at ease and establish a positive emotional connection. Smile at your audience before you begin; let them see that you're a real person and a pleasant one.

Close with…

The end of your presentation should be as strong as the opener. For your close, create a mental image of your critical message:

- Refer to your opener to create a frame for your presentation
- End with a vivid, positive picture
- Tell the audience exactly what to do to resolve the situation or solve the problem you've discussed

The following close from a fundraising speech combines a restatement of the main point with a call for action, telling the audience what to do:

> Plain and simple, we need money to run the foundation, just as you need money to develop new products. We need money to make this work. We need money from you. Pick up that pledge card. Fill it out. Turn it in at the door as you leave. Make it a statement about your commitment…make it a big statement.[5]

LO4   When you write out your opening and closing, remember that listeners can take in only so much information; then they disengage and tune out. Use the *KISS* formula: *Keep it short and simple.* As you can see in the example above, speaking style uses shorter sentences and shorter, simpler words than writing does. Oral style can even sound a bit choppy when it is read. Oral style uses more personal pronouns, a less varied vocabulary, and much more repetition.

LO3 LO5 How Should I Use Visuals?

Use a variety of visuals to emphasize your main points. Keep them simple and specific.

People understand and retain information better when they both *see* and *hear* the facts; they understand and remember best when they *see*, *hear*, and *do*. However, your topic or your time may preclude having your audience practise what you're preaching.

Whatever your topic, your choice of visual support can add emphasis and excitement. You can use dramatizations, demonstrations, questionnaires, quizzes, video clips, and role-plays.

The best presentations, however, depend on the speaker's preparedness and rapport with the audience. For North American audiences, your face is your number-one visual aid. Making eye contact with audience members is vital. And audience rapport comes from creating stories that speak to people's values and beliefs.

The best visuals are simple, clear, and specific. Illustrations should reinforce your message honestly and ethically (Module 19). Whenever possible, put people in the picture—doing or using whatever you're selling (Module 19). Keep text to a minimum. Use images and graphics immediately familiar to your audience. And when in doubt…leave it out.[6]

What About PowerPoint?

Design and rhetoric experts agree that PowerPoint™ slides—once attention-grabbers— are now misused and overused in presentations.[7]

When using slides, prepare well-designed visuals only as memory devices for your audience. With complicated material, provide handouts.

PowerPoint slides aren't the only way to involve the audience. Dan Leebar persuaded UPS to switch to Valeo clutches by disassembling the competitor's clutch and showing part by part why Valeo's product was better.

To create effective presentation visuals, use these guidelines:

- Use a sans-serif font (e.g., Arial, Helvetica, Technical) to maximize text readability.
- Use a minimum 24-point type to maximize readability (Module 5).
- Keep it simple.
- Use clear illustrations—charts, graphs, tables—whenever possible.
- Make only one point with each visual. Break a complicated point down into several visuals.
- Give each visual a title that makes a point connected to your presentation's main point.
- Limit the amount of text: no more than five lines per slide or five words per line.

To present your visuals effectively, use these guidelines:

- Have a friend/colleague manage the visuals for you, so you can concentrate on your ideas and your delivery.
- Use your visuals as enhancement, not competition.
- Use no more than one visual or slide per minute.
- Put up your visual (or have your friend/colleague put up the visual) only when you are ready to talk about it.
- Leave the visual up until your next point.

See Module 19 for information on how to present numerical data through visuals and see Figure 23.2 for more information on using PowerPoint.

Visuals work only if the technology they depend on works. When you give presentations in your own office, check the equipment in advance. When you make a presentation in another location or for another organization, arrive early so that you'll have time not only to check the equipment but also to track down a service worker if the equipment isn't working. Be prepared with a backup plan if you're unable to show your slides or videotape.

And because PowerPoint presentations have become commonplace, you must engage your audience in a variety of other ways:

- Students presenting on intercultural business communications demonstrated the way Chinese, Japanese, and Canadians exchange business cards by asking audience members to role-play the differences.
- Another student discussing the need for low-salt products brought in a container of salt, a measuring cup, a measuring spoon, and two plates. As he discussed the body's need for salt, he measured out three teaspoons onto one plate: the amount the body needs in a month.

FIGURE 23.2   PowerPoint Slides for an Informative Presentation

a.
b.
c.

d.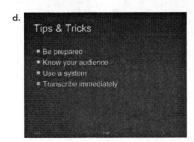
e.

As he discussed the amount of salt the average diet provides, he continued to measure out salt onto the other plate, stopping only when he had 500 grams of salt—the amount in the average North American diet. The demonstration made the discrepancy clear in a way words or even a chart could not have done.[8]

- Some presenters use quizzes, game formats, and dramatizations to encourage audience members to share their expertise with others.
  - ✔ To make sure that his employees understood where money went, the CEO of a specialty printing shop printed up $2 million in play money and handed out big cards to employees marked "Labour," "Depreciation," "Interest," and so forth. Then he asked each "category" to come up and take its share of the revenues. The action was more dramatic than a colour pie chart could ever have been.[9]
  - ✔ Another speaker trying to raise funds used the simple act of asking people to stand to involve them, to create emotional appeal, and to make a statistic vivid:

"[A speaker] was talking to a luncheon club about contributing to the relief of an area that had been hit by a tsunami. The news report said that 70 percent of the people had been killed or disabled. The room was set up with ten people at each round table. He asked three persons at each table to stand. Then he said, "You people sitting are dead or disabled. You three standing have to take care of the mess. You'd need help, wouldn't you?"[10]

LO6   EXPANDING A CRITICAL SKILL

Finding Your Best Voice

Paralanguage—*how* we say what we say—accounts for more than 30 percent of the meaning in our messages. Next to your face, therefore, your voice is your most important presentation aid! Effective speakers use their voices to support and enhance content. Your best voice will vary pitch, intonation, tempo, and volume to express energy and enthusiasm.

Pitch

Pitch measures whether a voice uses sounds that are low (like the bass notes on a piano) or high. Voices that are low-pitched project more credibility than do high-pitched voices. Low-pitched presenters are perceived as being more authoritative and more pleasant to listen to. Most voices go up in pitch when the speaker is angry or excited; some people raise pitch when they increase volume. People whose normal speaking voices are high might need to practise projecting their voices to avoid becoming shrill when they speak to large groups.

To find your best pitch, try humming. The pitch at which the hum sounds loudest and most resonant is your best voice.

Intonation

Intonation marks variation in pitch, stress, or tone. Speakers who use many changes in pitch, stress, and tone usually seem more enthusiastic; often they also seem more energetic and more intelligent. Someone who speaks in a monotone may seem apathetic or unintelligent. Speakers whose first language does not use tone, pitch, and stress to convey meaning and attitude may need to practise varying these voice qualities.

Avoid raising your voice at the end of a sentence, since in English a rising intonation signals a question. Therefore, speakers who end sentences on a questioning or high tone—known as *uptalk*—sound immature or uncertain of what they're saying.

Tempo

Tempo is a measure of speed. In a conversation, match your tempo to the other speaker's to build rapport. In a formal presentation, vary your tempo. Speakers who speak quickly and who vary their volume during the talk are more likely to be perceived as competent.

Volume

Volume is a measure of loudness or softness. Very soft voices, especially if they are also breathy and high-pitched, give the impression of youth and inexperience. People who do a lot of speaking to large groups need to practise projecting their voices so they can increase their volume without shouting.

Sources: George B. Ray (1986), Vocally cued personality prototypes: An implicit personality theory approach, *Communication Monographs, 53*(3), 266–76; Jacklyn Boice (2000, March), "Verbal impressions," *Selling Power,* 69.

LO3 What Are the Keys to Delivering an Effective Presentation?

Turn your nervousness into energy, look at the audience, and use natural gestures.

Audience members want you to succeed in your presentation out of a vested self-interest: they don't want to feel uncomfortable for you. They also want the sense that you're talking directly to them, that you've taken the time and trouble to prepare, that you're interested in your subject, and that you care about their interest.

They'll forgive you if you get tangled up in a sentence and end it ungrammatically. They won't forgive you if you seem to have a "canned" talk that you're going to deliver no matter who the listeners are or how they respond. You convey a sense of caring to your audience by making direct eye contact and by using a conversational style.

Putting Your Nervousness to Work

Feeling nervous is normal. Indeed, we are genetically programmed to feel anxious about speaking in public: being aware of other community members' perceptions was an essential survival mechanism for our ancestors.[11]

But you can harness that nervous energy to do your best work. As one student said, you don't need to get rid of your butterflies. All you need to do is make them fly in formation.

To calm your nerves as you prepare to give an oral presentation, try the following:

- Be prepared: analyze your audience, organize your thoughts, prepare visual aids, practise your opening and closing, check out the arrangements.
- Practise, practise, practise.
- Use positive emphasis to reframe what you're feeling. Instead of saying, "I'm scared," try saying, "My adrenaline is up." Adrenaline sharpens our reflexes and helps us do our best.
- Visualize your success: see yourself moving naturally and confidently around the room; see people jumping up, smiling and clapping, as you end your presentation.
- Focus on what you know you have done to succeed. "I've practised the presentation; I know it really well; I've checked out the room, know where to put the screen; I've prepared for most questions."
- Use only the amount of caffeine you normally use. More or less may make you jumpy.
- Avoid alcoholic beverages.

Just before your presentation, use relaxation techniques:

- Consciously contract and then relax your muscles, starting with your feet and calves and going up to your shoulders, arms, and hands.
- Take several deep breaths from your diaphragm.

During your presentation, be sure to do the following:

- Pause and look at the audience before you begin speaking.
- Concentrate on communicating well.
- Channel your body energy into emphatic gestures and movement.

Using Eye Contact

Look directly at the people you're talking to. Speakers who looked the most at the audience during a seven-minute informative speech were judged to be better informed, more experienced, more honest, and friendlier than speakers who delivered the same information with less eye contact.[12] An earlier study found that speakers judged sincere looked at the audience 63 percent of the time, while those judged insincere looked at the audience only 21 percent of the time.[13]

The point in making eye contact is to establish one-on-one contact with the individual members of your audience. People want to feel that you're talking to them. Looking directly at individuals also enables you to be more conscious of feedback from the audience, so that you can modify your approach if necessary.

Standing and Gesturing

Stand with your feet far enough apart for good balance, with your knees flexed. Unless the presentation is very formal or you're on camera, you can walk if you want to. Some speakers like to come out from the lectern to remove that barrier between themselves and the audience.

Build on your natural style for gestures. Gestures usually work best when they're big and confident.

Using Notes and Visuals

Unless you're giving a very short presentation, you'll probably want to use notes. Even experts use notes. The more you know about the subject, the greater the temptation to add relevant points that occur to you as you talk. Adding an occasional point can help to clarify something for the audience, but adding too many points will overwhelm the audience, destroy your outline, and put you over the time limit.

Put your notes on cards or on sturdy pieces of paper. Use prompts (opening and closing sentences, then your points, large font, highlighting, reference to visuals) that work for you. Practise your presentation using your notes, and make whatever changes increase your comfort level.

During your presentation, look at your notes infrequently. Direct your eyes to members of the audience. Hold your notes high enough so that your head doesn't bob up and down like a yo-yo as you look from the audience to your notes and back again.

If you know your topic well, you won't need to look at your notes, and you'll feel more confident. You can focus on being yourself and establishing rapport with your audience.

Get out of the way of your visuals: stand to the side of the screen, and *face the audience, not the screen*. Never read your visuals; the audience members can read for themselves. If your talk is lengthy, and the topic complicated, prepare handouts for your audience. Many people expect speakers to provide a copy of their slides at the end of the presentation.

Keep the room lights on if possible; turning them off makes it easier for people to fall asleep and harder for them to concentrate on you.

LO3 LO5 How Should I Handle Questions from the Audience?

Use PAIBOC to anticipate audience questions. Be honest. Rephrase biased or hostile questions.

Prepare for questions by listing every fact or opinion you can think of that challenges your position. Treat every objection seriously and try to think of a way to deal with it. If you're talking about a controversial issue, you may want to save one point for the question period, rather than making it during the presentation. Speakers who have visuals to answer questions seem especially well prepared.

During your presentation, tell the audience how you'll handle questions. If you have a choice, save questions for the end. In your talk, answer the questions or objections that you expect your audience to have.

During the question period, acknowledge questions by looking directly at the questioner. As you answer the question, expand your focus to take in the entire group.

If the audience may not have heard the question, or if you want more time to think, repeat the question before you answer it. Link your answers to the points you made in your presentation. Keep the purpose of your presentation in mind, and select information that advances your goals.

If a question is hostile or biased, rephrase it before you answer it. "You're asking whether…" Or suggest an alternative question: "I think there are problems with both the positions you describe. It seems to me that a third possibility is…"

If someone asks about something that you already explained in your presentation, simply answer the question without embarrassing the questioner. Even when actively participating, audiences remember only about 70 percent of what you say.

If you don't know the answer to a question, say so and promise to get the information and respond as soon as possible. Write down the question so that you can look up the answer before the next session. You may want to refer the question to your audience, which both involves and flatters them. If it's a question to which you think there is no answer, ask whether anyone in the room knows. When no one does, your "ignorance" is vindicated.

At the end of the question period, take two minutes to summarize your main point once more. (This can be a restatement of your close.) Questions may or may not focus on the key point of your talk. Take advantage of having the floor to repeat your message briefly and forcefully.

LO7 What Are the Guidelines for Group Presentations?

In the best presentations, voices take turns within each point.

Plan carefully to involve as many members of the group as possible in speaking roles. The easiest way to make a group presentation is to outline the presentation and then divide the topics, giving one to each group member. Another member can be responsible for the opener and the close. During the question period, each member answers questions that relate to his or her topic.

Employability Skills

In this kind of divided presentation, be sure to do the following:

- Plan transitions.
- Strictly enforce time limits.
- Coordinate your visuals so that the presentation seems a coherent whole.
- Choreograph the presentation: plan each member's movement and seating arrangements as the group transfers from speaker to speaker. Take turns managing the visual support so that each speaker can focus on content and delivery without worrying about changing slides or transparencies.
- Practise the presentation as a group at least once; more is better.

The best group presentations appear fully integrated; together, the members of the group complete the important tasks:

- Writing a very detailed outline
- Choosing points and examples
- Creating visuals
- Identifying and answering possible objections and questions

Then, *within* each point, speakers take turns, and different speakers field the questions they have prepared for.

This presentation is most effective because each voice speaks only a minute or two before a new voice comes in. However, it works only when all group members know the subject well, and when the group plans carefully and practises extensively.

Whatever form of group presentation you use, introduce each member of the team to the audience at the beginning of the presentation and at each transition: use the next person's name when you change speakers: "Now, Jason will explain how we evaluated the Web pages."

As a team member, pay close attention to your fellow speakers; don't ever have sidebar conversations with others in the group. If other members of the team seem uninterested in the speaker, the audience gets the sense that that speaker isn't worth listening to.

MODULE SUMMARY

- Most oral presentations have more than one purpose. People present to inform, persuade, and build goodwill.
- Oral presentations need to be simpler than written messages.
- In a **monologue presentation**, the speaker delivers the content without deviation.
- In a **guided discussion**, the speaker presents the questions or topics that both speaker and audience have agreed on in advance. The speaker serves as facilitator to help the audience tap its members' own knowledge.
- A **sales presentation** is a conversation using questions to determine the buyer's needs, probe objections, and gain commitment to the purchase.
- Adapt your message to your audience's experiences, beliefs, and interests.
- Use the beginning and end of your presentation as points of emphasis.
- Use visuals to reinforce your main idea; make the visuals clear, simple, and relevant.
- Use a direct pattern of organization: put your strongest reason first.
- Limit your talk to three main points. After your opener, **provide an overview of the main points** you will make. Give a clear signpost as you transition to each new point. This verbal signal is an explicit statement of the point you have reached.
- Even the most seasoned speakers feel nervous when giving a presentation. Such anxiety is natural and normal. To reduce apprehension about presenting,

- Be prepared: analyze your audience, plan your content, prepare visuals, practise, create notes, check out the presentation room and arrangements.
- Drink your usual amount of coffee; avoid alcohol.
- Visualize scenarios of your presentation success.
- Reframe your nervousness into positive affirmations.
- Just before your presentation
  - Consciously contract and then relax your muscles, starting with your feet and calves and moving up to your shoulders, arms, and hands.
  - Take several deep breaths from your diaphragm.
- During your presentation
  - Pause and look at your audience before you begin to speak.
  - Concentrate on communicating confidently.
  - Use your energy in strong gestures and movement.
- Establish rapport with the audience members by making direct eye contact, and using a conversational style.
- Treat questions as opportunities to give more detailed information. Connect your answers to the points you made in your presentation.
- Repeat the question before answering it if you think that the audience may not have heard it, or you want more time to think. Rephrase hostile or biased questions before you answer them.
- The most effective group presentations result when the group writes a very detailed outline, chooses points and examples, creates visuals collaboratively, and, within each point, allows members' voices to trade off one another.

ASSIGNMENTS FOR MODULE 23

Questions for Critical Thinking

23.1 What strategies do you use to overcome presentation anxiety?

23.2 When and how would you use images or a video clip in a brief presentation? What copyright laws apply to such use?

23.3 How do you create interesting PowerPoint slides? How do you test for audience reaction?

23.4 Think of a public speaker/orator you find impressive. What specific strategies does this person use to design and deliver effective presentations?

23.5 How would you begin to outline your presentation? What questions would you ask yourself to decide on your organizational pattern?

Exercises and Problems

23.6 Evaluating Monroe's Motivated Sequence as a Presentation Guide

Watch any of the many videos (for example, at www.youtube.com/watch?v=k0ED3PckYaM) on Monroe's Motivated Sequence, a five-step pattern of persuasion.

As your instructor directs

Create a short (two-to-five-minute) presentation, supported by appropriate visuals, on your opinion of the quality of the video and the usefulness of the pattern.

23.7 Making a Short Oral Presentation

As your instructor directs

Make a short (two-to-five-minute) presentation, supported by appropriate visual aids, on one of the following topics:

a. Explain how what you've learned in classes, in campus activities, or at work will be useful to the employer who hires you after graduation.

b. Profile someone who is successful in the field you hope to enter and explain what makes him or her successful.

c. Describe a specific situation in an organization in which communication was handled well or badly.

d. Make a short presentation based on another problem in this book, such as the following:

- Explain a "best practice" in your organization.
- Tell your boss about a problem in your unit and recommend a solution.
- Explain one of the challenges (e.g., technology, ethics, international competition) that the field you hope to enter is facing.
- Profile a company you would like to work for and explain why you think it would be a good employer.
- Explain your interview strategy.

23.8 Making a Longer Oral Presentation

As your instructor directs

Create a five-to-twelve-minute individual or group presentation on one of the following. Use any appropriate visual communication, *excluding slides*, to make your talk powerful.

a. Show why your unit is important to the organization and either should be exempt from downsizing or should receive additional resources.

b. Persuade your supervisor to make a change that will benefit the organization.

c. Persuade your organization to make a change that will improve its image in the community.

d. Persuade classmates to donate time or money to a charitable organization (Module 10).

e. Persuade an employer that you are the best person for the job.

f. Use another problem in this book as the basis for your presentation.

23.9 Making a Group Oral Presentation

As your instructor directs

Make a five-to-twelve-minute presentation using communication visuals on one of these topics:

a. Show how cultural differences can lead to miscommunication.

b. Evaluate the design of a Web page.

c. Recommend an investment for your instructor.

d. Recommend ways to retain workers.

e. Present brochures you have designed to the class.

f. Share the advice of students currently in the job market.

23.10 Presenting to Global Audiences

What tips can you give your peers about presenting to pluralistic audiences?

As your instructor directs

Create a twelve-to-fifteen-minute group presentation with communication visuals on presenting to a global audience:

- What specifically should presenters be aware of/sensitive to?
- How can presenters compensate for cultural diversity?
- What North American presentation norms should presenters particularly avoid?

23.11 Creating a Presentation Skills Evaluation Matrix

As your instructor directs

Together with four peers, create an evaluation guide to assess your class presentations. Begin by brainstorming the components of a presentation, such as content, delivery, visuals, time, organization, audience relevance, and so on. Create a table with headings (e.g., *Excellent, Good, Needs Improvement*) and beside the criteria describe the behaviours you would expect to see.

Use collaborative software to show your evaluation guide to the rest of the class.

POLISHING YOUR PROSE

Choosing Levels of Formality

Some words are more formal than others. Generally, business messages call for a middle-of-the-road formality, not too formal, but not so casual as to seem sloppy.

Formal and Stuffy	Short and Simple
ameliorate	improve
commence	begin, start
enumerate	list
finalize	finish, complete
prioritize	rank
utilize	use
viable option	choice

Sloppy	Casual
befuddled	confused
diss	criticize
guess	assume
haggle	negotiate
nosy	curious
wishy-washy	indecisive, flexible

What makes choosing words so challenging is that the level of formality depends on your purposes, the audience, and the situation. What's just right for a written report will be too formal for an oral presentation or an advertisement. The level of formality that works in one discourse community might be inappropriate for another.

Listen to the language that people in your discourse community use. What words seem to have positive connotations? What words persuade? As you identify these terms, use them in your own messages.

Exercises

In each sentence, choose the better word or phrase. Justify your choice.

1. On Monday, I [took a look at/inspected] our [stuff/inventory].
2. [Starting/commencing] at 5 p.m., all qualifying employees may [commence/begin] their [leave times/vacations].
3. Though their [guy/representative] was [firm/stubborn], we eventually [hashed out/negotiated] a settlement.
4. Call to schedule [some time/a meeting] with me to [talk about/deliberate on the issues in] your memo.
5. The manager [postponed making/waited until she had more information before making] a decision.
6. Rick has [done his job/performed] well as [top dog/manager] of our sales department.
7. In my last job, I [ran many errands/worked as a gofer] for the marketing manager.
8. Please [contact/communicate with] [me/the undersigned] if you [have questions/desire further information or knowledge].
9. This report [has problems/stinks].
10. In this report, I have [guessed/assumed] that the economy will continue to grow.

Check your answers to the odd-numbered exercises in the Polishing Your Prose Answer Key.